David Dutton is Ramsay Muir Emeritus Professor of Modern History, University of Liverpool, and the author of books and articles on twentieth-century British history, including *A History of the Liberal Party in the Twentieth Century* (2004) and *The Politics of Diplomacy: Britain, France and the Balkans in the First World War* (I.B.Tauris, 1998).

Liberals in Schism

A History of the National Liberal Party

David Dutton

Revised paperback edition published in 2014 by I.B.Tauris & Co Ltd
6 Salem Road, London W2 4BU
175 Fifth Avenue, New York NY 10010
www.ibtauris.com

Copyright © 2014, 2008 David Dutton
First published in hardback by Tauris Academic Studies, an imprint of
I.B.Tauris & Co Ltd, 2008

The right of David Dutton to be identified as the author of this work has been
asserted by the author in accordance with the Copyright, Designs and Patent
Act 1988.

All rights reserved. Except for brief quotations in a review, this book, or any
part thereof, may not be reproduced, stored in or introduced into a retrieval
system, or transmitted, in any form or by any means, electronic, mechanical,
photocopying, recording, or otherwise, without the prior written permission of
the publisher.

ISBN: 978 1 78076 047 6

A full CIP record for this book is available from the British Library
A full CIP record for this book is available from the Library of Congress

Library of Congress catalog card: available

Contents

	Preface	vii
	Introduction	1
1	Origins, 1916–31	7
2	Crossing the Rubicon, 1931–35	41
3	Years of Consolidation, 1935–39	81
4	The War Years and Beyond, 1939–47	124
5	The Long Road to Extinction, 1947–68	157
6	Conclusion	203
	Notes	217
	A Note on Sources	244
	Index	246

*For Margaret Hair
In warm friendship*

Preface

With only a slight exaggeration I can claim that my interest in the National Liberal party is as old as my interest in British politics. I have a vague recollection of the first General Election of which I was at all conscious – one in which the National Liberals were still active. Counting the results, rather in the way that I spotted trains or collected stamps, I felt that I understood the difference between Labour ('them') and the Conservatives ('us'). My father helpfully explained that the Liberals, of whom there were not many, came somewhere between the other two. But the existence of a number of National Liberals, to whom the suffix 'and Conservative' was confusingly added, defied my comprehension. Whether any parental guidance was offered I cannot now recall but, in any case, it is likely to have passed over the head of a nine-year-old political tyro. Many years later these infant enquires were rekindled by work on a biography of Sir John Simon, the man who did more than any other to bring the party into being. And, as the majority of my historical research has been focused over the years on the fortunes of the Conservative and Liberal parties in the twentieth century, it seemed reasonable that I should now attempt to chart the history of that group which in many ways represents the intersection of these two political traditions.

In writing this book I have incurred a number of debts which it is a pleasure to acknowledge. Once again, my good friends Philip Bell and Ralph White subjected the entire work to wise and constructive scrutiny, saving me from many errors. I am grateful for the support and advice of Lester Crook, Kate Sherratt and Elizabeth Munns at I.B.Tauris. Matt Cole, Mark Egan and Gaynor Johnson have helped at various points in my research. Those who took an active part in the activities of the National Liberal party are now, sadly, a diminishing band, but for granting interviews or answering written enquires I am grateful to the late Lord Gilmour of Craigmillar, Lord Heseltine, Dr Glyn Tegai Hughes, the late Viscount Muirshiel of Kilmacolm, Sir John Nott and the late Lord Renton of Huntingdon. I owe a particular debt of gratitude for the help of the staff in the many libraries and archives in which I have worked. I hope others will not be offended if I single out the team at the Denbighshire Record Office, housed in the Old Gaol in Ruthin, not only for their invariable good humour and for introducing me to an invaluable collection of papers, but also for affording the unique opportunity of carrying out research from within a former prison cell! Peggy Rider typed the entire manuscript cheerfully, accurately and promptly; Gill Wilson and Paula Mills gave crucial help in the latter stages of gestation; and Tim Johnson, with expert advice from Matthew Brown, took the fear out of the production of camera-ready copy. To all I offer my warmest thanks without in any way seeking to transfer ownership of those errors of commission and omission which no doubt remain in the finished work, and for which the author accepts full responsibility.

For permission to quote from original material of which they own the copyright or which is in their care, the author wishes to thank the following: the Hon. Leo Amery; the Earl Baldwin of Bewdley; the Bedfordshire and Luton Archives Service; Mr Robert Bernays; the University of Birmingham and the Chamberlain family; the Bodleian Library, Oxford; Cambridgeshire Archives and Local Studies; the Master, Fellows and Scholars of Churchill College, Cambridge; Mrs Joanna Clement-Davies; the Conservative Party Archive; the Denbighshire Record Office; the Durham County Record Office and Captain J. Headlam; the Hon. Mrs Susan Fairbairn; the Flintshire Record Office; the Baron Harlech; Manchester Archives and Local Studies; Mr Vince Morris and the Vale of Clwyd Conservative Association; The National Archives; the Viscount Runciman of Doxford; Dr Tom Shakespeare; the Director of Culture, Sheffield City Council; Mr John Simon; the Hon. Margaret Simon; the Viscount Tenby; the Baron Teviot; the Viscount Thurso, MP; Walsall Local History Centre; West Yorkshire Archive Service; the Earl of Woolton. Every effort has been made to trace the owners of copyright material. If any copyright has been inadvertently transgressed, the author trusts that his apologies will be accepted.

David Dutton
Liverpool, August 2007

Introduction

The Right Honourable Gentleman, a happily forgotten satirical novel by Roger Fulford, was published in 1945. Its leading character, Augustus Stryver, is a self-seeking careerist who is ready to abandon all political scruples in order to further his own career. Having at one time declared, amidst insistence that principle and honour were dearer to him 'than life – and more sacred than God', that any pact, alliance or understanding with the Conservatives would be fatal to his party, he suddenly became a supporter of the idea of National Government in 1931.[1] Stryver, suggests Fulford, was not drawn to this position by any old-fashioned conception of the need for the state to discharge its financial obligations, still less by any feelings of misplaced anxiety about those classes of society who were totally dependent upon the economic stability of the country:

> Augustus saw things more clearly and more personally. He saw nothing of the possible danger to his nation, he saw only the opportunity for himself. A coalition would save him. A party truce would prevent the Tories from fighting his seat. He would hold his seat and still be MP for Felixborough. Lady Lyndhurst would still treat him on the old terms of friendship and equality.[2]

Soon thoughts of an under-secretaryship 'surged through his excited mind' and Stryver gladly accepted junior office in the Conservative-dominated government. After all, 'as soon expect a child to give up its finest toy on Christmas morning as Mr Stryver to decline office on grounds of party or personal loyalty'.[3] In the end, however, this political charlatan got his just reward. He resigned after being caught up in an affair and his political career came to an abrupt end. Stryver, of course, was a Liberal National.[4]

Fulford's work is fictional, but his depiction of the Liberal National party is not far removed from that found in most surveys of the politics of this period. The Liberal Nationals have received little more than a cursory footnote from historians. They were, as Lord Boothby once said, 'neither National, nor Liberal nor a party'.[5] As Lord Samuel remarked of one leading Liberal National, 'his Conservatism cancels out his Liberalism and his Liberalism cancels out his Conservatism. His politics are left with nothing but the hyphen.'[6] Yet such dismissive judgements are difficult to reconcile with the reality of the historical record. The Liberal National party would enjoy an independent institutional existence for the best part of forty years. It was not formally wound up until 1968. Unless its survival over this period was a remarkably elaborate and prolonged political hoax, its presence compels historical recognition. Indeed, the election of more than 30 candidates in the General Elections of 1931 and 1935 gives some credibility to the claim that the Liberal Nationals were the most important 'minor' party in mainland British politics over the entire course of the twentieth century. To date, however, the history of the party has been the subject of a curious neglect.[7] The contrast with the British Union of Fascists, which came into existence at much the same date, could not be more stark. Though the BUF failed to return a single MP to Westminster, it has spawned, and continues to spawn, a veritable library of research, debate and analysis.

Three main factors may be offered to explain this historiographical blindspot. In the first place this is a classic case of history being written by the victors. The prevailing image of the Liberal Nationals has been set by writers whose sympathies lie with the orthodox Liberal party. Fulford himself was active in Liberal politics over a period of more than 40 years, standing three times for parliament and producing *The Liberal Case* for the General Election campaign of 1959.[8] Notwithstanding forty years of apparently remorseless decline and despite flirting with political extinction in the decade after the end of the Second World War, that party survived. Indeed, if it has not yet returned to the status it enjoyed at the beginning of the twentieth century, its modern incarnation, the Liberal Democrats, has become once again a force in the political land both at Westminster and in local government across the country. The struggle between Liberals and Liberal Nationals to establish their respective claims to be the authentic voice of British Liberalism was decided, decisively, in favour of the former. But for much of the period covered in this study, this was by no means a pre-ordained outcome. During the middle decades of the twentieth century it appeared entirely plausible that Liberalism would only be able to subsist in some sort of partnership with one of the great parties of the Conservative-Labour duopoly. In essence this was the position of the Liberal Nationals. It was therefore always in the interests of the Liberal party to deny the Liberal Nationals' authenticity – to deny their claims to be a political party and certainly to deny their claims to be in any sense 'Liberal'. Ridiculing the Liberal Nationals was part of the Liberal party's stock repertoire for at least 20 years. Edward Martell's handbook for Liberal speakers, produced for use in the General Election of 1950, contained a collection of quips that might be used at the expense of a Liberal National (or, by then, National Liberal) opponent. A National Liberal, it was suggested, was 'one who is Liberal to save his soul and National to save his seat'. Alternatively, in the words of the Liberals' former leader, Archibald Sinclair, a National Liberal had 'neither eyes to see, nor tongue to speak, nor ears to hear, save as his local Conservative Association directs him'.[9]

Any more serious assessments tend to start from the premise that the Liberal Nationals quickly transmogrified into Tories, and thus forfeited the right to separate treatment and recognition. By the autumn of 1933, writes Roy Douglas, who worked as a Liberal activist and parliamentary candidate through the darkest days of British Liberalism before turning to write his party's history, the Liberal Nationals 'had become Conservatives for all practical purposes'.[10] When the mainsteam Liberals left the National Government in September 1932, confirms Robert Skidelsky, the Liberal Nationals 'stayed on to become Tories'.[11] Standard works of reference tend to acknowledge the Liberal Nationals' separate identity at the time of the General Election of 1931 (when, in fact, their existence lacked clear institutional definition), but then subsume their statistics within those of the Conservative party at all subsequent elections.[12] Both the jibes and the more serious evaluations contain a grain of truth. The Liberal National tradition did ultimately disappear within the embrace of Conservatism. The name was employed in many constituencies long after it had ceased to have any particular relevance or meaning. Yet, at the very least, the proposition that a group of politicians, not to mention those who worked and voted for them, so quickly abandoned those Liberal political beliefs which, in many cases, went back over a period of decades, demands closer scrutiny and analysis.

In the second place the fact that the Liberal Nationals owed their very existence to their support for and participation in the National Government of 1931–40 has undoubtedly worked to their historiographical disadvantage. Damned for responsibility for the twin evils of mass unemployment and supine appeasement, this government was for long the victim of a twin assault from the right and left of historical writing, 'almost as frequently taunted with being socialistic as it was, from another quarter, denounced as reactionary'.[13] Writing, he claimed, as 'a student of modern history', but just as much in fact as a committed Liberal partisan, Ramsay Muir judged the administration of the 1930s to be 'the worst, the weakest, the most timorous and the most incompetent Government that Britain has known since the days of Lord North'.[14] Robert Boothby, no doubt dissatisfied with this assessment from a 'cautious' academic, went a little further. It was 'by far the worst Government this country has ever had. By comparison, the Government of Lord North was a shining example of patriotism, wisdom and courage.'[15]

For many, of course, the root of the problem was that the National Government was not really 'National' at all, but a sham behind which the country was conducted towards military and economic disaster by a Conservative party which self-consciously excluded its own most distinguished talents. Britain, writes Arthur Marwick, 'was in for a spell of one-party government'.[16] Branson and Heinemann agree, suggesting that the National façade initiated 'what were in effect Conservative-led governments for the rest of the decade'.[17] The Liberal Nationals, by sustaining this sham and for their complicity in the government's disastrous policies, stood condemned. Three Liberal Nationals take their places among the infamous cast-list of Cato's *Guilty Men*, the celebrated polemical tract which did more than any other published work to fix historical orthodoxy about the 1930s.[18] Liberal Nationals thus slip easily into Auden's 'low dishonest decade' or, according to Isaac Foot, 'the most squalid episode in our politics', from which the orthodox Liberal party had at least the good sense to distance itself.[19] Even when Marwick found something positive to say about the National Government, tentatively suggesting that it offered 'a central point around which the exponents of the ideas of political agreement could cohere', his focus was on the tiny National Labour group rather than the more numerous contingent of Liberal Nationals.[20] Now, however, as historians take a more sympathetic and understanding view of the politicians and policies of the National Government, it is also time to reassess one of its most important component parts.

The third point of explanation is more personal. The most significant single figure in the creation of the Liberal National party was Sir John

Simon. Indeed, in its earlier years the party he helped create was often referred to simply as the 'Simonites'. He lead the party from its formation until 1940. At one level Simon's political career is one of distinction. He was the only man in the twentieth century to occupy the four great offices of state in the British constitution beneath the premiership – Foreign Secretary, Home Secretary, Chancellor of the Exchequer and Lord Chancellor. His political career encompassed the entire first half of the twentieth century. He first held ministerial office in 1910 and only laid down the seals for the last time in 1945. But Simon was among the least popular and most criticised politicians of his age and the opinions of his contemporaries have exercised a marked influence upon the judgements of many later historians. The assessment, for example, that he was the country's worst Foreign Secretary since Ethelred the Unready remains close to the historiographical consensus.[21]

Many of those who knew Simon developed an intense antipathy towards him, prompting almost a competition in denigration. The Conservative minister Alfred Duff Cooper confessed that he hated Simon, while the diarist and National Labour MP Harold Nicolson described him as a 'foul man' and likened him to 'a toad and a worm'.[22] For Churchill's acolyte, Brendan Bracken, the appropriate comparison was with Uriah Heap.[23] The diplomat Sir Ronald Lindsay compared Simon to an adder, while for Anthony Eden, who worked alongside him in the National Government, he was merely 'snaky'.[24] The veteran Fabian Beatrice Webb judged him to be among the most unpleasant personalities she had ever met.[25] 'Some people', recalled the Oxford scholar A.L. Rowse with commendable understatement, 'made quite a thing of disliking him.'[26] Thus the major episodes in his career have tended to be interpreted in terms of Simon calculating his every move with a view to personal advantage and advancement. 'I am always trying to like him', confessed Neville Chamberlain, 'and believing I shall succeed when something crops up to put me off. He has a certain air of – what is it – *shyness* which is rather disconcerting in a man of the first rank.'[27] It was a reputation which followed him to the grave. As *The Times* recorded at the time of his death, he had 'a certain coldness of approach and a reserve which sometimes tended, however unjustly, to suggest that he had hidden motives'.[28] It was never likely that a political party created by such a man would attract a favourable or sympathetic interpretation.

For all that, it is argued below that the Liberal National party did exert a significant impact over the course of British politics in the middle decades of the twentieth century. The party was crucial to sustaining the 'National' identity of the governments presided over by Ramsay MacDonald, Stanley Baldwin and Neville Chamberlain, providing ministers at both junior and senior level. Perhaps more importantly, it helped determine the sort of Conservatism which dominated the era, in particular enabling Baldwin to fulfil the aspirations he had conceived in the 1920s and to move his party's centre of gravity appreciably to the left, thereby excluding Tory die-hards from access to power. In the years after the Second World War, with the National Government confined to history, the influence of the Liberal Nationals was inevitably reduced. In any case, they had now lost much of their pre-war momentum as well as their organisational identity. But they remained an important factor in the Conservatives' on-going efforts to broaden their electoral appeal beyond their core vote as the only means, in the context of a mass working-class electorate, of ending the Labour party's hold on power. At the same time the Liberal Nationals contributed significantly to the on-going erosion of support for the already declining orthodox Liberal party. Not only did they present, at least before 1939, an alternative and, to many, viable version of the Liberal creed, but they also tended to take over physically the surviving infrastructure of the Liberal party in a range of constituencies across England, Scotland and Wales, a process which it took mainstream Liberalism at least a generation to overcome.

At a number of levels, then, the Liberal National party mattered. Speaking in the House of Lords early in 1951, Lord Samuel, a former leader of the Liberal party, referred to the three political parties in British politics. He was interrupted to be reminded that there were in fact four as he had forgotten the Liberal Nationals. 'I will tie a knot in my handkerchief', replied Samuel with scarcely concealed irony.[29] What follows is a belated attempt to justify that interruption.

1

Origins, 1916–31

The Liberal National party owed its existence to differing opinions within the ranks of British Liberalism about how to react to Ramsay MacDonald's minority Labour government of 1929–31. Thirty years after the event, a party publication offered a succinct description of the issues at stake:

> The consequences [of allowing Labour to take office] were disastrous for Britain and for the Liberal Party. Under the Labour Administration the volume of trade dropped alarmingly, the steel industry was brought almost to a standstill, the numbers of unemployed rose from little more than one million to little fewer than three million, the Unemployment Insurance Fund became bankrupt, and the budgetary situation impossible. Britain was brought to the verge of economic collapse. The majority of Liberal MPs soon found that they could no longer continue their support of the Labour Administration.[1]

As will be shown below, resulting splits led eventually to the emergence of a new political party. But the Liberal National defection also needs to be set in the context of the previous decade of the Liberal party's history. The years since the end of the First World War had been characterised by ongoing internal division, the lack of a clear sense of direction and purpose, defections to other parties and mounting frustration at the party's impotence within the political nation. Such factors pre-disposed British Liberalism to the sort of seismic upheaval which occurred at the end of the Labour government in 1931.

This is not the place to rehearse the copious literature on the impact of the First World War on the fortunes of the Liberal party. Suffice it to say that the governing party of 1914, with almost a decade of distinguished administration to its credit, had been reduced by the end of the conflict to virtual third-party status, a position formally recognised in 1922 when Labour successfully laid claim to the style and privileges of the country's 'official opposition'. The outcome of the Coupon Election of December 1918, held just weeks after the guns fell silent, could hardly have been worse from a Liberal point of view. The party itself was still divided following the catastrophic falling-out of David Lloyd George and Herbert Asquith in December 1916. One hundred and thirty-three coalition Liberals, supporting Lloyd George, were returned to parliament, but they were comfortably outnumbered by 335 Conservatives. Only 28 independent Liberals, under the leadership of Asquith, took their seats when the Commons reassembled, overtaken now by 63 Labour MPs and a further ten elected as Labour supporters of the government.[2] By the time of the next General Election in 1922, the forces of Liberalism remained divided but their combined total of 116 MPs – 54 Asquithian 'Wee Frees' and 62 Lloyd Georgeite National Liberals – was significantly less than Labour's tally of 142 seats.

It is difficult to overstate the significance of these developments, especially in the context of a political system whose structure and operation favour the interests of no more than two serious contenders for power. As the third party in the state the Liberals faced questions which had not really confronted them before. Their failure to produce coherent and unanimous answers to these questions goes a long way to explain the parlous state into which the party had descended by the time of Ramsay MacDonald's second administration in 1929. Describing the impact of the election of the first cohort of Labour MPs in 1906, George Dangerfield famously suggested that the Liberal party had been outflanked. 'It was no longer the Left.'[3] Few would now accept Dangerfield's thesis in anything like its original form. Whatever its pre-war problems, the Liberal party before 1914 largely retained control of the political agenda, seemed capable of responding effectively to the aspirations of a mass working-class electorate and remained the dominant partner in the Progressive Alliance which it had formed with Labour and which had proved remarkably successful in keeping the Conservatives (Unionists) out of power. Applied to the 1920s, on the other hand, Dangerfield's assessment is fundamentally correct. The Liberal party no longer was 'the Left' and, in the context of an enormously strengthened Labour party, theoretically committed now to a socialist constitution, it was not sure that it wanted to be 'the Left' or even associated with it.

Fundamental to the Liberals' post-war predicament were the twin problems of poor leadership and divided counsels. The shattered Asquithian remnant, without even Asquith's presence – he having lost his seat at East Fife after a tenure of more than 30 years – seemed devoid of ideas for the future, intellectually bankrupt and bound together by little more than personal loyalties and historic memories. The selection of Donald Maclean to act as sessional chairman pending Asquith's return to the Commons was unlikely to fill the void to any great advantage. At a time when radical voices were looking to create a land fit for heroes to live in, Maclean seemed to want to return to the ideas of an earlier age, insisting that a future Liberal government would need to impose rigid and detailed economy measures. 'They would go right back to the Gladstonian policy of saving the pence and even the ha'pence.'[4] Not surprisingly, Charles Masterman, one of the ministerial architects of the pre-war 'New Liberalism', judged that 'the poor old Liberal Party is dead or dying'.[5]

Even when Asquith engineered a return to the Commons at a by-election in Paisley in 1920, it is doubtful whether he did his party any service by holding on to the leadership. Drained by the trials of war and increasingly dependent on drink, it is hard to escape the conclusion that he was now but a shadow of the man who had held the premiership through eight tumultuous and generally constructive years. But Asquith would retain the party leadership until 1926, a critical period during which Labour made remorseless gains at Liberalism's expense. 'The trouble is', suggested Lloyd George in 1924, 'that when you have a policy ready and Asquith launches it, it will freeze on his lips; all kindling warmth and hope will die out of it; he will present it accurately, but without sympathy.'[6]

Lloyd George was the obvious alternative leader to Asquith. But his own conduct in the post-war years did little to enhance his leadership credentials. On the one hand the longer the Coalition government continued, the clearer became the dominant Conservative voice in its direction. In this process Lloyd George lost any lingering claim to be the leading standard-bearer of British radicalism, a title few would have denied him before 1914. Many Liberals already nurtured a visceral hatred of the Prime Minister, convinced that by his actions in 1916 and ever since he had deliberately sought to wreck their party. If such figures needed any confirmation of their beliefs, Lloyd George's ever-growing dependence on the Tories provided it. By contrast, right-leaning Coalition Liberals were less concerned by this development, particularly as they tended to regard blocking Labour's route to power as their primary objective. But these men were in turn bewildered and alienated by the course taken by Lloyd George after the break-up of the Coalition in October 1922. By the middle of the decade he was clearly moving leftwards again, losing the support of those who had stayed with him in the years of the Coalition without necessarily recapturing the allegiance of those who had been appalled by his cohabitation with the Conservatives.[7]

Reunion was the *sine qua non* of any hope that the Liberal party would recover its sense of direction and purpose. Despite an increasing realisation at the party's grassroots that this was the case, it ultimately took an outside agency – the conversion of the Conservative leader, Stanley Baldwin, to the cause of tariffs prior to the General Election of 1923 – to effect some sort of reconciliation between Liberalism's warring factions. As in 1903, free trade still had the capacity to forge a sense of common identity among those who subscribed to the Liberal faith. But for many the process of reunion was difficult and could never be complete. There were, suggested Herbert Gladstone with his long experience of the party's local organisation, important men in most constituencies who 'could never be brought to accept Lloyd George and who would go out of active politics if he were once more brought in in an important position'.[8] Asquith himself clearly found the experience of sharing a platform with his former rival a painful one. 'I have rarely felt less exhilaration', he confided, 'than when we got to the platform amid wild plaudits and a flash-light film was taken, "featuring" me and LlG separated only by the chairman – an excellent local Doctor.'[9] A year later Lloyd George was still arguing that only if past grievances were forgotten could a Liberal revival take place. If this were not done, he warned Asquith's formidable wife Margot, 'then neither of us will live to see the day when liberalism will become again a dominant force in the national life'.[10]

The General Elections of 1922 and 1923 revealed that the Liberals were already falling into the third party trap, with all the disadvantages that this status imposes. Even in 1922 the Lloyd George and Asquith factions combined had secured almost 30 per cent of the vote but less than 20 per cent of the seats in the new House of Commons. Moreover, the British electoral system makes it difficult for a party to escape from this predicament. A third party is no longer the alternative government in waiting and is likely to see its strength further eroded as the electorate seeks to cast its vote for a genuine contender for power. Increasingly, prominent

Liberals began to speak a new language of politics which reflected the party's changed status. The triumph of Liberalism, suggested Lloyd George, did 'not necessarily depend upon a single party'. The possibility of converting other parties to Liberal principles and proposals also needed to be considered.[11] E.D. Simon, a prominent figure in the party's Summer Schools, appeared to agree. 'I don't know whether there is much chance of the Liberal party surviving', he conceded, 'but Liberal opinion must survive whatever happens to the party.'[12] Meanwhile, one of the party's leading intellectuals, Ramsay Muir, moved rapidly from a denunciation of multi-party coalitions as encouraging corrupt political bargains to the advocacy of the 'true representation of voters' through a system of proportional representation.[13]

For the time being, however, in the context of an unreformed electoral system, the most to which Liberals could realistically aspire was to hold the parliamentary balance between the other two parties. This, however, would force the party to decide on which way it inclined – had it in fact evolved into a party of the centre-left or of the centre-right? One of the most striking features of the Liberal decline of the 1920s was the way in which the party suffered defections to both the Conservatives and Labour. Moreover, as the central organisations of Liberalism weakened, local constituency associations were increasingly left to their own devices, a development which encouraged an existing tendency towards particularity and diversity. In consequence, Liberalism took on a variety of guises across the country. In general, however, and irrespective of what might be happening at Westminster, the trend in local politics during the 1920s was for the Liberal party to enter arrangements with the Tories, often involving the sacrifice of its own identity, in anti-socialist pacts.[14]

The General Election of 1923 brought this left-right dilemma into the open. The Conservatives remained the largest single party (258 seats) but, after an election fought specifically on the issue of tariffs, they were comfortably outnumbered by the combined free trade strength of Labour (191) and the Liberals (159). Asquith judged that this was a victory for free trade and that Labour, as the larger of the two free trade parties, should be given the chance of forming a government. Thus, with only a limited amount of advance planning and certainly no attempt to hammer out an agreed legislative programme, Liberal support enabled Labour to take office for the first time in its history in January 1924. But that support had to be active. As the Conservatives could on their own out-vote Labour, mere Liberal abstention would expose the new government to an early demise.

Many Liberals certainly approved of what Asquith had done, but others harboured grave doubts. 'The Liberal Party is divided on the question of supporting Labour', reported Lloyd George. 'Quite a number of the "important and influential" emphatically dislike it, but if Ramsay [MacDonald] were tactful and conciliatory I feel certain that the party as a whole would support him in an advanced Radical programme.'[15] For many this represented the opportunity to recreate the Progressive Alliance of the pre-war era. As Labour unfolded its legislative programme, E.D. Simon enthused about the 'immense field of constructive work in which we could fruitfully co-operate'.[16] Some even fooled themselves into believing that the Liberals could again hold the whip hand in such a partnership. But others recoiled from Labour's programme, particularly from the faintest suggestion of socialism. Percy Harris, MP for Bethnal Green South-West, remembered 'a distinct cleavage of thought' that emerged at every party meeting. 'The old Coalitionists were always looking for excuses to vote with the Tories, while the Independent Liberals were pressing for radical reforms and were only too glad to support legislation of a kind they had been advocating for years.'[17] In such a situation it proved virtually impossible for the party whips to assert any real discipline. Even on the initial vote which brought down Baldwin's government and opened the way to a Labour administration, ten Liberals had gone into the Tory lobby. Prime Minister MacDonald watched the Liberal performance in a mood of amused contempt and interpreted it as a struggle for the party leadership. It was 'really being badly conducted as such quarrels by small men usually are. None of the claimants attend the H. of C. very regularly, but when they do they plume themselves vulgarly (interrupt, cock their heads in the air, smile with superior airs – and have a good Liberal press next morning).'[18]

During the months of Labour government the Liberal party did little to enhance its standing. The parliamentary party regularly divided three ways between support for, opposition to and abstention from the measures put forward by the government. Such a spectacle made it difficult to take the Liberals seriously as a participant in the political arena. There was growing talk of the party being crushed between the upper and nether millstones of its political opponents. The Conservative party increasingly took on the appearance of the natural home for those who feared the advent of socialism, while Labour enhanced its claim to be the obvious vehicle of radical progress. When the government came to a premature but predictable end over its mishandling of the so-called Campbell Case, Lloyd George voiced his regret at what he regarded as a lost opportunity. Labour, he believed, could have formed a working alliance with Liberalism with the potential to provide 'a progressive administration of this country for 20 years'.[19] Such an assessment revealed a fundamental misunderstanding of the Labour party's position.

Indeed, the period of MacDonald's government served to highlight the attitude of both Labour and the Conservatives to what was now the third party in the state. Both had given considerable thought to the implications of three-party politics that had not been matched by the Liberals themselves. Labour had decided upon a political strategy which ruled out the sort of co-operation with the Liberals for which Lloyd George and others hoped. MacDonald in particular viewed one of the purposes of this first experience of Labour government as hastening the demise of the Liberals as a serious force in British politics. This objective could best be achieved by showing that Labour was a responsible and moderate party of reform, fully able to work in the national interest. His aim was not to re-create the pre-war Progressive Alliance but to replace it by a Labour party to which all progressive opinion could confidently adhere.[20] Any help which the Liberals offered to sustain Labour in power would be willingly accepted, but nothing would be proffered in return which might strengthen them. 'The first Labour government', writes Ross McKibbin, 'cannot be understood other than in these terms.'[21] Labour's Hugh Dalton was quite brutal about his party's goal. 'I hope we shall be able to avoid giving the Liberals either Proportional Representation or Alternative Vote in this Parliament. Then they mayn't live to ask for either in the next.'[22]

Such thinking was fully paralleled inside the Conservative party. In the early post-war years many Tories had seen partnership with the Liberals as the best way to respond to the 'impact of Labour', the only way in fact to prevent Labour coming to power. Asquith's decision to present MacDonald with the keys to 10 Downing Street, however, inevitably occasioned a major reappraisal. Leo Amery, advising Baldwin, was every bit as clear-sighted and frank in relation to the Conservatives' course as was Dalton about Labour's ambitions:

> My whole object in this and subsequent talks and letters has been to convince him that our main object in the immediate future is the destruction of the Liberal Party and the absorption of as much of the carcase as we can secure ... One of the three parties has to disappear

and the one that is spiritually dead and has been so for thirty years or more is the natural victim.[23]

* * *

The General Election of 1924 was a predictable disaster. Strapped for cash, the Liberal party managed to field just 340 candidates, effectively disqualifying itself from the outset as a serious aspirant for power. The party's campaign was itself undistinguished. 'I doubt', wrote Charles Hobhouse, a former cabinet minister, 'if [the Liberal party] any longer stands for anything distinctive.'[24] Deriving no benefit from its interlude of holding the parliamentary balance, the party looked increasingly irrelevant. The real contest was between Labour and the Conservatives and the majority of the electorate seemed to appreciate this. Just 40 Liberal MPs were returned. Defeated at Paisley, Asquith determined to soldier on as party leader from the House of Lords, a decision which itself encapsulated Liberalism's growing futility.

Over the next three years the party gradually fell under Lloyd George's control. He faced a major crisis at the time of the General Strike in 1926, an event which again revealed not just differences of opinion within the party's ranks but a fundamental division between its left and right wings. While Lloyd George blamed the Conservative government for what had happened, Asquithians insisted that society had an obligation to defeat the strikers, with the distinguished lawyer and former minister, John Simon, going so far as to declare the strike illegal. Lloyd George's senior critics saw an opportunity to force him out of the party, but the grass-roots had no stomach for further blood-letting and insisted that some sort of accommodation be reached. When illness finally forced Asquith's resignation in the autumn, Lloyd George's succession was not seriously challenged. But acceptance of his leadership was motivated above all by the most practical of considerations. The party was desperately short of money and Lloyd George, still controlling the profits of his ill-gotten Political Fund, was the only person capable of providing it. In the words of one leading Asquithian, 'as for money, the answer is simple, there ain't none'.[25] On such a basis, however, the Lloyd Georgeite take-over of the party could never be complete, even though the new leader made the shrewd appointment of Herbert Samuel as chairman of the party organisation with a clear brief to build bridges between the warring factions. On Lloyd George's appointment as sessional chairman of the parliamentary party after Asquith's defeat at Paisley, 11 right-leaning MPs led by Walter Runciman had formed the rather inappropriately named 'Radical

Group', effectively renouncing Lloyd George's authority. Now, in January 1927, the former Foreign Secretary Edward Grey took the lead in organising a group of dissidents into the Liberal Council, with officers and funds separate from those of the party. The stated aim of the new body was 'to enable Liberals who desire to uphold the independence of the Party to remain within it for the furtherance of the aims of Liberalism', a form of words designed presumably to highlight Lloyd George's inability to achieve such ends.[26]

In the period before the General Election of 1929 Lloyd George poured both his money and his energy into reviving an almost moribund party. Under his leadership the party took on a clearer sense of identity than at any time since before the First World War. That identity, notwithstanding his earlier years in coalition with the Conservatives, was of a radical party of the left, building upon the New Liberalism of the pre-war era in order to respond to the social and economic needs of modern, industrial Britain. Out of this energy and activity came *Land and the Nation*, the report of the Land Enquiry Committee, published while Asquith was still nominally in charge in October 1925. *Towns and the Land* followed in November and focussed on policy for urban areas. But of altogether more importance was the so-called 'Yellow Book', *Britain's Industrial Future*, published in February 1928, which formed the basis for the party's campaign in the General Election of the following year. All told, it amounted to something of an intellectual renaissance, staking out a clear position for the Liberal party between the protectionism of the Conservatives and Labour's theoretical commitment to socialism, with ideas that would become the common currency of political debate after the Second World War.

The problem was that it was not an image to which all Liberals could subscribe. Some openly, some covertly opposed the interventionism and high expenditure which Lloyd George's proposals entailed and which ran counter to their deeply entrenched understanding of Gladstonian Liberal principles. In September 1928, shortly after the publication of the Yellow Book, John Simon warned the party not to go into the next election 'like a cheap-jack in the fair', offering a 'patent remedy' for the immediate cure of unemployment.[27] In the privacy of his diary, Richard Holt, former MP for Hexham, was more explicit:

> Lloyd George has made things very difficult for sober minded Liberals by a reckless promise to cure unemployment in 12 months. All sorts of public works financed by loan which will only add to the

difficulties of all legitimate trade by enhancing prices and wages. It is a terrible misfortune to have him on our side.[28]

Meanwhile, in pamphlets such as *Liberalism As I See It*, Runciman propounded an alternative economic strategy based on the classic Liberal principles of retrenchment and free trade, and designed specifically to counteract Lloyd George's attempts to move the party in a collectivist direction. He was 'against trying to work on borrowed money [because] to do so compels you to pay the penalty at some time or other'.[29] Yet, for the time being, Lloyd George was in the ascendant. The party won an encouraging series of by-elections between March 1927 and March 1929, albeit largely in rural areas at the expense of an increasingly unpopular Conservative government and with little impact upon the erosion of the party's urban support to Labour which had been proceeding unchecked throughout the decade. The Liberal party's future prospects would be heavily dependent upon its performance at the next general election.

* * *

'All of the features which a political party needs for victory', writes Roy Douglas, 'seemed to be present: unity; a sense of purpose; enthusiasm; personalities; money; organisation.'[30] Such an assessment requires serious modification. The appearance of unity was plain to see. A campaign poster featuring Lloyd George, Grey, Samuel, Simon, Runciman and Lord Beauchamp was designed to suggest that the Liberal family had at last put its petty feuds behind it, the better to confront the nation's problems. The sense of purpose was real enough. Even Lloyd George's severest critics seemed ready to acknowledge that he had breathed new life into an almost moribund party and to give him the benefit of the doubt, at least for the time being. Richard Holt, standing in North Cumberland, had been one of the leader's most strident opponents. But even he, if never really converted to the philosophy which underlay 'We can conquer unemployment', the policy document based on a Keynesian programme of public works which provided the basis of the Liberals' campaign, conceded that 'LlG has touched the popular imagination and that we ought not to throw cold water on his schemes'.[31] Yet Liberalism's unity of purpose was shaped very much around Lloyd George's personal vision of the right course for the party to follow and was unlikely to survive for long in the event of a further electoral setback. Indeed, just beneath the surface picture offered for public consumption, all was far from well. To his secretary and mistress Lloyd

George confided at the beginning of 1929: 'I am fighting with an army paralysed by divided generalship. It is cankered with jealousy and suspicion.'[32] Samuel had been only partially successful in his efforts to win over the members of the Liberal Council. Grey and others were reluctant to appear on the same platform as their leader, while Runciman, 'an embittered malcontent who could never be reconciled to Lloyd George, no matter what the latter did',[33] professed his loyalty but really hoped to see enough like-minded Liberals elected to be in a position to take control of the party away from Lloyd George after the election.

The leader himself had no real expectation of a Liberal victory and his thoughts still focussed on some sort of co-operation with the Labour party. The very existence of the Liberals, he suggested to C.P. Scott in December 1928, would force Labour to come to terms by depriving it of any hope of an independent majority in the new House of Commons. Labour and the Liberals could 'go together a long way along the road to progress' and it was 'very sad' that they should fight each other 'for the benefit of the reactionaries and the revolutionaries'.[34] Such ideas have permeated the thinking of key Liberal strategists for the last hundred years, from Herbert Gladstone at the time of the 1903 electoral pact to Paddy Ashdown in the run-up to the General Election of 1997. Given the Liberal party's composition at the end of the 1920s, however, any move to repeat the tactics employed in 1924 would be almost certain to re-open fundamental divisions in its ranks. Of this Lloyd George was apparently fully aware. He 'said that if any attempt were made in the next Parlt. to induce the Lib. Party to support a Socialist Govt. the Party would be split from top to bottom'.[35]

Much then depended on the outcome of the General Election. The results gave little cause for comfort. The Liberal party's representation went up to 59 MPs, compared with 40 in 1924. More than five million voters had given their support, 23.4 per cent of the total. But such figures only served to confirm that the Liberals were firmly locked into third-party status. Support was spread too thinly to be fully effective within the existing electoral system. After the heightened expectations of the last two years, the party was inevitably overcome by a mood of gloom and disillusionment. The almost immediate defection of William Jowitt to Labour where, with somewhat indecent haste, he was rewarded with the office of Attorney-General, and of Freddie Guest, who had lost his Bristol seat, to the Tories, was symptomatic of the fate of the party as a whole and of its failure in the post-war era to carve out its own distinctive identity within the political spectrum. The goodwill directed towards Lloyd George, even on the part of some of his least natural allies, was unlikely to survive for long. Crucially, the party had to decide once more how it would respond to a minority Labour government. There was one important difference from the situation that had existed at the end of 1923 which should have worked to the Liberals' advantage. With 288 seats in the House of Commons Labour was now, for the first time in its history, the largest single party. Liberal support would therefore be less vital to the new government's survival. Even so, it is doubtful whether the party used this second opportunity of holding the parliamentary balance to any greater effect.

At the first party meeting after the election pledges of support and loyalty to the leadership were offered from all shades of opinion. But Lloyd George's predisposition to look sympathetically upon the new government was almost bound to lead to further dissension. Ever since the General Election of 1924, at which Asquith had lost his Commons seat, and more particularly since Asquith's retirement from the leadership in 1926, Lloyd George had sought to move the party in a distinctly more radical and anti-Conservative direction than had been the case at any time since before the First World War. Frances Stevenson, as well placed as anyone to assess Lloyd George's aims, believed that he intended to co-ordinate and consolidate all the country's progressive forces against Conservatism and reaction. 'Thus he will eventually get all sane Labour as well as Liberalism behind him.'[36] To a large extent, then, Lloyd George's attitude had not changed since the time of the last Labour government. Here though was the danger, for neither had MacDonald's whose basic strategy of destroying the Liberal party remained intact. A diary entry from November 1928 summed up the Labour leader's thinking. 'If the three-party system is to remain', he noted, 'it is obvious that the question of coalition in some shape or form has to be faced.' Therefore, 'our immediate duty is to place every obstacle we can in the way of the survival of the three-party system'.[37] So, unless the course of events moved MacDonald from this position, it would not be easy for Liberals to derive any advantage from again holding the balance of power. At least Lloyd George seemed determined to take a tougher line towards Labour than had Asquith five years earlier. MacDonald 'must not imagine he could have Liberal support for the asking'.[38] The Liberals would look to secure a reform of the electoral system, 'a speedy redress of this glaring wrong'. Yet even this suggestion of a firmer approach failed to please all Liberals, especially those who, against all evidence to the contrary, still believed in the possibility of re-creating the pre-war Progressive Alliance. E.D. Simon, who had recaptured the seat of Manchester, Withington, found Lloyd George's tone 'threatening', instead of 'looking forward to legislation in the fruitful field which is common to both parties'.[39]

Over the first months of Labour government two distinct points of view emerged within the parliamentary Liberal party – or rather two extremes between which individual Liberal MPs took up their particular stances. On the one hand there was a readiness to look benignly on the programme of the new administration. The raising of the school leaving age and the continuation of the Wheatley housing subsidy were, judged E.D. Simon, 'two really important things' which showed that Labour would pursue social reform in a totally different spirit from the previous Conservative government. In these two instances the government was doing 'exactly what a good Liberal Government would also have done'. It was therefore in the national interest to keep Labour in power to carry out 'an effective progressive policy'. It was true that the strictly party interest was more complicated since it would be Labour which would derive the credit from a constructive period of government. Even so, the electorate would not take kindly to any move by the Liberals to turn Labour out, as it would judge that it had not been given a fair chance. In Simon's opinion the majority of the parliamentary Liberal party took this view. But there were also 'perturbing signs' of a different attitude among Liberals who did not want 'economic equality' and who hoped that the government would go too far and afford the opportunity for Liberal criticism. Among this second group Simon named George Lambert, Tudor Walters and Sir Ian Macpherson, two of whom would be among the defectors to the Liberal National camp.[40]

Such divisions were not new. They represented a re-opening of the fundamental dilemma confronting Liberalism in the age of three-party politics, which had been temporarily concealed during the party's fleeting revival during the late 1920s. Granted that the only realistic short-term aspiration open to the Liberals, now that they had become the third party in the state, was to hold the balance of power, would they prefer to use this position to uphold a minority Conservative or a minority Labour government? To this very basic question the party was unable to respond with a single voice. While E.D. Simon looked kindly upon what he thought was 'in effect a moderate Liberal Government', some of his colleagues clearly favoured the Tory option.[41] Dr Henry Morris-Jones, MP for Denbigh, found himself 'getting more and more inclined towards

Conservatism'. His experience of the Labour government quickly disillusioned him. 'I have seen what a Labour majority would be like. They are crude and insufferable and bring into the atmosphere of debates in this old House some of the manners of our town councils in big industrial areas.'[42] Similarly, Walter Runciman felt 'great sympathy' for many Conservatives, especially those of the younger generation. 'We can aim at the same thing, almost at the same methods' as such 'excellent fellows' as Ralph Glyn and Harold Macmillan, though Runciman admitted that the Tories' renewed flirtation with protection would inevitably pose problems.[43] But at this stage Runciman's position remained flexible. The important thing was to effect a break with Lloyd George and this might just as easily lead to some sort of realignment with Ramsay MacDonald and moderate Labour colleagues as with the Conservatives.[44]

Fissures soon began to appear in the façade of Liberal unity as the Labour government brought forward its legislative agenda. These divisions foreshadowed in broad outline, though not always in every detail, the split of 1931 which would give birth to the Liberal National party. On the second reading of the government's Coal Mines Bill in December, 44 Liberals followed the instructions of the leadership and went into the opposition lobby, two voted with the government and a further six abstained. But there was an element of bluff in this apparent display of independence, as the party knew that it was in no condition to force another general election. The state of party organisation and the morale of its workers were such that it could not risk pulling the rug from beneath the government and precipitating a dissolution. As a result, this particular anti-Labour demonstration was only authorised after it had been ascertained that sufficient Conservatives were absent from the Commons to ensure that the government would not be defeated.[45] The important point about the Coal Mines Bill vote was the evidence it gave of renewed Liberal division which, as Lord Beauchamp, the party's leader in the upper house, fully recognised, would 'once more give the enemy an opportunity to mock'.[46] But Lloyd George, while accepting that the power and influence of the party in the present parliament would depend upon its cohesion, was reluctant to take action against the rebels.[47] Almost certainly, his indulgence at this stage was a fatal mistake. 'This three-way division was to become an embarrassingly common characteristic of parliamentary Liberalism over the next few years, one which diminished the party's reputation and effectiveness.'[48] Lloyd George was still hoping to keep Labour in office long enough to bring about an agreement on electoral reform and he held talks with leading members of the cabinet in early February 1930. But MacDonald's private diary entry shows how difficult it would be to extract the sort of concessions which Lloyd George sought. 'The bargain proposed really amounts to this', noted the Prime Minister. 'We get two years of office from the Liberals and give them in return a permanent corner on our political stage.'[49]

Over the course of 1930 the divisions within the Liberal party became more obvious. For many these were important primarily in confirming their disillusionment with the current state of the party and their conviction that a radical remedy was required. 'The struggle is rather a difficult one', noted Clement Davies, newly elected MP for Montgomeryshire. 'The position in the House is well nigh hopeless ... I feel that the Party as a Party is dead. There is neither health nor spirit in us ... When the time comes for us to go to the country we will go without a policy and without a party, and the result will be that less than a handful will come back next time.'[50] Morris-Jones was equally blunt: 'Liberal party is almost done for in my opinion ... finished as a separate party in the state'.[51] The whole position of the parliamentary party, confirmed E.D.Simon, was 'most disappointing. The Party is not in any way organised. There is no consultation or consideration of policy.'[52]

Herbert Samuel later recalled that the Liberals' weekly meetings were not happy occasions, with about a third of the parliamentary group openly distrustful of Lloyd George, another third his definite adherents, while the remainder 'tried to keep the party together and to guide it along what seemed to us the right lines of policy'.[53] The position was scarcely helped by the apparently inconsistent course followed by Lloyd George himself, which left his party both confused and suspicious of his real intentions. As E.D. Simon put it, at the outset Lloyd George announced

> a policy of general support of the Labour Government. This lasted until the second reading of the Coal Bill when he ... endeavoured to beat the Government. From that time came a phase of pretty active opposition to the Government until Lloyd George's Naval Treaty speech, when he announced that he had changed his mind, and that we ought not to defeat the Government on any essential issue. He then co-operated with the Government for a few months ... Then came, quite suddenly last week, another swing-round, and the attempt to defeat the Government on the Finance amendment ...[54]

There was in fact more consistency in Lloyd George's strategy than Simon appreciated, but his efforts to force a bargain out of Labour involved secret negotiations and tactical reversals which only a leader enjoying the full confidence of his party could have successfully executed. By the summer of 1930 the problem was acute. As Morris-Jones noted, the party was

> in a ferment and nearly crumbling. Members complain that they never know where they are with LlG. One day he wants us to refrain from embarrassing the Govt: another he says we must vote against them. Prominent members say that he does not take the party into his confidence, treats us like a lot of children … A crisis is imminent.[55]

Calls for party unity had little impact. A meeting on 21 July 1930 heard the chief whip, his voice 'broken with emotion', declare that the party was doomed unless it could act together. George Lambert (South Molton) insisted that he could not vote consistently for the government for fear of losing his seat at the next election. Harry Nathan, MP for Bethnal Green North-East, who would later defect to Labour, said that the party was 'done for'. Its organisation was falling to pieces and the disunity of the parliamentary party was communicating itself to the party outside Westminster. He 'did not see how we could fight the next election as a party'. Frank Owen, MP for Hereford, appealed to Lloyd George to take fellow Liberals more into his confidence, while Archibald Sinclair threatened that he would have to consider whether he could remain in the party any longer if matters continued as they were going.[56] It was a sorry picture. Henry Morris-Jones saw little chance of improvement:

> We promise to act as a united party. Division lobby shows we cannot and I question whether anything will alter us for it is inherent in our position. There are 3 parties and only 2 lobbies.[57]

The very diversity of Liberal thinking, once seen as one of the party's strengths, was now contributing to its undoing.

By the second half of 1930 John Simon, former cabinet minister and eminent lawyer, had emerged as the leading Liberal critic of Lloyd George's strategy. The intellectual poverty of Labour's response to the mounting scourge of unemployment convinced him that only unequivocal dissociation on the part of the Liberals from the doings of the government could save them from guilt by association. In late October, just before the opening of the new parliamentary session, Simon wrote to Lloyd George about his current feelings on relations with the Labour government. He argued that, after 17 months in power, the government had proved a total failure in almost all respects. As a result, the Liberals were deriving no benefit from keeping it in office, but were exposing themselves to the charge that their one concern was to save their own skins by avoiding another general election. Simon gave notice that, should the government try to repeal the trade union legislation enacted by the last Conservative administration, he would not be able to support it, but would join with the Tories in any resulting vote of confidence. 'We are in danger', he concluded in a telling indictment of Lloyd George's whole strategy, 'of carrying offers of assistance to the point of subservience and I do not believe that this is the way in which Liberalism is likely to become a more effective force in national and imperial affairs.'[58] Rather than considering each issue on its merits, Simon had made up his mind that the Liberal party should try to bring the government down at the earliest possible opportunity. Lloyd George, by contrast, continued to argue that Labour should be kept in office until there had been a revival of world trade sufficient to invalidate Conservative calls for protection or until the Liberals had managed to extract a commitment to electoral reform. The publication of Simon's letter in the press brought this latest, and possibly terminal, episode in the Liberal party's longstanding civil war into the public arena.

The reality of the party's disarray became clear when parliament reassembled and the Conservatives put down a motion on the King's Speech. The official Liberal line was to abstain, but five MPs including John Simon and the chief whip, Robert Hutchison, voted with the Tories, while four more went into the government lobby. After defying the discipline for which he himself bore primary responsibility, Hutchison had little option but to resign from his post. Yet only 30 Liberal MPs bothered to attend the meeting called to select the chief whip's successor. Meanwhile, Lloyd George continued to pin his hopes on extracting concessions from the government. In September he and Samuel held talks with MacDonald at which the Liberals demanded electoral reform in return for their continued support. The Labour cabinet agreed only to undertake further investigation into the Alternative Vote. This was not proportional representation, but was seen as a step in the right direction or, as the *Manchester Guardian* put it, 'a good starting off point for more comprehensive reforms'.[59] MacDonald tried to persuade Lloyd George that the Alternative Vote would result in significant electoral gains for the Liberals at the expense of the

Conservatives.[60] Yet the government's sincerity is open to question. Any change to the voting system would take at least two years to implement and might then be at the mercy of a new administration; but MacDonald's government would have had its survival guaranteed by Liberal support during this period.

Leading party members gathered on 20 November to hear Lloyd George propose a formal two-year pact with Labour. John Simon spoke forcefully against such an idea:

> I said that even if such a plan was entered into, and was carried through for two years, at the end of that time no Liberal candidate could have a chance against a Labour candidate. He would not be able to criticise the Government for his Party would have been doing nothing but keep them in. The Government was already discredited and I could see no reason in our putting Liberal assets into a bankrupt concern.

As 'expert investigation' had suggested that the Alternative Vote would be of no great advantage to the Liberal party, Simon was at a loss to understand Lloyd George's continuing enthusiasm for a pact with the government.[61] The meeting broke up in confusion with little having been established apart from the extent of intra-party dissension. Warned that Lloyd George was now trying to capture the Liberal Candidates' Association to strengthen his hand in negotiations with the government, Simon prepared for a showdown.[62] By the time that the debate was resumed a week later, he had enlisted the support of Lord Reading, soon to become the Liberal leader in the House of Lords. Thus, when Lloyd George put forward a modified version of his plan which would have amounted to a one-year deal with Labour coupled with the immediate introduction of the Alternative Vote, both Simon and Reading voiced their opposition:

> A one year's arrangement would only amount, in the end, to a bargain for two years, for it would be said in 12 months' time that various things were on the way, and we must not unhorse the Government before they were secured. We both expressed ourselves as gravely concerned at the idea of any bargain at all.

Sensing that the mood of the meeting was against him, Lloyd George sought refuge in obfuscation, prompting Reading to confess that he did not know what the outcome of the discussion amounted to or whether what was going to be pursued was an understanding or not. 'Something was said at the end by L.G. about the difference between an agreement and an understanding' and the meeting ended with no clear picture of how Lloyd George would now proceed.[63]

Simon now faced a choice of continuing to give nominal backing to a strategy which he regarded as profoundly mistaken, striking out on his own in the near certainty of courting political oblivion or exploring the possibility of an accommodation with his erstwhile political enemies. In the circumstances it was hardly surprising that he began to put feelers out to leading Conservatives. His thinking needs to be put in a broader context of growing disillusionment with the existing British party political structure, a mood that would soon give rise to calls for experiments in all-party government and to a minor growth of political extremism. 'Amongst the younger generation in all parties', suggested J.L. Garvin of the *Observer*, 'the strongest sentiment is in favour of "clearing out all the Old Gangs".'[64] Significantly, Reading had told Simon that the possibility of a National Government, headed perhaps by the veteran Tory Lord Derby, was now being discussed in certain quarters and that Simon's membership of such an administration was widely favoured. Simon met with Neville Chamberlain on 1 December, the object of the meeting being 'to ascertain how strongly I felt about the necessity of terminating the life of this Government', and whether any form of co-operation with the Conservatives was possible to this end. The two men seemed to be in agreement as regards the parlous state of the country which necessitated the 'frankest talk'. Simon mentioned the idea of a 'broad-bottomed Administration', but insisted that, as far as Liberals were concerned, this would depend on the extent to which such a government would promote tariffs and whether it would carry a reasonable measure of electoral reform. At the same time he indicated that Reading, himself and a sizeable number of other Liberals were no longer irreconcilable on the issue of protection. Simon also sought assurances from the Conservatives. It would be much easier if Liberals who took the same view as he did could be informed that they would not be opposed by Conservatives at the next election. Simon believed that, in the event of the Labour government being brought down, the King might invite Baldwin to form a coalition. The two men did not discuss the composition of such a hybrid administration, but Chamberlain got the clear impression that Simon would not object to being included.[65]

A few days earlier, seven Liberal MPs, representing predominantly agricultural seats, including Hutchison, Lambert, Macpherson and Roderick Kedward, MP for Ashford, had supported the motion of a Conservative backbencher deploring the government's failure to take action in relation to cereal dumping. Simon's own apparent weakening in his commitment to free trade soon provoked comment among those who remained faithful to the old Liberal doctrines. 'I can't make out what he is after', noted Leif Jones. 'He seems to be bent on turning the government out, even if it involves the return of a Protectionist Government.'[66] Yet it was not clear whether Chamberlain's idea of Conservative-Liberal co-operation was exactly what Simon had in mind. According to the former:

> The whole argument rests on the assumption that the continued existence of the Liberal party is a national interest, and that a coalition between Liberals and Conservatives would be able to hold the fort for at least ten years. I doubt if either of these assumptions could be sustained.[67]

For his part Simon now seemed ready to make a complete break from his Liberal colleagues. In advance of a party meeting scheduled for 11 December, he warned Sinclair, who had succeeded Hutchison as chief whip, that he would have to insist upon Liberal opposition to any move to change the Trade Union Political Levy from a contracting-in to a contracting-out basis. If the party preferred ambiguity, he would reluctantly go his own way.[68] At the meeting itself the atmosphere was palpably tense. 'One could sense it.' Simon, studiously courteous towards Lloyd George, argued that the Liberal party had secured precisely nothing out of 18 months of Labour government and would get nothing in the future. More probably, indeed, it would find itself dragged down with Labour. But Simon was not a man who readily inspired others. The meeting gave hints of some of the later problems he would experience as a party leader. As one broadly sympathetic observer noted:

> The matter of JS's speech was good and I agreed with nearly all of it. But he was pleading as a Barrister and he was studiously over-polite and over-courteous in matters where he felt deeply. He only got two or three 'hear hears' in a gathering of about 34.[69]

In the event an open rupture was avoided. Simon, perhaps concerned at the amount of support he could command within the parliamentary party, seemed now to hesitate. Having reiterated his criticism of the Liberal strategy of sustaining the Labour government in power, he withdrew his resolution on the Political Levy and left the meeting. Morris-Jones assessed the balance of forces within the party: 'Conclusion – about 90 per cent of the Lib. Party will go to almost any length to keep the Government in office until the Electoral Reform bill is thro' even if it takes 2 years'. Still in the dark about Lloyd George's negotiations with the government, Morris-Jones judged that, although there might not be a written pact, there was 'unquestionably an understanding'.[70] Two days later Simon told his constituents in Cleckheaton that they should not be surprised to find him in future exercising an independent judgement and following an independent line in public affairs. Chamberlain was hopeful that Simon would soon be forming an independent group 'which will work with us'.[71]

In the first months of 1931 the Liberal party visibly collapsed as a unified force in the House of Commons. The parliamentary party gave every appearance of a disorganised rabble. While Simon continued to negotiate with the Conservatives about the possibility of a free run at the next general election for himself and those Liberal MPs prepared to follow him, Lloyd George moved closer to Labour, telling George Lansbury that 'the great majority of our party are in accord with yours in the general line of advance for the next ten years'.[72] The new chief whip despaired of his task in trying to assert a measure of discipline over the warring factions. 'I am all for the party being independent and having a mind of its own', he conceded, 'but if individual members claim the same right, it is impossible for us to work effectively in the House of Commons.'[73] When the government introduced legislation designed to undo key provisions in the 1927 Trades Disputes Act, another clash was inevitable. The party meeting called to determine the Liberal approach to the government's bill was 'the most antagonistic to the party leadership' of any Morris-Jones had attended. Sinclair threatened to resign if there were further public splits and advised his colleagues that the party was in no position to fight a general election. 'We had neither the money nor the candidates.' Lloyd George confirmed that, while he too opposed the bill, it would be 'suicide' to defeat the government at the present time. He suggested that the party should declare its opposition to Labour's proposals but abstain at the bill's crucial second reading. With Simon again leaving the meeting early, this course of action was approved by a vote of 32 to 10.[74] Simon, however, refused to be bound by this majority decision. In a major Commons speech he clashed publicly with Lloyd George and called for the 'humane slaughter' of the government's bill. He was, thought Morris-Jones, 'brilliantly clever' but 'over suave and over courteous'. 'Personally I instinctively feel the insincerity when he is most suave.'[75] But the key issue remained, as before, the number of Liberal MPs whom Simon could rally to his cause. 'Simon's following was first estimated to be 30 and came down by stages to six who followed him into the Tory lobby tonight', recorded MacDonald on 28 January.[76]

At least many Conservatives had been impressed by Simon's contribution to the debate. George Lane Fox doubted whether he had ever done better. 'There was not a dull moment and, though very closely reasoned, his speech was not so subtle and hair-splitting as some of his speeches have been.'[77] In the minds of a number of leading Tories Simon had become the key figure in the determination of events. Austen Chamberlain organised a dinner with Philip Sassoon, Robert Horne and Simon, with the purpose of putting 'fire in the belly of the latter'. His message was, 'you are a great figure. I want you to be a great force. To be that, you must do as my father did in '86: organise as well as speak.'[78] The feeling was clearly in the air that a major split in the Liberal ranks was now a distinct possibility, comparable to the defection of the Liberal Unionists nearly half a century earlier. Edward Grigg, the former Liberal MP for Oldham, convinced that Lloyd George was 'going left ... with a vengeance', had also entered into negotiations with the Tories and was hopeful of organising a 'Liberal-Unionist party'.[79]

A mood of expectation surrounded Simon's every move. According to the political columnist in *Punch*, he had become 'the biggest man and the most formidable debater' in the House of Commons. His prestige at Westminster was 'tremendous'.[80] 'J.S. has the ball at his feet', confirmed Morris-Jones. 'His reputation in the country is very high.' And yet a problem remained. 'What it is to have a reputation – a brave courageous Liberal and yet every member of the party knows that he has no courage. If he had he could sweep the board.'[81] It was inherent in Simon's nature to move cautiously. After a public declaration that, if Liberalism was to be merely a variant of socialism, as the party's continuing support for the discredited Labour government seemed to imply, there was no reason for its independent existence, he renewed his negotiations with Neville Chamberlain. The latter was disappointed that Simon had, as yet, not marshalled his Liberal supporters into a coherent body, but noted with approval his intention to speak out in public against the government and against Lloyd George's policies of increased public expenditure.[82]

If Simon was going to make any further progress, one particular bullet had got to be bitten and that was tariffs. He gave the first public indication of a change in his thinking on this matter in an interview with the editor of the *Sunday News* at the beginning of March, 1931. He had, he stressed, no intention of abandoning essential Liberal principles, but neither did he wish to become 'a sort of indoor servant to Socialism'. A telling sentence implied a significant change of heart. 'I, at any rate, am not going to shut out of my mind the consideration of fiscal measures which may be found to be necessary, even though they involve steps which in times of prosperity and abounding trade Liberals would never contemplate.' The phraseology was convoluted, but its meaning clear. Simon was no longer wedded to the principle of free trade.[83] Two days later, and symbolically in Manchester, the historic seat of free trade, he asserted that the limits of direct taxation had now been reached and invited his audience to consider the fiscal measures they might be obliged to adopt.[84] A letter to Lord Reading was more explicit. He now stressed that his conversion to tariffs was a matter of practical necessity rather than economic doctrine. The government's prospective budget was alarming; a series of loans to the Unemployment Fund had all but eaten up the Sinking Fund. It was to be hoped that expenditure could be reduced, but economies would take time. He had no intention of professing enthusiasm which he did not feel, but 'I do not think I can go to Economy meetings and talk generalities without making the observation which the very disturbing facts of the financial situation are forcing upon me'.[85]

After Simon's Manchester speech the pace of Conservative-Liberal negotiations quickened. Neville Chamberlain had a 'satisfactory discussion' with Hutchison and Lambert, after which the two Liberals agreed to draw up a statement of their position and have it signed by as many Liberals as possible with a view to publication. Thereafter Chamberlain hoped to try to get Conservative opposition withdrawn in the constituencies of the signatories. 'If this succeeds', he suggested, 'it might have a wonderful effect on Liberal opinion both in and out of the House.'[86] Lloyd George's position was shaken when his tactical manoeuvring over the Trade Union Bill appeared to backfire. Believing they had the government's tacit approval to do so, Liberals helped pass an amendment at the committee stage only to find themselves sharply criticised by the government for their action. This was followed by a further outbreak of disunity over a clause in the Electoral Reform Bill which proposed the abolition of University seats. When only 19 Liberals obeyed their whip and the clause was defeated, Sinclair offered his resignation. 'LlG looked angry after Govt. defeat. He cannot deliver the goods.'[87] But the next day's party meeting found the Liberal leader in defiant mood. Denying that he had been offered a post in the Labour government, Lloyd George nailed his colours to the mast:

> He said we cd. not go on like this, said a small united party cd. do much and be a great power and force but he had no use for a disorganised rabble. He said that certain proposals wd. be put before us on Tuesday for our consideration and acceptance and those who cld. not agree to them cld. go their own way.

Morris-Jones believed Lloyd George would now try to tie down as many MPs as he could to give conditional support to the government and to split the party into those who were pro-Labour and those who were pro-Tory.[88] *The Times* reported that supporters of Lloyd George were openly declaring that a purge of the party would do no harm. No one now seriously believed that a working arrangement could be devised which would be satisfactory to both factions. Yet it was by no means certain that Simon and those who thought like him were prepared to leave the party to Lloyd George's mercies. They were more inclined to present themselves as the only true Liberals left and to argue that, if Lloyd George agreed to any working arrangement with the government, this would confirm that he had aligned himself with the Socialists. 'A critical position', the newspaper concluded, 'has been reached in the affairs of the Liberal party.'[89]

The party meeting held on 24 March was, Morris-Jones suspected, probably the longest in its history. Including a one-hour adjournment for dinner, it lasted for more than six and a half hours. All Liberal MPs, except those prevented by illness, were in attendance and it soon became clear that Lloyd George would have to fight to save his leadership of the party. He warned his colleagues of the danger of a general election and the return of a Conservative government. But those MPs, led by Leslie Hore-Belisha, who spoke in favour of the party's independence 'got loud cheers in spite of LlG saying that he would resign if the declaration [in favour of supporting any government which backed Liberal policy] were not carried'. In the end the leader won the day by a vote of 33 to 17. Morris-Jones summed up the prevailing mood as being in favour of independence and against a pact with either of the other two parties.

Lloyd George's personality was as strong as ever, but 'party getting more and more restless and antagonistic. Assertion of independence much stronger and issues debated on results.'⁹⁰ Most, but not all, of the dissenting minority, including Hore-Belisha, Geoffrey Shakespeare, Ernest Brown, Leslie Burgin and Murdoch Macdonald, would in due course become members of the Liberal National group. Five of the dissidents, suggested *The Times* – Simon, Hutchison, Macdonald, England and Pybus – were now ready to co-operate with the Tories to remove the government from office at the earliest opportunity, and to their number could be added George Lambert who had not voted in the final division on Lloyd George's motion.⁹¹ Sinclair now believed, perhaps prematurely, that Simon had secured the necessary assurances from the Conservatives about Tory abstentions at the next election. At all events, Simon seemed more confident than before about the future development of events. Dining two days later with Leo Amery, an old friend from their shared time at All Souls in the 1890s, he talked openly about his aspirations for the future. His hope, it appeared, was to join a future government, preferably as Foreign Secretary – 'an ambition which it had never occurred to [Amery] that he cherished'.⁹²

A final parting of the ways now appeared to be imminent. But any positive Tory response was likely to be dependent upon the size of the Liberal defection which Simon could engineer. By early April Neville Chamberlain was becoming impatient at Simon's reluctance to act. 'I got him so far as to say that he would certainly join a Committee of Liberals (if they would call themselves Independents and not Unionists) to vote against the Govt., but he did not seem to think he could count on more than *four* to join.' Chamberlain did not see how he could make an appeal to local Conservatives to withdraw candidates and sacrifice their organisation 'for a single vote and an ineffective one at that'.⁹³ But by the middle of the month potential numbers looked more promising. Chamberlain now believed that ten Liberals were ready to join a new independent group at once, with the prospect of a further dozen if satisfactory constituency arrangements could be reached. 'Twenty-two would be worth talking about.'⁹⁴ In the event it was the government's proposed land tax, a cause to which Lloyd George had attached himself before the First World War, which brought matters to a head. A party meeting on 7 May saw further wrangling with Lloyd George criticising Simon for opposing the government's proposals before they had even been published. In such a situation Simon was no match for his opponent. 'With LlG in a room he seems to shrink into his shell.'⁹⁵ The following day Chamberlain reported that Simon had turned up at the Commons with a speech prepared against the government's proposals, but went away without having delivered it. 'So like him … Simon won't give a lead.'[96] But events at the National Liberal Federation in Buxton a week later may have emboldened him. A resolution moved by Leslie Hore-Belisha to reaffirm the 'absolute and unfettered independence of the Liberal party' in opposition to Lloyd George's on-going negotiations with the government was defeated but received significant support. At all events, Simon spoke out in the Commons on 19 May against the government's proposed land tax. It was, he suggested, 'quite impossible' for a Liberal to support land taxes, except for tactical reasons. They represented a 'very definite test of our relations to Socialism'.[97]

Finally, accompanied by Sir Robert Hutchison and Ernest Brown, Simon formally resigned the Liberal whip on 26 June. The occasion of the breach was the Liberals' confused and divided parliamentary tactics over the land tax proposals and the success of Philip Snowden, Labour's Chancellor of the Exchequer, in exposing the hollowness of the party's position. As the chief whip rightly stressed in his published acknowledgement of Simon's withdrawal, the imposition of a land tax of a penny in the pound on capital values was scarcely a matter for resignation.[98] But what Simon could no longer tolerate was his party's continued disunity which had once again enabled the Labour government to avoid parliamentary defeat. The Liberal party, by its 'pitiful exhibition', had reached a 'lower depth of humiliation than any into which it had yet been led'.[99] *The Times* offered its support for what Simon had done:

> It is small wonder that some Liberals, seeing the disintegrating confusion to which their party has been reduced by the subordination of principle to tactics, have decided to make a stand for a Liberalism which is more modern, more constructive and more courageous … Whatever may be the electoral fate of the nucleus of untrammelled Liberalism which they propose to create, the results of the recent by-elections, the contempt with which the official Liberal Party is regarded by allies and opponents in the House of Commons and the discords existing even among the more docile section of that party are all facts which show that, failing the practical assertion of independence, there will soon be no Liberal Party left at all.[100]

Yet it seemed possible that Simon and his two colleagues had miscalculated. Their resignation of the whip failed to precipitate a mass exodus from the party. Simon's efforts to persuade Hore-Belisha to join him – 'if three or four of us do this at the same time, during *this weekend*, we should form a nucleus which would grow' – were unavailing.[101] Hore-Belisha explained that in his opinion it would be more sensible to remain inside the party, not least because Lloyd George was so keen to see the dissidents depart.[102] Indeed, it was possible that Lloyd George and those who felt like him would themselves soon quit the party and join Labour, thus leaving Hore-Belisha and his followers in control of the Liberal machine.[103] The possibility of Lloyd George's migration to Labour has to be taken seriously. Though the evidence is slender, with important documents now missing from his surviving private papers, it seems that by the summer Lloyd George was in talks with the government about a formal coalition which would have seen him become Leader of the House and Foreign Secretary or Chancellor.[104] Even more intriguingly, there is a suggestion that Hore-Belisha was contemplating joining the so-called New Party, the ideologically confused grouping which represented a staging post on Oswald Mosley's journey from mainstream politics to overt fascism. He had 'joined us in spirit', noted Harold Nicolson on 22 July, 'and hopes to bring with him a group of Liberals. He will remain in the Liberal camp for the present and work for us there.'[105]

Hore-Belisha's uncertain intentions merely compounded Simon's problems. The latter's personality also remained a stumbling block. According to the *Sunday Observer* around ten Liberal MPs shared Simon's views but some of them, while agreeing that the policy of supporting the government would lead to Liberal annihilation at the next general election, would have preferred Hore-Belisha as their leader.[106] Then, there was the response in the constituencies to consider. While Simon, Hutchison and Brown claimed that they spoke for Liberalism in the country, the reaction of their local associations would be critical in determining the outcome of their rebellion. Brown, MP for Leith, was the first to test the water. His rejection of the whip would, he suggested, make no difference to his relations with his constituents, except that he would fight the next election as an independent Liberal out of his own resources. The chairman of the Leith Liberal Association was quick to offer his full support.[107] At least the reaction of Lloyd George was entirely predictable. Seldom since the days of his famous Limehouse speech on the House of Lords had he used such venomous language. On 3 July, during the third reading of the government's Finance Bill, Lloyd George launched his attack, comparing Simon to a teetotaller who had turned to drink. He did not, he said, in the least object to Simon changing his opinion, 'but I do object to this intolerable self-righteousness ... Greater men ... have done it in the past, but ... they, at any rate, did not leave behind them the slime of hypocrisy in passing from one side to another.'[108] At least by the end of the debate on the Finance Bill it was impossible to ignore the extent of the Liberal party's disarray. Both in the final vote on third reading and in an earlier division on a Conservative amendment the party was hopelessly divided. Still, however, it was not easy to discern the shape of the future Liberal National party. Among those supporting the government were Clement Davies, William Edge and Frederick Llewelyn-Jones; Ernest Brown, Godfrey Collins, Robert Hutchison, Murdoch Macdonald and John Simon went into the opposition lobby; while Hore-Belisha, Geoffrey Shakespeare, Robert Aske and R.J. Russell abstained. All of those named would eventually find their way into the Liberal National ranks. The tactical machinations of individual MPs no doubt made sense to themselves, but they invited ridicule and contempt from impartial observers.

*   *   *

Had events been allowed to follow their natural course, it seems likely that there would have been an attempt by the Conservative party, and such dissident Liberals as Simon could muster to his cause, to bring down the government in the autumn session of parliament. As it was, such a possibility was quickly overtaken by the dramatic collapse of the Labour cabinet at the end of August. With the pound under severe speculative pressure, and unable to agree on a package of economy measures to balance the budget which necessarily included a cut in unemployment pay, the cabinet authorised MacDonald to tender their collective resignations. In the event the Prime Minister re-emerged from inter-party talks, facilitated by the King, with a commission to form an all-party administration to tackle the country's mounting economic crisis. With Lloyd George indisposed by illness, the Liberals were represented in these negotiations by Herbert Samuel. Indeed, pressure from the King for an immediate decision effectively ruled out wider consultation with the parliamentary party.[109] Recent events determined the nature of Liberal representation in the resulting National Government. In a ten-man emergency cabinet there were places for Samuel and Lord Reading as Home and Foreign Secretary respectively. The Liberal party was also well represented in posts which would normally have merited cabinet rank, with a position even found for the veteran Marquess of Crewe who, at 73 years of age, resumed his ministerial career as Secretary of State for War. By contrast, Simon could hardly expect preferment through an organisation which he had so recently renounced, but it is striking that other prominent figures such as Runciman, Hore-Belisha and Godfrey Collins were also excluded, the victims it seemed of Lloyd George's veto, delivered via Samuel from his sick-bed.[110] As Morris-Jones put it, 'the influence of LlG' had excluded from office 'all those patriotic Liberals who foresaw the coming crises'.[111] This selection may have been significant in determining their future allegiance, but for the time being it appeared that the Liberal dissidents might have badly misjudged the situation.

There was at least a chance that the national crisis would relegate the internecine disputes of the Liberal party to the political long grass. The meeting of MPs, peers and candidates held on 28 August was the most harmonious for many months, 'quite a remarkable demonstration of unity'.[112] From a sick-bed in Churt and an engagement in Scotland Lloyd George and Simon sent their respective messages of support and goodwill. Resolutions of confidence in the leadership were moved by Kedward and Hore-Belisha, while Ernest Brown announced that he was ready to 'come back to the Party'.[113] All could rejoice that Liberals were once again occupying governmental office, while Simon and those who thought like him could feel vindicated by the way in which the Labour government had been found wanting in the country's hour of need. That government which had provoked such divisions within the Liberal ranks had now been consigned to the pages of history. But, as has been argued above, contrasting attitudes to the Labour government concealed a more profound crisis of identity which had beset the post-war Liberal party. To this extent its problems had now been postponed but scarcely resolved, especially as the newly formed National Government was only meant to be a temporary expedient. 'There is no question of any permanent coalition', stressed Baldwin on the very day that the new administration was formed. 'The National Government has been allotted a definite task [of balancing the Budget and restoring confidence in sterling] and on its completion it is understood that Parliament will be dissolved as soon as circumstances permit, and that each of the parties should be left free to place its policy before the electors.' To his own followers, indeed, he promised 'a straight fight on tariffs'.[114]

In all the circumstances it was hardly surprising that the Liberals' internal harmony shown on 28 August was of short duration. Simon lost no opportunity to emphasise an almost embarrassing willingness to help the Prime Minister. Not only did he offer to move a vote of confidence in the new government, but he even suggested that, should MacDonald feel obliged to resign his seat at Seaham Harbour because of pressure from his constituency Labour party, he would be prepared to stand down in Spen Valley in MacDonald's favour.[115] Events soon conspired to shift the balance of advantage back towards Simon The national financial crisis continued to worsen. News of a minor disturbance in the Royal Navy at Invergordon sent shock-waves through the already fragile façade of international confidence, resulting in renewed withdrawals of gold on a massive scale from London. This, in turn, made it less likely that the emergency could be resolved, as originally believed, merely by balancing the budget. Then, on 19 September, the cabinet was forced to abandon the Gold Standard whose maintenance had been at the very basis of the government's formation. Meanwhile, Geoffrey Dawson, editor of *The Times*, having first sounded out Baldwin, used his newspaper to suggest that the next election should, contrary to earlier commitments, be fought by the National Government.[116] Around this proposition two opposing Liberal camps began to coalesce. Simon was now encouraged to believe that the possibility of a tariff election would be sufficient to force Samuel and his Liberal followers out of the administration. In such a situation it would be important to show that an alternative group of Liberals was ready to take their place to maintain the government's 'National' identity. With Neville Chamberlain declaring publicly that the Liberals deserved to be wiped out for having sustained Labour in office, but at the same time praising Simon and his followers for opposing this strategy, the prompting could scarcely have been clearer.[117] In fact, Chamberlain's private comments would have offered Simon less cause for comfort. The Liberal party, he warned, would have to face up to 'the fiscal decision'. That decision 'will split it from top to bottom, and ... will end it, the two sections going off in opposite directions; and bring us back nearly to the two party system'.[118]

Nonetheless, Simon used a speech in the House of Commons on 15 September to make his boldest statement yet on the question of tariffs:

> I find myself – I take no pleasure in it – driven to the conclusion, as I can see it, by a pure course of deduction and reasoning, that if it is true that our broad condition has changed in connection with our

overseas trade, if it is true that even when you bring in the whole sum total of invisible exports and add it to our sales, you cannot make a figure which pays for our imports; if it is further true that it is absolutely necessary to stop the consequences which might follow, I ask myself and I ask my colleagues ... , if these facts are true, is there any alternative but to insist upon putting at once some block in the way of the flow of free imports?[119]

Quite suddenly, the mood was changing. 'Staunch free traders now in favour of a Tariff', noted Morris-Jones, 'and it seems certain to come.'[120] Baldwin had already sensed that the whole country was 'tobogganing' towards protection.[121] *The Times* suggested that perhaps as many as 30 Liberal MPs had now 'put their free trade views into cold storage'.[122] The financial situation seemed only to confirm the error of Lloyd George's ways:

> the Liberal party or the majority of it – now represented in the National Government – bear a heavy responsibility for our present situation. They encouraged Labour in its policy of trying to keep up its election promises of increased expenditure on the social services. They were responsible for helping Labour in passing the clause in the unemployment Insurance scheme which abolished the genuinely seeking work clause and added 200,000 people on to the state dole. A small section of it lead by Sir John Simon – about six in all – must be excluded from this responsibility, for they have seen the rocks ahead some time ago.[123]

If, however, the minority was now to claim its reward, Samuel and his colleagues would have to be dislodged from their privileged position inside the government. Events moved rapidly to transform the temporary expedient of national government into a more permanent arrangement. The spectacle of party politicians sinking their differences in the broader interests of the country as a whole met with clear popular approval. The Conservatives became determined to hold an election to secure a mandate for tariffs as soon as possible. If this had the effect of driving Liberal free traders from the government, so much the better. Members of the Conservative Business Committee, the shadow cabinet of the day, meeting on 24 September, were 'all agreed as to the great importance of pitching our tariff demands high enough to make sure of getting rid of Samuel and, if possible, Reading'.[124] Since early September MacDonald had also been moving towards the idea of a long-term programme which would probably include protection. Now, the departure from the Gold Standard had removed the strongest argument against an early election. Indeed, it could be argued that it would be best to get the election over as quickly as possible to enable the government to prepare for an extended battle to prevent a steady depreciation in the value of the currency. Simon, moreover, used material provided by his Tory friend and arch-protectionist, Leo Amery, to argue against the idea that a devalued pound had removed the need for tariffs.[125] Samuel, by contrast, vigorously backed by the still side-lined Lloyd George, remained vehemently opposed to an early election, partly in the expectation of Liberal losses and partly because it would be likely to result in the endorsement of tariffs. It had been difficult enough, MacDonald told Hore-Belisha, to come to a decision with the old Labour cabinet, but it was no easier now that Samuel was involved. Hore-Belisha responded that he could provide evidence that Samuel and his followers no longer represented the parliamentary Liberal party's views on tariffs and he presented the Prime Minister with a memorial signed by those Liberal MPs who were prepared to offer unqualified support for any measure necessary in the interests of the finance and trade of the country.[126] By 23 September this memorial had been signed by 29 MPs. In most cases this represented a clear commitment to tariffs, though Runciman stressed that in his case, while he would not rule out any step to deal with the present emergency, he still set his face against a permanent protective tariff.[127] Invited by Hore-Belisha and Geoffrey Shakespeare, Simon now agreed to lead a new parliamentary group of more than two dozen Liberal MPs. Immediately, he began to seek funds to reassure his followers that, in cutting themselves adrift from the party machine, they were not consigning themselves to electoral disaster.[128]

By the end of the month the House of Commons had become 'literally a beehive of rumours and intrigue'. Morris-Jones described the sorry condition of a party which he regarded as 'finished':

> Liberal members of the Government with Samuel at their head – in order to keep their offices and their seats – are swallowing the poison which a week ago they were saying would ruin the country. Simon and others who have predicted and warned the country of this crisis [are] being outmanoeuvred by those who helped to bring it about ... Politics is a hard game – everybody is now out to save his own skin.[129]

On 3 October *The Times* noted that, until Samuel made up his mind on the issue of an election, the question of inviting the co-operation of Simon and his colleagues did not arise, though MacDonald was in the strong position of knowing that 'however the situation develops he can rely upon the support of a substantial section of the Liberal members of the House of Commons'.[130] Simon made his position clear in a statement to the press:

> I cannot help feeling that the game of formula hunting has gone on long enough. The reality of the national crisis is not in dispute, and in such circumstances the best course is for the country to put its confidence in the Prime Minister, which I feel sure it is quite ready to do. That is the course that I mean to follow. I have the best of reasons for knowing that this is also the view of many other Liberal members of parliament and we are forming an organisation at once for the purpose of carrying it into effect.[131]

Liberal party headquarters expressed 'complete equanimity' about Simon's actions, claiming that he was already so distanced from the party as to render this latest move of little relevance. He had become, it was suggested, a 'Conservative endeavouring to keep one foot in the Liberal camp for purposes best known to himself'.[132] Yet such a display of studied indifference could not hide the fact that the Liberal party now faced its gravest crisis since the Asquith-Lloyd George split of 1916.

Two decisive meetings were held on the evening of 5 October. On the one hand the cabinet decided to call a general election without further delay. Almost until the last moment Samuel seemed likely to resign. Then, according to the Lord Chancellor's diary entry, 'suddenly Samuel said he agreed and in less than 90 seconds we decided to stick together when it had appeared hopeless. I was never so surprised in my life.'[133] The formula which produced this last minute accord was the decision to seek authority from the electorate for whatever policies were needed to restore the national finances, the so-called 'Doctor's Mandate'. The parties would be free to make their separate – and, in the case of the Samuelite Liberals, different – appeals to the country beneath the umbrella of a general statement from the Prime Minister to which all ministers would assent. Then, with the cabinet meeting still in progress and its outcome unknown (although Simon must at least have been considering the possibility of Samuelite resignations), a 'secret conclave' of 22 Simonite Liberals gathered at 9.30 p.m. No invitations had been extended to Liberal members of the government. The following resolution was passed unanimously: 'This meeting of Liberal members of Parliament resolves to form itself into a body to give firm support to the Prime Minister as the head of a National Government and for the purpose of fighting the General Election.' *The Times* listed those present as Hore-Belisha (Plymouth Devonport) in the chair, Simon (Spen Valley), Sir Robert Aske (Newcastle East), Sir Robert Hutchison (Montrose Burghs), Sir Murdoch Macdonald (Inverness), Sir William Edge (Bosworth), Sir Godfrey Collins (Greenock), Ian Macpherson (Ross and Cromarty), Rev. Roderick Kedward (Ashford), George Lambert (South Molton), Ernest Brown (Leith), Col. Abraham England (Heywood and Radcliffe), Geoffrey Shakespeare (Norwich), Arthur Harbord (Great Yarmouth), Dr Leslie Burgin (Luton), Thomas Ramsay (Western Isles), Cecil Dudgeon (Galloway), Richard Russell (Eddisbury), Frederick Llewelyn Jones (Flintshire), Henry Morris-Jones (Denbighshire West) and James Blindell (Holland-with-Boston).[134] That evening Simon wrote to the Prime Minister to convey the news. The purpose of the new body, he said, was to give MacDonald full support in any steps he decided were necessary and to support one another and any other likeminded Liberal candidates at the election. 'We shall', Simon concluded, 'call ourselves Liberal Nationals.'[135]

2
Crossing the Rubicon, 1931–35

Sir Ivor Jennings has rightly pointed to the difficulty of dating the origins of a political party with any degree of precision:

> We must remember that in Britain a party is not a legal entity except in the sense that any association having funds vested in trustees or a committee is a legal entity ... If a party were a legal entity created by a charter or legislation, like a college or a public company, we could give it an age and celebrate its birthday.[1]

In this respect, the Liberal Nationals pose fewer problems than the great political movements which evolved, slowly and uncertainly, over the course of the eighteenth and nineteenth centuries. It is clear that the meeting held on 5 October 1931, which set up a separate parliamentary group, issuing its own manifesto and proposing to sponsor candidates at the forthcoming election, had brought some sort of new body into being. Whether that body truly merited the title of 'party' is, however, another matter. The distinction is not merely a question of semantics. It is unlikely that many of the MPs involved yet believed that they were engaged in an irreversible parting of the ways which would permanently separate them from the mainstream party. By 1931 splits and divisions had become endemic in the ranks of the British Liberal party. Against the background of bodies such as the 'Radical Group' of 1924 and the later 'Liberal Council', it would not have been unreasonable to interpret the events of 1931 in a similar light.

Granted the Liberals' now longstanding tradition of disunity, the temptation is strong to trace a consistent pattern of allegiance between this latest outbreak of division, which ultimately produced the Liberal National party, and the earlier processes of schism which had begun with the celebrated split in December 1916 between the two giants of Edwardian Liberalism, David Lloyd George and Herbert Asquith, and their respective followers. The effort is, however, only partially rewarding. A line does exist linking these two moments in the Liberal party's history, but it is far from straight. For one thing the two principals had themselves pursued inconsistent and sometimes paradoxical courses which were too erratic to sustain a single and coherent body of support. Lloyd George, the pre-war radical and by any definition on the left of the Liberal spectrum, had gone into partnership with (or, as many saw it, become the prisoner of) the Conservative party, an alliance and an inclination which lasted at least until the fall of the Coalition government in October 1922. Only latterly, his erstwhile radicalism apparently revived, had he reorientated himself towards the political left, becoming the leading advocate of sustaining Ramsay MacDonald's minority Labour government in power and even, it seemed, entering negotiations which could have led to his own membership of that government. In the process, however, he had confused and alienated many of those Liberals who had readily followed him into alliance with the Tories during and after the war.

Meanwhile, his rival Asquith, a right-wing Liberal Imperialist in the days of the Boer War, had found himself in 1916 – *faute de mieux* – the somewhat reluctant champion of traditional Liberalism in the face of Lloyd George's apostasy in accepting the Tory embrace. Though Asquith had retired from active politics in 1926 and died two years later, those who took up the leadership of the anti-Lloyd George faction had themselves followed paths that were almost as inconsistent as that taken by the hated Welshman. John Simon, whose role in the schism of 1931 was clearly pivotal, had in the early 1920s felt considerable affinity with the Labour party. Though 'Socialism would make a man into a machine', he told his Spen Valley constituents in 1922, when it came to practical business he had always found that the immediate objects he wanted to pursue were objects which Labour men and women also wanted to pursue. 'He had found it so throughout all his public life.'[2] Over the next few years, however, Simon had embarked upon a political odyssey which would eventually take him, and the Liberal National party, into unending partnership with the Conservatives. He condemned the General Strike of 1926 as not only illegal, but as opening up the possibility that every trade union leader guilty of inviting workers to breach their contracts would be liable to damages 'to the uttermost farthing of his personal possessions'.[3] Then, as has been seen, he had become one of the most trenchant critics of the performance of

MacDonald's government after 1929 and of Liberal moves to maintain it in office. So while the fissures created by the Lloyd George-Asquith split were profound and long-lasting, it was almost impossible for the Liberal party's divisions to remain entirely consistent over the following decade and a half of kaleidoscopic confusion.

By the start of the 1930s it was the tradition of dissension and disunity within the Liberal party which was the important factor rather than any ideological consistency attaching to these divisions. Though the dissenting Liberals of 1931 were predominantly right-leaning in their political orientation, they came nonetheless from all sections of the party. Amongst the most prominent, Simon and Runciman had been committed supporters of Asquith, but both Ernest Brown and Robert Hutchison, who resigned the Liberal whip with Simon in June, had been followers of Lloyd George. So too were Leslie Hore-Belisha and Geoffrey Shakespeare. Indeed, the latter had served in Lloyd George's secretariat before being elected as a Coalition Liberal in 1922. But they had become exasperated by Lloyd George's attitude towards the Labour government of 1929–31. Sir William Edge had even served as a trustee of the Lloyd George Fund. By contrast Sir Charles Barrie and Godfrey Collins had sat as Asquithian MPs at the time of the earlier schism. George Lambert, the long-serving MP for South Molton, was in many ways *sui generis*. Though not in receipt of Lloyd George's coupon in 1918, he had been selected as party chairman of the Coalition Liberal MPs in a move designed to build bridges with the Asquithians. Most strikingly, he opposed any form of state intervention. On the other hand, the member for Montgomeryshire, Clement Davies, was thought of as a radical interventionist.

Not surprisingly, the motives of such a disparate group varied enormously. Some Liberal National converts were no doubt moved by the desire to save their political skins. It would, for example, be unrealistic to think that electoral calculations and the prospect of a Conservative withdrawal did not enter the thinking of A.E. Glassey, hanging on to his East Dorset constituency by just 277 votes, as he made a last-minute commitment to the Liberal National camp. In the event the Conservative candidate stayed in the contest and Glassey lost his seat. It seems equally likely that Leslie Hore-Belisha, MP for Plymouth Devonport, had one eye on the mood of his electorate and was pushed into defection by the decision of the Labour government to reduce the size of the Royal Navy.[4] For others, including in all probability Runciman, simple hatred of Lloyd George and all his doings was sufficient to determine their conduct. Lloyd

George himself was rather taken aback to be told that the Simonite defection could largely be explained in these terms. 'Nearly all of them had at one time or another had their backsides kicked by L.G. L.G. had forgotten, but they hadn't.'[5] But for many more the decision to join the Liberal National group was a logical and carefully considered response to their experience of the failure of Liberal politics over a period of years.

Yet the lack of a single and easily identifiable point of principle, based on intellectual or ideological commitment, to explain the schism of 1931 ultimately made it possible for the Liberal, rather than the Liberal National, interpretation of the events of that year to take hold. Quite simply, the defection of the Liberal Nationals soon came to be seen as unprincipled. Such an interpretation largely persists to this day. Typically, they have been presented as self-serving renegades, concerned only to save their parliamentary seats and prepared to sell their political souls to the Conservative devil in order to gain a finger-hold on the seat of power. They are seen as 'traitors, knaves or dupes, men whose tenure of office relied on their political masters and who toed the Tory line in order to survive'.[6] Two key factors confirmed this impression. The first was the reputation Simon himself already enjoyed for insincerity and self-centred careerism; the second, the attitude of the defecting MPs to the issue of free trade and protection.

Simon's distinction as a lawyer may have made it more difficult for him to be fully successful as a politician, for he always gave the impression of being able to speak to any brief. The game of logical argument sometimes seemed more important to him than matters of conviction and principle. 'There is left the impression', noted a perceptive observer in the *Evening Standard*, 'that his real opinion might possibly be quite different, but that for great and good reasons he thought it necessary to support the other side.'[7] But what may have been necessary on a client's behalf in the courts of law gave him a reputation in the political sphere for lacking sincerity. Lloyd George's stinging rebuke at the time of Simon's resignation of the Liberal whip merely confirmed what many in the political world had long believed. Even the *Isis* of his undergraduate days in Oxford had drawn attention to 'an affectation of intense earnestness which is (with or without cause) unanimously derided as insincere'.[8] Similarly, a cabinet colleague had remarked upon the element of careerism in Simon's make-up in the early months of the First World War. 'He has his ear always on the ground and, though he will not advocate principles in which he does not believe, he will certainly push aside those in which he was trained if they happen to stand in the way of political advancement.'[9] In later years observers as varied as Margot Asquith, Beatrice Webb, Aneurin Bevan and Neville Chamberlain reiterated the same complaint. Bevan put it most succinctly – 'nobody believed he believed'.[10] 'Everything this brilliant man does', confirmed one veteran observer of the political scene, 'seems shifty or even worse; he has a lamentable reputation as a twister.'[11] Such perceptions of Simon's character have served to colour interpretations of his actions in 1931, while those who acted with him were rapidly damned by association and attributed with similarly base motivations.

Both at the time and for many years afterwards Simon's conduct has been seen in terms of a desperate attempt to secure governmental office or as a means of persuading the Conservatives not to put up a candidate against him in Spen Valley. His detractors present him manoeuvring skilfully through the slimy trail of hypocrisy painted by Lloyd George, with no aspiration other than to secure advancement for himself. It is certainly true that, as the crisis of 1931 developed, Simon did see the possibilities of personal gain and sought to take advantage of them. A deeply ambitious man, this once rising star of Liberal politics had passed the best years of his political life in the ranks of opposition, since resigning as Home Secretary over the issue of conscription at the beginning of 1916. 'I do not want to waste the rest of my public life', he confessed in November 1930, 'and wish I saw the road by which I might be of more general service.'[12] But Simon's opposition to Lloyd George's strategy of keeping the Labour government in power had been pursued fairly consistently over a period of 18 months before that government's demise. Over most of this period he cannot have foreseen that the outcome of any crisis would be a national government in which the need for all-party support would enhance his own claims to office. Indeed, it was more likely that a failed Labour government would be succeeded by a Conservative one and, if ambition alone had motivated him, Simon might have been better advised to join the Tories as many fellow Liberals had done over the previous decade. History suggested that a breakaway group, and still more a new political party, would soon head towards political extinction. In any case, by resigning the Liberal whip, Simon had effectively disqualified himself from selection for a post in a Conservative-Labour-Liberal coalition. In fact, Simon's actions were probably more principled than his critics have allowed. His disagreement with Lloyd George about how to treat the Labour government was genuine enough. It grew out of conclusions he had rightly drawn from the experience of 1923–24. Over the course of the previous decade he had come to see socialism as the ultimate political evil. At the same time he came to believe that the Conservative party of Stanley Baldwin could foster at least some of the Liberal values that he held most dear. Yet any benefit of the doubt which Simon's conduct may have merited was probably sacrificed by his conversion to the Tory policy of protection. 'This made me an outcast from free-trader circles', he later recalled, 'and for a time my heterodoxy appeared to them almost as a moral perversion.'[13]

Any political party may sometimes need to examine and even change its key beliefs and policies if it is to survive and, more importantly, prosper in changing times. But free trade was not just one policy within the Liberal pantheon. For many it was the very essence of what it meant to be a Liberal, the unique rallying cry which had gathered together the party's warring factions after 1903 and again when Baldwin raised the spectre of protection in 1923. Free trade for Liberals, writes David Marquand, 'was what the Thirty-Nine Articles were for the Church of England: though individual Liberals might have doubts, the Liberal Party could not abandon it without destroying the chief justification for its existence as an organised body'.[14] That Simon and those who followed him should have challenged this particular article of faith was bound to arouse hostility and contempt. Protection was seen as a Conservative policy and the fact that the Simonites seemed ready to embrace it merely confirmed that their main purpose was to curry favour with the Tory enemy. Lloyd George cruelly asserted that protection was 'one of the subjects to which Sir John has lent one of his countenances'.[15]

Some Liberals never wavered from the straight path of doctrinal purity on this issue. Looking for someone to carry the party's colours at the next election, the executive committee of the constituency association in the Exchange division of Manchester insisted that 'the first essential character in any candidate must be his strength in the principles of Free Trade'.[16] Yet Simon was by no means the first or only Liberal to question the continuing relevance of this doctrine in the modern world – and by no means all these Liberal heretics would follow him into the Liberal National camp. Indeed, 'the march of protectionist ideas in 1930–31 made more headway than in the whole of the previous quarter-century'.[17] These months saw a groundswell of opinion ranging from the Conservatives to Oswald Mosley's New Party and from the TUC to the Federation of British Industries that protection was the only answer to the country's problems. In the face of a deepening economic crisis, more than two million registered unemployed, a looming budget deficit and a severe adverse balance in the country's trading account, it was surely only reasonable that even the most sacred of economic principles should be re-examined. Locked into a collapsing world economy, there was a growing feeling that Britain was doomed unless the commitment to free trade was abandoned. The unrelated E.D. Simon, MP for the Withington division of Manchester, was among the first Liberals openly to question the prevailing orthodoxy. In what the *Liberal Magazine* dismissed as a 'regrettable outbreak', Simon suggested that free trade was causing Britain to lose its share of world markets to Germany. Most leading Liberals reacted with a mixture of contempt and horror but, significantly, the economist Hubert Henderson offered his congratulations for this 'fiscal indiscretion'.[18] Perhaps the most prominent convert was the great economist John Maynard Keynes, a life-long free-trader who managed to change his mind without incurring the charge of cynical careerism so readily levelled against the Liberal Nationals. Keynes first declared his conversion in the evidence he gave to the Macmillan Committee on the working of the banking and financial systems in February 1930. Writing in the *New Statesman* in March 1931, he explained that only tariffs could offer the protection needed against a falling exchange rate and a loss of business confidence, if his policy of expanding demand were to be carried out successfully.[19] Similar reasoning motivated other Liberals who had no obvious prospect of political advantage attaching to their conversion to protectionism. Coming down from Oxford, where he had been president of the University Liberal Club, the young David Renton was among those who became convinced that the scale of unemployment, and the widespread dumping of cheap foreign imports which contributed to it, compelled a change of course.

For some Liberals it was not a case of abandoning a life-long belief for all time, but simply of reacting to the realities of the world situation as it then existed. Looking back more than a decade later, Clement Davies recalled that the breach had occurred 'on what I thought then was a very narrow and out-of-date question, namely – FREE TRADE'. As he further explained, 'Not that I do not think Free Trade is essential but, as all the other countries were now fixing quotas and prohibiting trade in excess of the quota, I felt that we had to take some counter-measures in order to bring these other countries to a sense of reality.'[20] Walter Runciman's thinking moved along very similar lines. As a hitherto committed free-trader, he was prepared to accept tariffs for the time being in order to use them as a bargaining counter to reduce the general level of tariffs world-wide. Significantly, even many of those who remained within the mainstream Liberal party, such as Lord Lothian, accepted the logic of this argument and the division between the two Liberal factions on this issue was never as clear-cut for most of the 1930s as some of the rhetoric of political debate suggested.

* * *

The Liberal Nationals met again on 6 October and found their number enhanced by the addition of three more MPs – Percy Pybus (Harwich), Dr Sidney Peters (Huntingdonshire) and Edgar Granville (Eye). The defection of Pybus was significant, as he had been appointed Minister of Transport in September, soon after the formation of the National Government. Simon now became chairman of the organisation and it was decided to set up an executive consisting of Hore-Belisha (chairman), Geoffrey Shakespeare (secretary), Ian Macpherson, Godfrey Collins, George Lambert, Robert Hutchison, Ernest Brown and William Edge. Offices would open the following day at 145 St Ermin's, Westminster with Walter Hackney, until then secretary of the Manchester Liberal Federation, as chief organiser.[21] Simon later reflected that few political organisations had ever got into fighting trim so quickly.[22] Around 40 candidates took to the field, backed by a substantial fighting fund and central organisation. But the speed with which the apparatus of a political party came into being suggests that Simon at least had been planning this moment for some months.

The General Election campaign of 1931 was marked by considerable bitterness, particularly between estranged former colleagues from MacDonald's recent Labour cabinet. But relations between Simonite and Samuelite Liberals, who nowhere opposed one another, were relatively cordial. A speech at Cleckheaton on 12 October in which Simon criticised Samuel was a rare exception. To his electors in Spen Valley Simon put forward a reasoned justification of his recent conduct. He was, he said, 'utterly opposed' to what had passed for official Liberal policy over the previous two years on the grounds that it was leading to 'ambiguous courses' which would imperil 'every sound principle of government and finance'. Now the nation needed to make a fresh start. His own belief, 'reached after anxious study of the existing situation' was that some application of tariffs would be found to be necessary and 'in that case I am prepared to see them applied'.[23] In general, the distinction between the two Liberal groups was much less clear-cut, even to Liberal voters, than it later became. The words 'Liberal' and 'National' were often employed together to describe a candidate who was supporting the National Government, a position adopted, with varying degrees of enthusiasm, by all existing Liberal MPs except for the tiny family group around Lloyd George. Thus, even Samuel used the description 'Liberal and National candidate' in his address to the electors of Darwen.[24] Lists did exist to differentiate the two camps, but even these were not definitive and a few names appeared on both. Runciman insisted that his name was not to be included in any group when the press sought to clarify the confusion surrounding his position.[25] In a handful of cases Liberals did not make their allegiance known until after the election was over.

Few saw any value in emphasising divisions. After all, each candidate needed the support of as many Liberal voters as possible. Some saw ambiguity about their precise affiliation as the best means of achieving this. In Huddersfield both the local Liberal association and the voters who supported him had every reason to believe that William Mabane was an orthodox advocate of the mainstream Liberal faith. A telegram of support from Herbert Samuel and the appearance of the party's elder statesman, the former Foreign Secretary Viscount Grey, at his eve of poll rally seemed to bestow the imprimatur of legitimacy upon him. But Mabane would align himself with the Simonites as soon as he arrived at Westminster after his successful campaign. In Flintshire the sitting Liberal MP, Frederick Llewelyn Jones, who at the beginning of the year had seemed to support Lloyd George's strategy of seeking an accommodation with Labour, was now moving towards the Simonites. But his statement to the executive committee of the Flintshire Liberal Association was purposefully opaque. He appeared before the committee, he insisted, as a Liberal and nothing would induce him to break his association with the Liberal party. But he regarded the Prime Minister's manifesto for the forthcoming election as the most statesmanlike declaration ever made in such a situation and he was disappointed that Samuel had not felt able to add his signature to it.[26] Llewelyn Jones too would find his way – albeit temporarily – into the Liberal National group once the election was over. In Walsall Joseph Leckie, a local man with an impressive record of public service, stood as the 'National' candidate and conducted his campaign on the theme that a socialist victory would result in inflationary chaos and the collapse of the country's banking system. As late as 29 September he insisted that he was 'as strong as ever on Free Trade', although he would not carry his conviction 'to the last point' in the case of manufactured luxuries from abroad.[27] Just over a week later, however, Leckie announced that he had agreed with the Walsall Conservative Association to sign a statement to the effect that he would 'vote for any policy brought in by the National Government', a commitment that in many minds was bound to include tariffs.[28] Nonetheless, once safely elected, Leckie took his place – for the time being – among the Samuelites. 'I am one of yours, not Simon's', he assured his leader on 31 October.[29]

Perhaps the clearest indication of differentiation between Liberals and Liberal Nationals lay in the very different attitudes taken up towards them by the Conservatives. In theory, of course, both Liberal groups together with the Tories were partners in the same anti-socialist enterprise, but much depended on the attitude of local Conservative associations and the readiness of the party's headquarters to put pressure upon them to give way to Liberals in the national interest. In practice, this meant that a Samuelite Liberal was far more likely to face a Tory opponent than was his Liberal National counterpart. Conservative Central Office 'definitely understood that we were in conflict with the Samuelite Liberals', a perception shared by Ramsay Muir, the chairman of the National Liberal Federation. 'We need not look for any arrangement with the Conservatives', he wrote on 7 October. 'They will do their best to destroy us, except possibly in the constituencies where we alone have any chance of defeating Labour. There will be no pact and no coupons.'[30] Muir's forebodings were fully justified. Around 80 Samuelite candidates faced Conservative opposition, including a dozen sitting MPs and even four who held office in the National Government. Samuel himself was challenged by a Tory in Darwen, even though in his case the intruder was publicly disowned by Baldwin. By contrast, Hutchison was able to predict that just two sitting Liberal National MPs would face Conservative opposition.[31] In the event there were four Conservative-Liberal National contests, in East Dorset, Ashford, Nuneaton and the Western Isles, with that in Nuneaton not involving a sitting Simonite. When it appeared that the Tories might oppose Runciman, whose allegiance had yet to be settled, in St Ives, his friend the Prime Minister determined to intervene. The Conservatives' one concern, complained MacDonald, was 'an absolute majority. They are keeping as many Liberals and my Labour friends out of constituencies as they can ... Never let it be said that the Tory machine had a glimmering of national duty and sacrifice.'[32]

At the time, of course, neither relations between the two Liberal factions nor their respective dealings with the Tories lay at the heart of the electoral battle. This focused, almost universally, on the sense of national crisis and the claim that Labour had 'run away' from the grave problems confronting the country in the summer and could not again be entrusted with the reins of government. Not surprisingly, the Labour party was the most obvious casualty of the contest, arguably the first electoral setback it had incurred since its formation at the beginning of the century, though the country's first-past-the-post system greatly exaggerated the extent of its defeat. A mere 52 Labour MPs made their way to Westminster to face a total of 554 supporters of the National Government. Superficially, the Liberals had improved upon their performance of 1929. The assorted branches of Liberalism totalled as many as 72 successful candidates, an increase of 13 on the figure secured in the previous general election. But this numerical advance barely concealed the plight of the mainstream party. Precise figures were at first disputed and difficult to determine until individual MPs showed their true colours,[33] but it gradually became clear that four of the 72 were supporters of Lloyd George, while the Liberal Nationals claimed the allegiance of as many as 35, leaving only 33 Samuelites.

The mainstream Liberals had fielded 113 candidates, by far the lowest total in the party's history. In part, this reflected the need to give way to the Conservatives in the supposed national interest, but it was also a function of financial embarrassment. Lloyd George had demonstrated his opposition to the election by withholding funds. Thirteen seats won in 1929 were now lost, all to the Tories. All the party's compensating gains had been at Labour's expense, but many would be immediately vulnerable to any revival in Labour's fortunes. Overall, the Liberal vote had dropped by more than three million, largely because of the reduction in the number of candidates. Such statistics are difficult to interpret because of the peculiar circumstances in which the election was fought. It seems unrealistic to suppose that the potential reservoir of Liberalism in the country had dried up as dramatically as the 1931 results implied. After all, a little over two years earlier the united party had secured more than 23 per cent of the popular vote. It seems likely that many Liberal voters had simply jumped on to the prevailing anti-Labour bandwagon and registered their support for whichever non-socialist candidate was available. Indeed, laying claim to the 'Liberal vote' would be one of the key political themes of the next few years. But the fact that could not be escaped was that, as a parliamentary force, independent Liberalism was in danger of losing credibility. Advising an old friend who had served under him on the Western Front, Winston Churchill suggested that Archibald Sinclair should now 'carefully but ruthlessly' detach himself from the Samuelite group and 'establish solid

Tory or Simonite connections'. The Samuelites, he added, were 'wilderness headed'.[34] Having fewer MPs than even the Liberal Nationals would be at least symbolically important in the forthcoming contest – largely of words – between the two groups.

The Liberal Nationals, by contrast, had done remarkably well. Forty-one candidates had produced 35 MPs. The group made ten gains from Labour, but lost two of the three seats in which its sitting member faced Conservative opposition. Of course, all that these results had established was that in the anti-socialist mood of 1931 the electorate generally preferred to support a Liberal National candidate rather than a Labour one. The group's relative strength against the Samuelites had not been tested, while its generally cordial relationship with the Conservatives had unquestionably enabled it to pick up substantial numbers of Tory votes. For all that, the presence in the House of Commons of a new block of nearly three dozen MPs could not be ignored.

* * *

The year which followed the General Election of 1931 was of crucial importance in determining the relationship between the severed wings of the old Liberal movement and in transforming the Liberal Nationals into a genuine political party in their own right. One option, of course, was reunion. This might have given a vestige of credibility to the otherwise hollow claim of Walter Rea, soon to become the Samuelites' chief whip, that the Liberals were 'now once more the second largest' party.[35] Indeed, there was even an outside chance that a reunited Liberal party could have made some further progress at the expense of a Labour party that was now in disarray. Liberals performed surprisingly well in a handful of by-elections in the course of 1932, including retaining, against expectations, their seat in North Cornwall. In one sense reunion became more likely after the General Election, since leading Liberal Nationals were now given office, alongside Liberals, in the National Government. The once divisive issue of whether or not to prop up MacDonald's Labour government could now be relegated to a position of historical debate. 'It would be ridiculous', argued one journalist, 'if the two sections were to be disunited while sitting together as Ministers.'[36]

MacDonald discussed the question of posts with Simon on 1 November, as soon as the electoral dust had settled. Where his own career was concerned, Simon was not impeded by false modesty. He wanted a position at the heart of affairs, international, monetary and fiscal. Questions of status and pride ruled out the post of Minister without Portfolio and he would accept nothing inferior to Samuel who was already Home Secretary. In short, only the Treasury and the Foreign Office, from which, respectively, Philip Snowden and the veteran Liberal Lord Reading were ready to retire, seemed appropriate.[37] MacDonald, conscious of the weakness of his own position at the head of a group of just 13 National Labour MPs, grateful for Simon's unequivocal support during the campaign and anxious to emphasise the National character of his new administration, was keen to oblige. With the Treasury earmarked for Neville Chamberlain, Simon found himself appointed Secretary of State for Foreign Affairs, returning to government more than a decade and a half after he had last laid down the seals of ministerial office. Hore-Belisha had no doubts that Simon would look after himself, but was less confident that fellow Liberal Nationals would be rewarded. 'You would not comfortably hold high office', he suggested, 'in a government from which a fair proportion of those who had stood by you were excluded.'[38] In the event, Runciman went to the Board of Trade, supposedly to balance the committed protectionist, Chamberlain. Outside the cabinet there were junior posts for Pybus, Shakespeare and Ernest Brown. Hore-Belisha himself became Parliamentary Secretary at the Board of Trade. Logically, as long as both Liberal groups remained part of the same government – or both moved into opposition – there was always a possibility that they would come back together. What is, however, clear is that key figures in the Liberal National leadership, including Simon himself, stood very self-consciously in the way of reunion.

With the election out of the way the Samuelite Liberals held out an olive branch to their Simonite colleagues. Donald Maclean contacted Simon and suggested a meeting between the two of them and Samuel to discuss the general situation, offering the Home Office or Liberal headquarters in Abingdon Street as possible venues. Simon's first response was to plead a lack of time. He then asked for a more neutral meeting place before finally suggesting that any discussion 'would be better left for the time being'.[39] By 3 November *The Times* was able to report that the Liberal National group had decided to accept the government whip rather than that of any political party. Even so, the Samuelites still decided to send their whip to all those Liberal MPs whose candidatures at the election had been approved by their local associations, a stipulation which gathered in the vast majority of the Liberal National contingent. On the previous day no Liberal National had attended a meeting of the Liberal shadow cabinet, but an evening dinner helped give clarity to the group's parliamentary strength. Here, Hore-Belisha was host to 27 of his colleagues, while a further seven MPs, including Runciman, were unable to attend because of prior engagements.[40] When Henry Morris-Jones, MP for Denbigh, spoke in favour of attending a meeting of the Samuelite parliamentary party, he found feeling among his Liberal National colleagues 'too strong' and the breach between the factions 'yet too strained'.[41]

Speaking in Scarborough on 11 November, Ramsay Muir criticised Simon for his readiness to contemplate tariffs in order to ensure the absence of Conservative opposition in Spen Valley, but he seemed ready to forgive the Liberal Nationals for having 'kept their consciences in their seats'. A great many of Simon's followers were, he believed, 'genuine Liberals' and he did not think the split was 'really as serious as it appears to be'.[42] In like vein Samuel insisted that the door to reunion was still open – but the will to come through it appeared to be lacking. Simon himself –'in great spirits' – seemed more interested in his relationship with the Prime Minister, telling the dinner of his own followers that 'the great thing was to assure Ramsay that he had a solid block behind him irrespective of the Tories'.[43] Before the end of November the group had emphasised its growing autonomy by setting up committees to consider a wide range of policy areas – Finance and Trade, Health and Education, Agriculture, Labour and Pensions, Foreign and Imperial issues and Scottish affairs.[44] Then, early in the New Year came the first signs that the Liberal Nationals wished to extend their activities beyond those of a purely parliamentary group. A unanimous decision was taken to form a council and executive to represent Liberal National opinion in the country. As the group's chief whip, Geoffrey Shakespeare would welcome approaches from individuals in constituencies not fought at the General Election who now wished to be associated with the group's activities.[45]

Granted the size of the Conservative component within the National Government, it was inevitable that the question of tariffs would soon return to the agenda, and it was this issue which finally ensured that there would be no coming together of the disparate strands of Liberalism. A cabinet committee, which included both Simon and Samuel, worked on the matter over Christmas before tabling its proposals early in the New Year. The resignation of Samuel and others over the government's Import Duties Bill was only averted by Lord Hailsham's ingenious suggestion that, on this particular issue, conventional notions of collective cabinet responsibility should be set aside and individual members of the government allowed the liberty to 'differ'. Ministers took up predictable positions, for or against the government's proposal for a ten per cent tariff on a wide range of goods, though it was noticeable that at this stage Runciman and Simon supported the tariff as a 'temporary' expedient only. The former, in particular, viewed the government's plans without enthusiasm, as a distasteful necessity resulting from the prevailing economic climate. Among Liberal MPs there remained a degree of fluidity. A.C. Curry, the Liberal National member for Bishop Auckland, voted against the bill, while two MPs hitherto associated with Samuel, Dr J. Hunter (Dumfriesshire) and J.A. Leckie (Walsall) supported the government. Hunter, who was PPS to Archibald Sinclair, insisted that he could not go against pledges he had given during his election campaign.[46] Then, on 24 February, an amendment was moved in the Commons designed to exclude food from the list of commodities which would be subject to duties. The Samuelites voted *en masse* in support of the amendment; the Simonites were at this stage divided – ten following their Liberal colleagues and nine voting with the government.

Far from seeking the means to paper over these renewed signs of Liberal division, however, Simon privately expressed his contempt for Samuel's stance:

> He no doubt will claim that he has alternative plans, but can they produce concrete results this year or next? It is no good prescribing a long sea voyage as a cure for persistent hemorrhage; you must try to stop the bleeding. Samuel is not opposed to all tariffs, as his speech shows. He merely objects to a portion of the present scheme, but he has no right to be a Free Trader if he favours a different use of tariffs.[47]

Speaking in Norwich in March, Simon argued that the Liberal Nationals had shown the way by breaking through 'the tyranny of dogma'. They had contributed the sense of reality and the sense of moderation without which a truly national and progressive policy could never embody the fundamental good sense of the British people.[48]

Delegates from many constituencies now represented by Liberal Nationals attended the Samuelite party's National Liberal Federation meeting in Clacton in April. Some even voted for free trade resolutions, apparently accepting their MPs' assurances that protection was only a temporary measure designed to promote an all-round reduction in trading restrictions.[49] Over the summer, however, the Simonites took further steps towards finalising the breach. Simon's own vision of the future seemed to have little to do with any concept of Liberal reunion. Were British politics in the future, he asked, going to be the same as in the past?

> I have a feeling that, after the experience through which we have passed, both in peace and in war, it may very well be that there will emerge an outlook on current political questions which will not be confined to any one of the old political parties and in which we shall be able really to influence one another.[50]

July saw the establishment of the Liberal National Council as a 'rallying point' for Liberals up and down the country who wanted to give 'wholehearted support' to the National Government. With Hutchison as chairman of its executive committee, the new body was designed to co-ordinate relations with the Conservatives and to act as a fund-raising machine to gather the money needed to finance candidates at future elections. It was part of a concerted effort by the Liberal National leadership to present their group as the true standard-bearers of Liberalism in the country. The press release announcing the setting up of the Liberal National Council argued that its purpose was to represent the predominant Liberal sentiment in the land, just as Liberal National MPs did in the House of Commons.[51]

Yet it is clear that at this stage many Liberal Nationals remained apprehensive about the future and that they were still wary of cutting all links with the historic Liberal party. Morris-Jones wrote in his diary of the possibility that a 'separate organisation' could be handed over 'to the Tories when the time comes'. He feared that 'we may find ourselves nobody's children 'ere long'.[52] In like vein, Hore-Belisha warned that if the Conservatives once, 'like strong chickens, get on the back of us, the weak chickens, they will continue their pecking to the death'.[53] Such fears were not without foundation. The Conservative party's attitude towards the Liberal Nationals was determined by dispassionate calculations of what was in its own political and electoral interests. The overriding aim must be to retain the support of those Liberal and Labour electors whose votes had contributed to the overwhelming majority secured in 1931. 'The longer that collaboration can be maintained both in Parliament and in the country the better, and we ought to do our utmost to cultivate a National rather than a Party spirit in politics with that object in view.'[54] Whether such thinking would involve the Liberal Nationals maintaining a long-term separate identity was, however, another matter. Tory Central Office believed that the

Simonites were likely to join with the Conservatives before long, 'thus forming a very strong combination'.⁵⁵ Neville Chamberlain, for one, was keen to hasten the departure of the Samuelites so as to leave a 'far more homogeneous' government. It would then be possible to 'move towards the fused party under a National name which I regard as certain to come'.⁵⁶ But the Liberal Nationals' two leading ministers, Simon and Runciman, were altogether more optimistic about their group's prospects.

The crunch came when the government's delegates, with Chancellor of the Exchequer Neville Chamberlain taking the lead, succeeded in negotiating the Ottawa Agreements in August which set up a scheme of Imperial Preference. For Samuel and fellow free-traders this was a step too far. As Prime Minister, MacDonald was anxious to keep the Samuelites inside the government in order to sustain the claim that this was an all-party administration and thus to justify his own position at its head. 'If you go', he implored the Liberal leader, 'I am no longer the head of a combination ... I should be regarded as a limpet in office.'⁵⁷ But Samuel was already aware of a growing body of Liberal opinion in the country which opposed continuing participation in the government.⁵⁸ Back in April, for example, the Manchester Exchange Liberal Association had passed a resolution looking 'forward to the day when Sir Herbert Samuel and his colleagues in the Ministry resign office and again champion the cause of Liberalism in the country'.⁵⁹ For his part, Simon was equally keen to see Samuel depart, pressing the case that the presence of the Liberal Nationals alone would be sufficient to uphold the government's 'national' credentials. 'The PM needs all the Liberal help he can get', he told Runciman, 'and deeply appreciates anything we can do to stand by him and prevent submergence in the Tory flood.'⁶⁰

Runciman now set out the position for Chamberlain's benefit. The Chancellor, already convinced that Samuel was 'emphatically not a man to go tiger hunting with', needed little persuasion.⁶¹ Runciman's understanding was that, unless ratification of the Ottawa agreements was postponed until after the forthcoming World Economic Conference, Samuel 'and his henchmen, one and all, will go out'. 'In my view', he continued:

> such damage as may be done will be mainly in altering the nature of the Government, and that can be met in two ways; First, by filling the gaps at once, that is to say on the 29th [Samuel had scheduled his resignation for 28 September], and thus give the impression that Samuel and his associates are not irreplaceable, and, second, by filling

Liberal undersecretaryships with Liberal Nationals, of whom we can name at least ten who are quite up to these jobs. The three Cabinet posts [Samuel, Archibald Sinclair and Viscount Snowden] are subject to other considerations: two of these, however, ought to continue to be as they are now – Liberal [by which, of course, Runciman meant that they should now become Liberal National]. This is partly for the look of the thing – preserving the broad base – and partly to keep alive loyalty to the government in circles which had Liberal antecedents.[62]

Consultations within the Liberal National group over the next few days revealed a growing appreciation of the enormous importance of what was happening for the future of British Liberalism, together with continuing uncertainty as to whether the Liberal Nationals could survive on their own. On 23 September Morris-Jones met, by appointment, with Shakespeare, the Liberal Nationals' chief whip, finding him 'much absorbed in crises'. Morris-Jones warned that, if the Samuelites did leave the government, 'we might be suspended in mid-air, subjected to hostility of Liberals and not absorbed by the Tories'. The imperative need, Shakespeare responded, was for a firm commitment from the Conservatives over future electoral arrangements and about the ministerial vacancies that would result from the resignation of the Samuelites.[63] Shakespeare now wrote to Simon. In its recognition that relations between the two Liberal factions were fast reaching a point of no return, this letter merits extensive quotation:

> I am not at all happy about the position. Assuming we continue our support of the Government, our lines of communication with the Liberal Party will be cut for ever. Ottawa will be our Rubicon. There can be no re-crossing. Those who refuse to accept the Ottawa Agreements and wear sheets of repentance will be permitted to sit with Samuel and [Geoffrey] Mander [Liberal MP for Wolverhampton East] in the seats of the Mighty. Those Liberals who accept the Ottawa Agreements to preserve National unity will be cut off root and branch from the Liberal Party. We shall be subjected to increasing difficulties in our constituencies. We shall be freely attacked by the Samuel Liberals and the Liberal machine; at Bye-elections we shall be expected to support Conservative candidates against Free Trade Liberals, and ultimately we shall be opposed by Free Trade Liberal candidates in our own constituencies. If we still

parade the name of Liberal it will really only be by false pretences, because it must be clear to everyone that there is no future for us but ultimate absorption in the Conservative Party ... If my forecast is correct, and I don't think it exaggerated, we shall perish miserably between the cross fires of Conservatives and Liberals, a nuisance for the former and a target for the latter.

As in his conversation with Morris-Jones, Shakespeare went on to outline the conditions upon which Liberal Nationals should insist in return for continuing to co-operate with the government. 'Unless we do this, we shall hand ourselves over gagged and bound to the Conservative Party.'[64] These conditions included assurances about the inclusion of Liberal measures in the government's legislative programme; the allocation of half or two-thirds of the posts that would be vacated by the Samuelites; a definite understanding regarding honours and other appointments; a guarantee that Conservatives would not oppose Liberal National candidates at the next general election; and a promise, important if the group were to have any chance of growth, that the selection of Liberal National candidates would be considered at future by-elections.

On the same day that Shakespeare wrote to Simon, Hore-Belisha communicated with Neville Chamberlain. His mood was more up-beat, but there were also striking similarities in his phraseology. The announcement of the Samuelite resignations, he suggested, should be accompanied by a statement that the government would now go forward with 'a fresh enthusiasm and clear purpose'. The Liberal Nationals were now 'among the wolves'. 'We shall have to fight and I think take the offensive for the soul of Liberalism, maintaining that we are in the Rosebery tradition.' The continuation of the National Government depended upon the Liberal Nationals' co-operation, which should not be taken for granted, and it was important that they should be 'fairly treated'. Otherwise, as Shakespeare had also argued, it would be like 'being asked unprotected to cross a Rubicon'.[65]

Simon was shrewd enough to recognise that the Liberal Nationals' bargaining position was nothing like as weak as calculations based on simple parliamentary arithmetic might suggest. Indeed, there were good grounds for thinking that it would be enhanced by the departure of the Samuelites, since such a development would leave the Liberal Nationals as the only real guarantee that the existing National Government would not degenerate into a purely Conservative one. This was a development which the two leading figures in the government, MacDonald and Baldwin, for their differing reasons were determined to resist – MacDonald because it would render his own position untenable; and Baldwin because of the internal dynamics of the Tory party.

Apprehensive Liberal Nationals met, in the absence of both Simon and Runciman, on 26 September at Shakespeare's house in Sloane Street. The meeting was supposed to be secret, but the press soon got wind of what was afoot. While the majority favoured continuing support for the National Government, dissatisfaction was expressed at the small number of progressive measures on the legislative agenda and members called for a clear deal with the Tories regarding electoral arrangements and the distribution of offices and honours. They were told that Simon and Runciman would 'fight to keep up the prestige and influence of our group'.[66] The following day Shakespeare found himself summoned to see the Prime Minister. After half an hour, during which he told MacDonald of the great concern within the Liberal National group at 'having to sever their connections of a life time', Shakespeare judged that 'we are now in a position to drive any bargain we want'.[67] The Liberal National chief whip probably over-estimated his own influence and certainly failed to recognise the extent to which the interests of MacDonald and Baldwin coincided with his own. At all events, Shakespeare received a 'severe reprimand' from Simon for overplaying his hand.[68]

When the cabinet met on 28 September the free trade ministers duly tendered their resignations. Simon gave the sort of duplicitous performance which his critics held to be his stock-in-trade, passing a scribbled note of pained regret to Samuel during the course of the meeting. The Lord Chancellor, Lord Sankey, made a record of Simon's contribution to the discussion. 'We are all acting under a great sense of responsibility and longing to do our duty', he recorded the Foreign Secretary as saying. The free traders' withdrawal 'will make a great depreciation of British influence'.[69] But a private letter to Lady Hilton Young probably came nearer to expressing Simon's true feelings: 'Samuel has chosen an amazing moment to go, for the whole world is now rocking and in the middle of an earthquake it will not be much good to howl "Ottawa"'.[70] Snowden was among those who doubted Simon's sincerity. As he later recalled: 'That same evening the Simonites had a dinner. Whether it had been arranged to celebrate the resignation of the Liberal Ministers and the transformation of the National Government into a Tory Government I do not know, but it was a strange coincidence that it should be held that evening.'[71]

In the meantime, Simon had met Baldwin on 27 September and he followed up his interview with a letter the following day. His main concern was with 'the prospective electoral position of the 35 Liberal Nationals who have taken the same line as Runciman and myself, and who represent a large body of Liberal opinion'. With the resignation of Samuel and his followers, 'the position of these friends of mine in their constituencies will be much more difficult and they will very soon be exposed to every sort of attack and pressure from the organisations who approve Samuel's démarche'. Simon suggested that the Commons division on the second reading of the bill implementing the Ottawa Agreements should be regarded as a litmus-test of loyalty. He hoped that Baldwin would agree that those Liberal Nationals who supported the government on this occasion could be assured that no Conservative candidates would be fielded against them at the next general election.[72] While Baldwin pondered these proposals, the Liberal National group at least found cause for satisfaction when the details were announced of the governmental reshuffle following Samuel's resignation. The appointment of Godfrey Collins, MP for Greenock, to succeed Sinclair at the Scottish Office meant that there were now three Liberal Nationals in the cabinet, and several other members of the group, including Leslie Hore-Belisha, who became Financial Secretary to the Treasury, and Leslie Burgin, secured promotion within the junior ministerial ranks. Liberal Nationals seemed well pleased with what Simon had secured. Shakespeare wrote to thank him for his 'terrific fight for the Group', while Runciman was 'amazed' at his 'astuteness in negotiation. He had never seen anything like it.'[73] Equally revealing were reports that rank and file Tories and the Conservative chief whip, David Margesson, were dismayed at the allocation of government jobs that had given the Liberal Nationals a disproportionate influence within the administration.[74] From the political sidelines, Lloyd George observed that the Tories would be 'more furious with this new Govt. than with the last. Many of them were looking for promotion when the Samuelites took flight from the hive ... Amery Winterton Page Croft Winston etc etc will be howling with rage.'[75]

Baldwin now sent Simon a 'letter of reassurance' about the position of sitting Liberal National MPs and, under further prompting, gave public voice to this in a speech at Blackpool on 7 October. His statement that those who supported the Ottawa Bill 'right through' should not suffer was, he told Simon, received with enthusiastic cheers. Though Baldwin had to insist upon the independence of local Conservative constituency parties to do as they saw fit, he felt 'entitled to assume that support will be forthcoming for those Liberal Members of Parliament who are prepared to give consistent support to the Government'.[76] Significantly, Simon had asked Baldwin to make no mention of a pact in his Blackpool speech, but simply to make a 'generous gesture'. At the same time, he remained exceptionally cautious about anything that stressed Liberal National independence 'lest we vex the Tories'.[77] He was even unenthusiastic about the publication of a monthly newsletter, an idea energetically supported by Hutchison, out of fear that it might be interpreted by the Conservatives as unnecessarily partisan. If it had to go ahead, then he suggested to Hutchison that it might be more appropriate to have a photograph of Prime Minister MacDonald rather than himself on the front cover of the first issue.[78]

For all that, with the help of MacDonald and Baldwin, the Liberal Nationals had taken a significant step towards separation from the historic Liberal party, while signalling their own institutional independence. The attitude of the government's two senior figures merits a further word of explanation. The position of the Prime Minister is readily understood. Separated from, and then expelled by, the Labour party which he had done so much to bring into existence and turn into a party of government, MacDonald had entered a political cul-de-sac as head of the National Government. His position was almost wholly dependent upon the continuing participation of non-Conservative elements within it. The departure of the Samuelites thus came as a considerable blow to him. 'The new Government', he wrote to the King, 'will also be, to all intents and purposes, a single-party administration, and I think Your Majesty will find that a Prime Minister who does not belong to the Party in power will become more and more an anomaly.'[79] But at least the strengthened Liberal National contingent provided the beleaguered premier with some comfort about the future.

Baldwin's attitude was more complex and, at the same time, less personal. For most of the 1920s, he, along with most thoughtful Tories, had been concerned that the arrival of a working-class political party had the potential, in the context of a greatly enlarged working-class electorate, to confine the Conservatives to permanent opposition. A Conservative party 'on the old lines' would 'have no future in the life of this country'.[80] Only a transformed party had a chance of survival. This meant attracting all those bodies opposed to socialism and reckless change – in practice, winning over a substantial part of the Liberal vote. This would come not just from a negative policy of anti-socialism but through a positive appeal based on constructive, moderate reform. Such thinking placed Lloyd George and all he stood for in the later 1920s beyond the political pale. But Baldwin sought to present himself as the true heir of the Asquithian mantle.[81] It was a perception which many shared. According to H.A.L. Fisher, Baldwin was 'not a Conservative but a Liberal with a heresy about protection'. The leader writer on the *Manchester Guardian* was of a similar opinion. The Conservative leader was turning his party into 'something like the Liberals of our youth'.[82] Baldwin was not an extreme Conservative, confirmed one Liberal National MP at the time of the Samuelite resignations, 'but in many ways is philosophically Liberal-minded'.[83]

The centrist, conciliatory brand of Toryism to which Baldwin aspired had almost been destroyed by the concerted campaigns of his right-wing critics during the period of the Labour government of 1929–31, which had come near to costing him the party leadership. Now, participation in a National Government enabled him to readjust the balance and outflank his opponents, giving the Conservatives 'a national rather than a party outlook'.[84] With their massive parliamentary strength the Conservative majority within that government had no numerical need of the 35 votes which the Liberal Nationals could muster to put their measures on to the statute book. But these Liberal Nationals helped Baldwin consolidate the sort of Conservatism in which he believed, steering the party according to his own instincts and away from the inclinations of the Tory right wing. Liberal National influence within the National Government should largely be measured in these terms rather than that of forcing the majority Conservatives into paths they would not otherwise have followed. That said, a 'Liberal' influence was sometimes evident in the actions of non-Conservative ministers in those departmental matters which did not normally come before the full cabinet and a plausible case can be made for the success of Walter Runciman in moderating the full-blown Tory policy on tariffs.[85] Progressive Conservatives had appreciated from the outset of the National Government the potential advantages of a Liberal presence in their midst. 'I think you will agree', wrote Samuel Hoare, the Secretary of State for India – who once described himself as 'a liberal amongst conservatives and a conservative amongst liberals'[86] – in January 1932, 'that from an Indian point of view, we are on much stronger ground with the Samuel Liberals in the Cabinet.'[87] After the departure of the Samuelites the value of the Simonites – only marginally less 'liberal' on the Indian issue – correspondingly increased. With one eye always on his critics on the right,

Baldwin once commented of his block of Liberal supporters, 'they are my body guard'.[88]

In the long term, Baldwin's plans did not necessarily involve maintaining the separate identity of the Liberal National group. A fused 'National party' might be the best means of permanently blocking a Labour recovery. As he explained to Thomas Jones, 'We shall put the tariff through and if it does well it will drop out of party politics very much like free trade did. Then leave suitable time to change the title of our Party to National, as there will be little which really divides us from the bulk of the Liberals.'[89] But such a realignment could be safely left to the future. Little would be gained by forcing the issue at the present time. Baldwin's eventual successor, Neville Chamberlain, who also looked forward to a future 'National Party' which would enable him to 'get rid of that odious title of Conservative which has kept so many from joining us in the past', developed a similar line of thought.[90] As he wrote to a family member in February 1932:

> Nor need you sympathise with me on not having a Conservative Government, since I have got just as much out of the present composite team as I wanted; and if I had owed my support to an extreme right-wing, I might have found them much more difficult to control.[91]

In short, the National Government, by laying a firm claim to the centre ground of British politics, represented for Baldwin and Chamberlain the best means of excluding both the Labour party and the Conservative die-hards from power. For the time being the Liberal National group could rest assured of their continuing political relevance.

By contrast, the position of Samuel's independent Liberals was now anomalous in the extreme. Though they had left the administration, they continued for the time being to sit on the government benches. Samuel was worried that, in crossing the floor of the House of Commons, he might lose some more of his supporters. As he later explained, 'If he had gone over when the Liberal Ministers resigned on Ottawa, the group would have been seriously split and all the enemies of the Liberal Party would have declared that he was leading it to final destruction.'[92] Furthermore, the Samuelites still seemed to assume that the Liberal National defections would not be permanent. Morris-Jones found them in late November 1932 making 'desperate efforts to win over Simonites'.[93] Speaking in Paisley a year later, Samuel once again declared that it was his aim to 'gather together all Liberals'. As has been seen, however, this was not likely to happen, not least because the Liberal National leadership did not wish it to. By the autumn of 1933, bombarded with complaints from Liberal organisations up and down the country, Samuel at last conceded that his own supporters could not continue to occupy places on the government benches. If they did so any longer, 'the party would fade away'.[94] But when the move did take place, the mainstream party suffered further damage, much as Samuel had feared. Joseph Leckie (Walsall), William McKeag (Durham), Robert Bernays (Bristol North) and J.P. Maclay (Paisley) all stayed on the government side of the House. Of these, Leckie had already aligned himself with the Liberal Nationals, McKeag did so formally in June 1934, Bernays' defection was delayed until 1936, until which time he continued to sit as an 'Independent' Liberal, while only Maclay contrived to remain a Samuelite.

Even now the Samuelites had some difficulty in differentiating themselves from the government, and therefore from the Liberal Nationals, on issues other than free trade, despite the efforts of Sinclair and others to do so. The National Government had taken over the traditional Liberal rallying cries of retrenchment and sound finance, without appearing unduly reactionary or illiberal. 'So long as Baldwin presses so far to the middle and is at war with his Die-hards', judged Sir William Sutherland, Lloyd George's former press secretary, 'it is not clear where Samuel is going to crash in with a separate identity and policy.'[95] After the Samuelites' first session on the opposition benches, *The Times*, which took a consistently supportive line towards the Liberal Nationals, offered a damning assessment. The independent Liberals, it claimed, belonged to an age that had passed. 'The ideas of 1906 have no bearing upon the conditions of 1933.' Their attempts to distance themselves from the government had left 'an astonished House of Commons with the impression that all they wanted was a little more land settlement, a few more houses and rather more talk about peace'.[96] Ironically, even the issue which had occasioned their resignations no longer seemed wholly compelling, with one leading Samuelite already declaring that 'the possibility of a world system of complete free trade has gone and probably will never return'.[97] Lord Lothian was one who managed to stay within the ranks of orthodox Liberalism, while at the same time accepting much of the Liberal National critique – that many of the Liberal party's historic objectives had been secured and that those which remained had been taken up by the National Government or at least by its progressive Conservative wing.[98] Not, in fact, until after the General Election of 1935 and the National Government's apparent renunciation of a League-based foreign policy at the time of the Hoare-Laval crisis would Liberals find much scope for carving out a distinctive identity.

Yet hindsight makes it possible to assert that the separation of the two Liberal groups was in practice now complete. In the years ahead there would be much talk of reunion and there remained those unwilling to accept the finality of the break. The *Liberal Year Book* failed to separate the biographies of members of the two factions before 1936. The two groups were allowed to maintain membership of the National Liberal Club without distinction. Anomalously, Runciman was re-elected in March 1934 as a Liberal Council vice-president. But, while individuals continued from time to time to move from one group to the other, the two maintained their separate existence. Many Liberals, particularly activists, now appreciated the distinction. Meetings of the Yorkshire Liberal Federation well illustrated the change. At that body's AGM in July 1932 one delegate moved the deletion of John Simon's name from the list of Federation vice-presidents. 'This proposal was not seconded and the vice-presidents were re-elected en bloc.' Eighteen months later it was a different picture. Now, when it was proposed that Simon should be included in the list of vice-presidents, 'only six voted in favour, an overwhelming majority voted against'.[99] For the Liberal party, however, the Liberal National defection amounted to far more than the loss of numerical strength in the House of Commons. If this had been all that was involved, the opportunity would have existed to disown the sitting member and replace him with a party loyalist at the earliest electoral opportunity. Instead, it meant in many cases the effective elimination of independent Liberalism as a viable political force from locations where a considerable Liberal tradition persisted. An institutional infrastructure was damaged or even destroyed, while an existing pattern of voting was lost.

By the late 1920s, of course, the condition of the Liberal party in many parts of the country was already parlous. A report drawn up for the Manchester Liberal Federation in January 1927 on the state of the party's organisation in the various wards of what had once been a citadel of classic free-trade Liberalism made depressing reading:

Cheetham – organization very poor
Levenshulme – local organisation fair
Longsight – organisation not very good
All Saint's – organisation poor

Beswick – local organisation very poor
St George's – organisation poor.¹⁰⁰

In associations where membership and attendance were already in steep decline, it only needed the allegiance of a small number of key individuals to determine the character of the local constituency party. Often loyalty to a sitting MP or candidate would be enough to effect this process, especially when such figures tended vigorously to insist upon their continuing 'Liberalism' after their defection to the Liberal Nationals.

In St Ives in Cornwall the Liberal organisation was almost moribund by the early 1930s. Financial subvention from the sitting member made it relatively easy for Walter Runciman to determine the outlook of his local association. Able also to rely on a strong personal following among his electorate, Runciman was in a position to transform the whole aspect of Liberalism in his constituency, recently described as 'a slow, mild, timid thing'.¹⁰¹ In Huddersfield the local Liberal party had been shocked to read in the press of Mabane's presence at Hore-Belisha's dinner for Liberal National members on 2 November 1931. The MP was obliged to attend a special meeting of the Huddersfield Association's executive committee. Here he sought refuge in obfuscation, reading out the text of a letter that he proposed to send to both Samuel and Simon. Its tone sought to blur the distinction between the two Liberal groups, to imply that complete reunion was only a matter of time and, indeed, to suggest that Mabane himself was well placed to bring this about. He admitted that his own thinking over the past 12 months had moved in the direction of the Simonite position but, while he was willing to work with the Liberal National MPs, it must be understood that he would not do so if this were to involve his severance from the rest of the party. The Huddersfield Liberal Association found Mabane's explanation of his conduct sufficiently convincing to endorse the terms of his proposed letter to Samuel and Simon.¹⁰² Mabane subsequently voted against the second reading of the Ottawa Agreements Bill on 27 October 1932, but then used the failure of Samuel and his colleagues immediately to go into opposition to justify distancing himself from the mainstream Liberal party. When, in November 1933, the Samuelites did finally cross the floor of the House of Commons, the Huddersfield MP remained firmly ensconced on the government benches. His action caused disquiet within the local party, but he comfortably won a vote of confidence at the association's AGM in March 1934.¹⁰³ Crucially, Mabane was successful in retaining the support of the association chairman, J.D. Eaton Smith, and of the Liberal party's local agent, Stanley Hickman.

At his adoption meeting in Montgomeryshire in October 1931, Clement Davies had insisted that, when he was satisfied that the country's financial emergency was over, he would no longer support the government. But whatever happened, he would be 'as always a Liberal through and through'. He was, he stressed, a free trader but, if the government said that tariffs were needed to save the country, he would vote with the government. Challenged as to whether he was a member of the Simonite group, his answer was 'both yes and no'. He belonged to a group of which Simon had become the most prominent member, but which he preferred to call the 'Hutchison Group'.[104] By the time of the Montgomeryshire Association's AGM the following February there was no further talk of the member abandoning his support for the government. But Davies was obliged to respond to further questions on the matter of tariffs. He 'very clearly replied, explaining the position and the meeting seemed fully satisfied with, and favourable to, the steps taken, and fully appreciated the very difficult situation in which he is now placed'.[105] Three years later the association's executive committee recorded their 'continued confidence' in the MP as 'a convinced Liberal'.[106] In this way the Montgomeryshire Liberal Association became in practice, if not in name (or even formal affiliation), the Montgomeryshire Liberal National Association. With Davies himself becoming by far the largest subscriber to the local party's funds and with meetings and general political activity declining after an uncontested election in 1931, it was relatively easy for the sitting member to determine the orientation of his local party.[107] A similar process occurred in Luton, represented by the Liberal National, Leslie Burgin. Looking back many years later, Sir Herbert Janes, a local Liberal activist and personal friend of Burgin, described what had happened with commendable simplicity. 'It was more or less accidental', he explained, 'that Luton is a National Liberal constituency.' 'It was due to our member, the late Dr Leslie Burgin, who was a National Liberal.'[108] The important point is that in Huddersfield, Montgomeryshire, Luton and most other Liberal National constituencies, the mainstream Liberal party virtually disappeared as an organised movement for the rest of the decade.

Even more significantly, the experience of Liberal National and Liberal constituencies was often similar. In Shakespeare's seat of Norwich Liberals and Conservatives joined forces in municipal politics in 1932 in a single anti-socialist party. Though quickly regaining their separate identities, the two parties maintained their electoral alliance for the rest of the decade.[109] Yet in Manchester, 'the spiritual home of radicalism and Free Trade', where, notwithstanding repeated reports of 'Simonite activities', the Samuelite party retained control, events developed in a very similar way. A meeting of Liberal councillors in July 1933 was informed that, although no formal pact existed, 'owing to the difficulty of securing candidates, an understanding had been arrived at that Conservative Candidates would not oppose Liberal Candidates and vice versa'.[110] The scope for confusion among Liberal voters was evidently considerable.

Perhaps not surprisingly, the Samuelite party was extremely reluctant to challenge Liberal National MPs and candidates in their constituencies. The experience of the East Fife by-election in February 1933 did little to encourage a change of heart. One problem was the official policy of the National Liberal Federation spelt out at the time of the North Cornwall by-election the previous July:

> It was earnestly to be hoped that all sections of the party would follow the unwritten but well-recognised understanding that the candidate chosen by a democratically constituted Liberal Association at a meeting properly convened for the purpose is the recognised Liberal candidate and ought therefore to be free from attack by any Liberal organisation.[111]

As in most instances in seats now held by Liberal National MPs the local associations still purported to be *Liberal* organisations, maintaining their affiliations to the National Liberal Federation, the effect of this policy was to allow what had become in practice Liberal National associations to go about their business unhindered. Even when the question was posed explicitly, the answer was the same. What would be the attitude, asked a member of the Manchester Liberal Federation's executive committee in April 1933, if one of the Manchester constituencies adopted a Liberal National candidate. 'The chairman replied that ... the policy of the Manchester Liberal Federation would be adhered to, and full and unqualified support would be given to any constitutionally adopted Liberal candidate.'[112]

When, therefore, the death of Duncan Millar, the Liberal National Member for East Fife, in December 1932 created a parliamentary vacancy, the local association went ahead and selected the Simonite, James Henderson Stewart, to fight the seat in the resulting by-election. Yet many

Liberals sensed a real opportunity to reclaim the initiative in Liberal politics, not least because this was the seat represented for 32 years by Herbert Asquith. Efforts were even made to persuade Asquith's formidable daughter, Violet Bonham Carter, to contest the by-election herself.[113] In the event, it was the *News Chronicle* journalist, David Keir, who rose to the challenge. Keir was not supported by Liberal headquarters, but he received the backing of such figures as the former Labour Chancellor, Lord Snowden, Ramsay Muir and Lloyd George. According to the last named, Keir's

> spontaneous enterprise, stimulated and inspired by a single-minded desire to revive the struggle for Liberal ideals, has already put heart into a distracted and perplexed Liberalism throughout the country. Liberals everywhere have been waiting for such a move. They have been depressed by our apparent acquiescence in the maintenance in power of a Government which has reversed every principle of steady progress for which Liberals stand.[114]

Asquith's defeat in 1918 had shown that East Fife was no longer the Liberal stronghold it had once been. Nonetheless, the party had emerged victorious from the General Elections of 1922, 1923 and 1929. The 1933 campaign therefore offered revealing insights into the now limited appeal of independent Liberalism. Keir concentrated upon his opposition to tariffs, while Henderson Stewart stressed the continuing need to maintain national unity which had brought the country through the most acute stages of the economic crisis and which was still needed to face the tasks ahead. *The Times* warned that the views of East Fife had changed on the question of free trade and that its farmers were unlikely to pay much heed to the 'doctrine of free imports, however capably it may be expressed'.[115] Yet few expected an outcome as decisive as that which occurred. Henderson Stewart retained the seat with a majority of over 9,000. Keir, who lost his deposit, came in fourth behind Labour and the candidate of the so-called Agricultural party.

Observers drew contrasting conclusions. Lord Stanley of Alderley, the president of the Lancashire, Cheshire and North-Western Liberal Federation, who, defying the official party line, had taken a prominent part in Keir's campaign, insisted that 'neither one defeat nor twenty will deter us from fighting for what we believe to be true Liberalism'. The important thing was 'to fight with every weapon at our disposal the insidious cancer of

Simony which is eating into the very vitals of Liberalism'.[116] The *Liberal Magazine* seemed to voice the same refrain, rejoicing with 'downright delight in the spectacle of a young Free Trader marching out to fight the combined hosts of Tories and Simonites'. It was 'a Charge of the Light Brigade; and Mr David Keir ... and his young comrades have covered themselves with glory'. But the journal went on to admit – perhaps for the first time – that there was more to the Liberal National position than the personal views of a group of MPs. Most Liberals in East Fife, it conceded, genuinely believed that supporting the National Government was the best option, and the same was true in 'a score or two of constituencies':

> Nothing is gained by hiding the fact under such words as 'machine' and 'caucus' ... It is important to face the fact that in these constituencies what we have to deal with is a genuine state of opinion in the minds of rank and file electors.[117]

In fact, the worst forebodings of the party leadership had been confirmed. Leaving aside Keir's humiliation, the by-election had drawn attention not only to the split between Simonites and Samuelites, but also to the divisions within the ranks of the latter. 'Time will show whether the Gods will destroy the Liberal Party', bemoaned Archibald Sinclair, 'but they have certainly driven it mad!'[118] This would be the last formal contest between the two wings of British Liberalism until the General Election of 1935.

Rather more frequent were situations in which Liberal Nationals found themselves supporting Conservative candidates in by-elections in which a Samuelite Liberal was also in the field. This caused considerable uneasiness among those who still found it difficult to accept that the breach between the two Liberal groups was now beyond repair. But the logic of the case was compelling. Adherence to the National Government inevitably meant supporting those candidates who backed it and opposing those who did not. The Liberal National executive met in February 1933 to discuss the situation that had arisen in the forthcoming by-election in Ashford in Kent. The situation was particularly delicate since the Liberal candidate had stood as a Liberal National at the General Election less than two years earlier. But the executive decided unanimously that 'we can't pick and choose'. The full parliamentary group gathered later in the day and were 'uneasy over it', but eventually agreed that individual members should be free to campaign for the Tory candidate if they so wished.[119] Simon himself had no qualms about acting in this way and was a frequent speaker on Conservative platforms. In response, the Samuelite party could do little more than issue pious, but ultimately futile, resolutions of protest. That moved by John Day, Liberal candidate for Tavistock, at the executive committee of the National Liberal Federation in February 1934 was typical:

> this Committee, representing organised Liberalism in all parts of the country, protests against the action of those 'Liberal National' members who, while still calling themselves Liberals, freely accept invitations from Conservative party associations to address meetings, organised and paid for by the Conservative party in support of official Conservative party candidates, and openly oppose and attack Liberal candidates in the constituencies. The Committee condemns action on the part of any claiming adherence to Liberalism.[120]

* * *

With the final departure of the Samuelite Liberals the National Government took on the essential form which it would retain, albeit under changing Prime Ministers, until its demise in May 1940. For many years this government was the victim of a hostile, left-leaning, historiographical consensus. 'The history of the National government', wrote C.L. Mowat in his standard work on the inter-war period published in 1955, 'was one long diminuendo. From its triumph in 1931 it shambled its unimaginative way to its fall in 1940 ...'[121] Part of its problem, critics argued, was that it was not really a National Government at all. 'A Government controlled by so overwhelming a majority of a single party', insisted Ramsay Muir, 'could not be anything but a party Government.'[122] By the latter stages of the Second World War it served a politically motivated purpose to attribute the government's seemingly disastrous failures specifically to the Conservative party. The National Government's title was presented as no more than a sham, 'a mere façade behind which the Conservatives governed Britain for the decade before the Second World War'.[123] 'Why not trust the Tories?' asked Aneurin Bevan in 1944, with his thoughts fixed on a post-war general election. The answer was simple. As the 1930s had shown, with the approach of peace the Conservative party would once more 'lie, deceive, cajole and buy time so as ... to snatch a reprieve for wealth and privilege'.[124] Nor has this perception of unqualified Conservative rule yet been entirely erased. David Marquand, in his definitive biography of Ramsay MacDonald, argues that until the Samuelite resignations the government had been a genuine coalition, 'albeit a hopelessly unbalanced one'. With their departure, however, it became 'a Conservative Government which happened to have a non-Conservative at its head and a number of other non-Conservatives attached to it'.[125] Michael Bentley even seems ready to delete the Liberal Nationals from the historical record. The loss of the free traders, he insists, 'left the Tory presence undiluted apart from persistent "National Labour" individuals such as J.H. Thomas ... and Lord Sankey'.[126]

The debate on the performance of the National Government lies largely outside the scope of the present discussion. But it is important to stress that the idea that this was a Conservative administration masquerading under false pretences is no longer tenable. The National Government was a reality and, in most respects, remained so throughout the 1930s. Philip Williamson makes the point well:

> The National government is often treated as a Conservative government in disguise, or even without disguise. It was not considered to be so by Churchill and the diehards, by Amery and 'whole-hog' protectionists, and by anti-statists and isolationists, all of whom thought that Conservatism had been compromised. Nor, on the other hand, was it considered to be so by the many Conservative MPs who owed their election to local pacts with Liberals and to non-Conservative votes. Nor was it by Baldwin.[127]

At its heart the National Government did not operate in the manner of a normal party administration. At least until the middle of the decade, and arguably beyond, there existed an informal group of ministers from the three component parts of the government – Baldwin and Chamberlain for the Conservatives, MacDonald and Thomas for the National Labour group and Simon and Runciman for the Liberal Nationals – operating as 'a team of colleagues rather than a meeting of party representatives'.[128] Indeed, early in 1935 the Prime Minister, acting on Chamberlain's prompting, formalised the meetings of the 'Big Six' by announcing the creation of a new General Purposes Committee of the Cabinet whose function would be to 'discuss matters which did not belong only to one Government Department'.[129] At its first meeting the committee decided to look into the question of the financing of public works schemes. From time to time MacDonald, prone at this stage of his life to bouts of depression, voiced gloomy thoughts about being overwhelmed by the Tories. 'Party Conservative pressure upon Government policy is becoming more insistent', he warned his National

Labour colleague Lord Sankey in July 1934. 'Pressure will be brought to bear upon me ... to produce a Cabinet with an adjusted balance.' It was, he believed, a difficult situation for 'those of us who do not mean to be absorbed in the Conservative Party'.[130] Yet on the whole the evidence suggests that the Conservative leadership did not seek to abuse their party's numerical superiority. Non-Conservative ministers maintained a disproportionate presence within the government's ranks throughout its existence. Indeed, when on an earlier occasion the Prime Minister had protested against 'right-wing Tories always getting their way and having no consideration for us National Labour and Liberals', he had received unexpected support from several Conservative ministers, including Baldwin himself.[131]

Simon, who regarded the Cabinet as 'the most united I have every known',[132] believed that the country might be witnessing a fundamental transformation of its political culture. It was not only 'in the composition and work of the Cabinet that party distinctions are being obliterated', he observed:

> the same thing is happening in the mind and attitude of the ordinary citizen. Party war-cries are being forgotten. Neither the free trader nor the protectionist thinks that he has a simple formula to bring back prosperity. Modern problems are at once so complicated and so novel that it has become absolutely necessary to cooperate together instead of to fight one another. This is the most significant change of all and, unless I am greatly mistaken (or unless the narrower type of Conservative stupidity prevents it), there will emerge a new kind of politics in this country extraordinarily different from that of 1906 or 1910.[133]

Certainly, the possibility of some form of political realignment occurring in the 1930s needs to be taken more seriously than has usually been the case. Robert Bernays, separated from the Samuelite Liberals but not yet committed to their Simonite critics, felt that party politics were becoming increasingly unreal. 'Men are in their own particular party far more by tradition and accident than by real conviction' and divisions between parties no longer corresponded with the key divides in national politics.[134] At the heart of any possible redrawing of party boundaries lay the Liberal party – or at least the Liberal vote. The distinction was a significant one. What was important, as Bernays recognised, was not Liberal votes in the House of Commons, but Liberalism's voting power in the country. The Conservatives had 'realized that we can keep several millions from voting Labour'.[135] From the socialist left, the young Aneurin Bevan saw politics as 'a race between the Conservatives shedding their right wing and the Labour party shedding their left in order to get the Liberal vote'.[136] Indeed, the ultimate destination of the five million electors who had voted Liberal in 1929 remained at the strategic heart of party politics throughout the 1930s. The previous decade had shown that, except in the sort of exceptional circumstances contrived in 1931, Liberals still had the capacity to render uncertain the outcome of any general election, even if they were no longer in a position to form a government themselves.

For some observers, formalising the coalition of 1931 offered the obvious answer. As time went on, noted Neville Chamberlain, the differences between the 'constituent parts of the Alliance become less visible'. Old problems 'which used to divide us' were passing away, to be replaced by new ones where 'we tend to think alike' or 'if we differ, the difference is not on party lines'.[137] In the summer of 1934 the Tory chairman, Lord Stonehaven, reported that around 100 Conservative MPs had signed a memorial in favour of fusing the 'National' parties.[138] Nor were all Liberal Nationals adamantly opposed to such a prospect. Writing at the time of the Samuelite resignations, Edgar Granville considered the possible creation of a 'Centre or National Party' to fight the next general election, but judged that this development was as 'yet a long way off'.[139] Hore-Belisha seems to have discussed the idea with both Baldwin and Chamberlain in terms of a rather shorter time-scale. 'If the opportunity were missed, the central Liberal vote in the country might be swayed back towards the left.'[140] This sort of realignment might then have prompted a breakaway on the political right, leading to the foundation of a 'new Conservative Party which is true to Conservative principles'.[141] In the event, of course, the majority of Liberal Nationals were determined to cling to their autonomy and fusion between Conservatives and Liberal Nationals would be long delayed, a victim also perhaps of the intrusion in 1939 of world war into the domestic political arena and its existing pattern of development.

For the time being the Liberal Nationals sought to consolidate their position as an independent component of the National Government. In April 1933 the decision was taken to set up a series of area organisations to act as liaisons between the Liberal National Council and the various regions of the country. The focus of these bodies would be propaganda and platform work and they would be available for consultation outside constituencies held by Liberal National MPs.[142] By October there were signs that the Liberal

Nationals were preparing to take part in the forthcoming elections to the London County Council.[143] In the meantime publication had begun of a monthly newsheet, *Liberal National View*, selling at 3d. per copy. The first issue contained a message from the Prime Minister and articles by Simon, Hore-Belisha and the Tory minister, Walter Elliot. By the end of the year Hore-Belisha was urging the establishment of a nation-wide organisation to champion the Liberal National point of view. Presiding over a meeting of the newly constituted area committees, Simon called for an organisation to be set up in every 'suitable' constituency.[144] To this end, Dr Joseph Hunter, MP for Dumfriesshire and at one time Lloyd George's Director of Liberal Campaigns, was appointed the Liberal Nationals' first national organiser in June 1934. In response, orthodox Liberals could do little more than ridicule their rivals' pretensions and emphasise every indication of tension in the Liberal National-Conservative partnership. It was the Liberal party, stressed the *Liberal Magazine*, which could boast more than 500 organised constituency associations of which 'at least 400' were 'in full active work'. This was a wildly optimistic gloss on the reality of a crumbling party infrastructure. But there was perhaps more truth in the Liberal claim that what the Liberal Nationals were really seeking to do was to protect themselves from the Conservative party – 'notoriously disloyal to annexes and honorary associates'. The Conservatives 'will always eat you up if you don't look out'.[145]

Amid the competing claims and propaganda of the two Liberal factions, there was one area in which the Liberal Nationals appeared to enjoy a clear advantage and that was the all-important factor of money. The Liberal Nationals were well financed in the early 1930s, enjoying the support of a number of wealthy benefactors including the motor manufacturer, Lord Nuffield, who contributed as much as £10,000 to the group's election fund in 1931. With a residue of £3,500 remaining in the coffers and income continuing to flow in after the election, Hutchison was confident that the Liberal Nationals' organisation would remain viable for at least the duration of the parliament. Some confusion surrounds the fate of funds donated by Nuffield via Hore-Belisha rather than directly to the group's headquarters, but the evidence suggests that shortage of money was not a factor in the mounting of the General Election campaign in 1935.[146] By contrast, the Samuelite party faced a financial crisis. Revenue from the subscription list of the Liberal Central Association had fallen by 1931 to about £500 per annum. Party headquarters were in effect being maintained by Lloyd George and his ill-gotten Political Fund and, before falling out with Samuel over the holding of an election while Liberals remained in the National

Government, Lloyd George had promised a sum of £30,000 for the next campaign. When, however, that election was held in circumstances of which he disapproved, Lloyd George withdrew his offer and the election was fought with a hastily raised war-chest of just £17,000. Thereafter, the loss of Lloyd George's subvention had serious implications for the continuing viability of the mainstream party. The death of Lord Cowdray, a generous party benefactor, in October 1933 compounded the problem. Increasingly, even promising by-elections tended to go uncontested. From the whips' office, Harcourt Johnstone bemoaned the 'worry and strain of trying to carry on the organisation of a political party without knowing for two months in advance whether the inevitable liabilities can be met or not'. He doubted whether he had 'ever in these ten miserable, discouraging years ... been so sorely tempted to chuck the whole thing and be a free man again'.[147] It was difficult in such circumstances to see how the Liberal party would ever regain the capacity to act as a potential party of government.

Inside the ranks of the Liberal Nationals themselves, however, underlying tensions persisted. Simon's leadership never enjoyed unqualified support. The plaudits he received at the time of the governmental reconstruction in the autumn of 1932 were seldom repeated. Indeed, it was often argued that Simon did not protect the interests of his fellow Liberal Nationals with sufficient vigour and that he was overly sensitive about offending the leadership of the National Government. Morris-Jones noted Hutchison's opinion in June 1934 that the party would 'fizzle out if he does not back us better'.[148] Simon's relations with some of his senior Liberal National colleagues were never easy. He and Runciman had little in common except a shared allegiance in earlier days to Herbert Asquith and they continued to view one another with scarcely disguised suspicion. If Simon were to leave the government, judged Runciman at the end of 1934, 'not 10' of the party would follow him and Runciman would not be one of them.[149] His relations with Leslie Hore-Belisha were also strained. In fact, Simon's Parliamentary Private Secretary, Edgar Granville, blamed Hore-Belisha for much of the press campaign against Simon, conducted 'with a view to his own advancement to Cabinet', which was progressively undermining the Foreign Secretary's position.[150]

Simon's role as Foreign Secretary was, indeed, part of the problem. He took on the job at a difficult time when Britain had to begin confronting the problems of military aggression and political extremism in Europe and the Far East, as the settlement constructed at Versailles started inexorably to fall apart. Moreover, the pressure of work and in particular his repeated absences at League of Nations meetings in Geneva ultimately told upon his health and certainly left him little time to attend to the duties of leading an embryonic political party. Not until 1933 did his junior minister, Anthony Eden, begin to take on more of the Foreign Secretary's responsibilities in Geneva. Even then, in March 1933, having just visited Mussolini in Rome, Simon had to hurry back from Geneva to take part in a parliamentary debate on the government's White Paper on India, for which his own past experience as Chairman of the Statutory Commission on the subcontinent's future made his presence desirable. There was no escaping the difficulty that 'no one can be in two places at one time'.[151]

Had Simon's performance in high office been deemed a success, the irritation of his neglected parliamentary followers might well have been assuaged. But the conduct of British foreign policy in the early 1930s earned few bouquets. Disgruntled Tories soon found in the Foreign Secretary's performance confirmation of their underlying conviction that the government should be pointed in a more explicitly Conservative direction. On coming into office Simon inherited an on-going diplomatic problem of major proportions in the Japanese invasion of Manchuria, which had begun in mid-September 1931. Simon had few viable options open to him granted the state of British military unpreparedness and the far-away location of the crisis. Nevertheless, no single aspect of his foreign secretaryship did more to damage his reputation than his handling of events in the Far East. Harold Laski's judgement, written early in 1933, was widely shared. Simon had 'done more than any other man since 1918 to destroy the prestige of the League by his scarcely concealed support of Japan in her rake's progress of imperialistic crime'. By his attitude the Foreign Secretary had 'done more to destroy the position of his country as the leader in the effort for peace than any other man in our time'.[152] From such onslaughts Simon's reputation never fully recovered. Nor were his efforts at the World Disarmament Conference which opened in Geneva in February 1932 well received. His diplomatic style was judged to be devious. He preferred a 'bad compromise to a straight solution'.[153] Personal charm was not his strength. 'You have no idea', noted one observer, 'how suave and bland Sir John Simon offended every nation in Geneva, in the sweetest and most naïve and friendly manner.'[154] William Ormsby-Gore confirmed that 'it is his manner that kills him here'. 'I don't dislike or think ill of Simon except when he tries to be kind.'[155] Almost certainly, Simon would have been removed from his post earlier than he was but for a reluctance on the part of MacDonald and Baldwin to weaken the non-Conservative component of the government.

These personal failings were also felt by many of his Liberal National colleagues. Despite having made a clear choice as between the divided Liberal factions, Morris-Jones preferred Samuel to Simon on personal grounds. The former was 'always the same and much more dependable and approachable than Simon'.[156] Simon would 'never be a great leader. He is too suave and apologetic.'[157] The Liberal MP Percy Harris well captured his personal shortcomings. Simon was 'a strange mixture':

> I think it is safe to say there is no man with a better brain ... But he has not the gift of making friends easily: he is just a little bit too clever and creates an inferiority complex in people who come into contact with him. He wants to be friendly and would like to be popular, but he has in the course of his profession so developed the critical faculty that it does not come natural to him to unbend to the level of the ordinary man.[158]

* * *

Notwithstanding such internal problems, three years into the life of the National Government the Liberal Nationals had evidently made substantial progress. Their organisation had expanded steadily since the improvised arrangements of 1931. They were now clearly more than a parliamentary group – indeed, the use of the title 'party' seemed no longer inappropriate. Difficulties, of course, remained. Their relationship with the Conservatives was to many still a cause for concern. In particular, a change in the Tory leadership might leave them 'stranded like fish that the floods have left behind, opening and shutting [their] mouths, waiting for the death that will come mercifully soon at the hands of the electors'.[159] For the time being, however, the presence of Stanley Baldwin at the head of the Conservative party seemed to offer considerable reassurance. The loss of the Liberal Nationals from the government might necessitate the inclusion of the sort of right-wing Tories whom Baldwin was most concerned to exclude.

On the other hand, the contest between Liberals and Liberal Nationals to lay claim to be the authentic voice of the historic Liberal creed was not so much unresolved as so far unengaged. Yet the probable balance of advantage was by no means as clear-cut as spokesmen for the orthodox party liked to claim. As *The Times* put it:

No one can pretend to know how many of the 2,300,000 electors who voted Liberal in 1931 should be counted as belonging to each group, nor how many would vote for each group if the total Liberal vote were to rise to the 5,300,000 which it reached at the election of 1929. But there is no reason to believe that Sir John Simon and Mr Runciman would be such orphans of any electoral storm as the other Liberals pretend.[160]

The Liberal Nationals could at least argue that they could exert some influence over the direction of government policy, and it was not just committed Simonites who claimed to discern the impact of Liberal values on the politics of the time. With tariffs now decided upon, judged Robert Bernays, there was 'no great question' on which Liberals could disagree with the National Government.[161] Those who still clung to the Samuelite party might dream of one day returning to power. But more realistically they seemed to have been sucked into an irreversible process of decline. In such circumstances it was at least arguable that the best hope for the Liberal creed was for its practitioners to seek to influence others. Liberals, suggested Simon, should not 'deplore the spread of Liberalism which had now got into so many people's blood that it had almost ceased to be the Liberals' own particular strain'.[162] *The Times* made the same point more brutally. Was it 'really impossible for Liberalism to have any effective say in the character of national policy unless Liberal statesmen are identified with cantankerous opposition to any Government except a Liberal Government and unless any idea later than 1914 is branded as treachery to Liberal traditions?'[163] On the answer to such questions would depend the long-term prospects of the Liberal National party.

3

Years of Consolidation, 1935–39

By the mid-1930s two very different interpretations of the Liberal National party were already in place. According to the mainstream Liberals, the Liberal Nationals were not in fact a party at all. The whole concept was built on sand and the organisation consisted of little more than a collection of self-interested individuals who had betrayed the real party to which they owed their preferment and who were now attempting to deceive the British electorate as to their true credentials. This point of view was well expressed by the Liberal leader, Herbert Samuel, as early as October 1932:

> That group was supported by no organisation in the country. It had failed in its attempt to establish such an organisation. It was a plant without root, stuck precariously in the soil; it would not flourish; it would soon wilt and wither. He did not believe there was a single Liberal Association throughout the land outside their own constituencies which would adopt as a candidate for parliament anyone holding the views of Sir John Simon and his friends.[1]

By contrast, the Liberal Nationals themselves argued that they had as much claim as any other body to the mantle of Liberalism and that their party, supported now by a solid and permanent infrastructure, represented the majority of Liberal opinion in the country. They were performing valuable work inside, and influencing the direction taken by, the National Government, while their former Liberal colleagues had reduced themselves to a position of impotent futility on the opposition benches. When the Liberal National movement had first started, conceded Simon, most people thought it might be a mere flash in the pan. But at the end of four years the majority of Liberal members who were elected to the present House of Commons were staunch and declared supporters of the National Government, receiving the National Government's whip, voting in the National Government lobby, and contributing every ounce of their influence and weight to sustaining the National Government's cause. This had been accompanied by an ever-increasing indication of support of representative Liberals in all parts of the country.[2]

The events of 1935, and in particular the imminence of another general election, would go a long way to put these rival assessments to the test.

A general election was in the air for most of the year, particularly following the reorganisation of the government in June. That reorganisation itself provided a significant illustration of the administration's 'National' credentials. It was all but inevitable that this would be the occasion for Ramsay MacDonald to step down from the premiership. The Prime Minister's powers were in visible decline. His eyesight was failing, his ability to concentrate waning and his former oratorical skills in danger of descending into rambling incoherence. 'His speech seems to have ceased to connect with his brain', recorded one MP as early as November 1932. 'He meanders on and on and at the end of a long sentence it is impossible to grasp what the fellow is driving at.'[3] It was also inevitable that he should be succeeded by Stanley Baldwin, a step which could not fail to underline the government's overwhelmingly Conservative composition. Baldwin, noted Simon, would make 'an entirely acceptable chief – he represents our general outlook completely and there is nothing of the high and dry Tory about him'.[4] This may have been true, but the significance for the National Government of a nominal Conservative in 10 Downing Street could not be escaped.

It was also highly probable that John Simon would be the leading casualty of any resulting cabinet reshuffle. As one senior minister put it to Baldwin in February, 'I can't disguise from you that I don't think we can carry on with Ramsay as Prime Minister or Simon at the F.O.'[5] The Foreign Secretary was widely regarded as the weakest link in the higher ranks of the government. 'As far as I can make out', Churchill reported to his wife, 'everyone of every party, official and political, wants to get rid of Simon.'[6] The argument that a serious situation might result from disturbing the existing balance of party representation inside the cabinet carried less weight than had once been the case. In April 70 Conservative MPs protested against Simon's continuing tenure of the Foreign Office.[7] The senior Tory backbencher, Austen Chamberlain, judged that he had become 'a positive danger ... Nobody in any quarter has any faith in him – least of all the Cabinet and F.O!'[8] Predictably, Lloyd George was also busy arguing that the Foreign Secretary's removal was essential if the European situation was ever going to improve.[9]

Simon's failings were now well established. His colleagues noted an inability to devise and carry out a clear-cut policy with undeviating conviction. 'I wish Simon had more "faith" in himself and in his task', confessed William Ormsby-Gore, 'and [did] not think quite so much what so and so in the Cabinet will say. He's astonishingly gifted, industrious and well meaning – but he's terrified of "Cabinet instructions".'[10] He could analyse international issues with perception and set out the pros and cons of every possible policy line. But he could also invariably see the drawbacks of any proposed course of action. The result was often close to paralysis. He suffered, as Eden put it, from 'too penetrating a discernment and too frail a conviction'.[11] Yet in his defence it must be added that Simon faced an unenviable task. It had fallen to him as Foreign Secretary to deal with a crisis in the Far East that represented the first major challenge to the international status quo of the post-war era, and with the advent to power of Adolf Hitler in Germany, all at a time when Britain's military resources were at their lowest ebb. No easy answers existed to the diplomatic conundrums of these years. 'The truth is', Simon reflected during his last months at the Foreign Office, 'that we are living through such difficult times that criticism is the easiest thing in the world and the least useful.'[12]

What to do about Simon, judged Neville Chamberlain, would be Baldwin's chief difficulty in the construction of the new government.[13] Discussing the forthcoming reconstruction with MacDonald on 30 April, the Conservative leader argued that the Foreign Secretary would either have to be moved or dropped altogether.[14] A fortnight later he seemed ready to offer him a sinecure office, to 'look after defence and be Deputy Leader H of C'.[15] In the event Simon did even better. He returned to the Home Office, a post he had briefly occupied during the First World War. Though this rated lower in the ministerial pecking order than the Foreign Secretaryship, steps were taken to emphasise that Simon was not being demoted – 'done in' to use Hore-Belisha's words.[16] The Home Office was now coupled with the deputy leadership of the House of Commons, a position previously occupied by Neville Chamberlain. It was all meant to emphasise the continuing reality of the National Government. Simon had to be kept on board if this idea was to retain any credibility. Liberal Nationals had interpreted the campaign to remove Simon as 'at bottom another move in favour of a pure Tory policy'.[17] But by the end of May Simon was able to reassure a Liberal National party meeting that he had received Baldwin's promise that the new premier would maintain the National Government, that the party's proportional strength in that government would not be diminished and that the Liberal Nationals would have an input into the policy upon which the government would campaign at the General Election.[18] Indeed, it was part of the bargain finally struck with the new Prime Minister that the elevation of a Conservative to the premiership should be balanced by the addition of an extra Liberal National to the cabinet. Ernest Brown now became Minister of Labour. Hearing details of the reshuffle, Leo Amery, still excluded from the government's ranks, judged that 'all the emphasis' had been laid on 'the retention of the "National"' i.e. the coalition character of the Government'.[19] Simon, by contrast, believed that the Liberal National contingent had 'done so well that they have more than earned their places'.[20] The presence of four Liberal Nationals in the Cabinet provided 'a good basis for the coming [election] campaign'.[21]

But even more compelling evidence that the government's 'National' designation was not merely cosmetic and that the Liberal National components within it were not simply the prisoners of the Tories – not just a 'poor ration of *foie gras* on a *tournedos rossini*' in Roy Jenkins's characteristically extravagant metaphor – comes from the attitude of the Conservative party itself.[22] Partnership with the National Labour and Liberal National parties enabled Baldwin to lead the Conservatives towards that centre ground of British politics which he himself found most congenial. The price to be paid, however, was growing unease on the right wing of his own backbenches. Many Tories criticised the government for succumbing to the charms of an effete liberalism – what one called 'MacStanleyism' – when it was perfectly capable, in terms of its strength inside the House of Commons, of pursuing a straightforward Conservative course. According to Amery, 'incompetents' had been put in charge 'at vital points' so that 'the "national" label may be justified'.[23] In like vein the *Morning Post* complained that the government had 'departed from some very good Tory principles in the past four years', while the Conservative journalist Collin Brooks noted growing dissatisfaction with the government's 'Socialist character'. 'There has been little or nothing said to suggest that Baldwin and his colleagues have any faith left in private enterprise.'[24] Churchill was more succinct. The country, he asserted, lacked two things. The first, reflecting his low opinion of Baldwin, was a prime minister and the second a Conservative party.[25]

Right-wing unease focused above all else on the issue of India as the government sought to give legislative enactment to the Irwin Declaration of 1929, which had promised to move India towards Dominion status within the Empire. The Government of India Act, which finally made its way on to the statute book in the summer of 1935, was the single most important – and controversial – piece of legislation put forward in the parliament of 1931. The bill occasioned 1,951 parliamentary speeches, a total of 35½ million words of debate on its 473 clauses, filling more than 4,000 pages of *Hansard*. India – the jewel of the Empire – was certainly important; but for many it was the symbol of something bigger – an unnecessarily timid and conciliatory brand of Conservatism which derived from contaminating the Tories' own ideological purity by on-going contract with Labour and Liberal politicians. So the right-wing revolt over India represented more than a single-issue campaign. It became a vehicle for those who wished to return to conventional party politics, or at least to a restructured National Government in which Conservative influence would be more visibly preponderant. As one Tory with recent experience of India had earlier explained, 'I'm afraid that [the disquiet over Baldwin's policy towards India] represents the position in our party on many things. Many think that S[tanley] B[aldwin] is weak and woolly, and is letting the Party down.'[26] Thus, India was but the starting point for the campaign of Churchill's erratic son, Randolph, when the latter stood as an independent Conservative candidate in a by-election in Wavertree, Liverpool in February 1935. The younger Churchill began his challenge with an attack on the administration's policy towards India, but soon broadened it out into an indictment of the National Government itself.[27]

* * *

One of the first domestic issues facing the new government was the timing of the general election. The process by which a decision was reached on this matter again showed evidence of a collective decision-making structure which indicated that the government's National credentials were more than merely nominal. Baldwin, MacDonald and Simon still enjoyed the status of the 'three leaders' of the government.[28] Several members of the cabinet, and in particular the Chancellor, Neville Chamberlain, were keen to secure a renewed mandate for a policy of rearmament in the face of a patently worsening international situation. Chamberlain received general support from Simon for the proposition that rearmament should be the central plank of the government's campaign. But he judged a speech on the subject by the new Home Secretary 'so vague and nebulous' that he felt obliged to take the lead himself.[29] Despite resistance from MacDonald, now Lord President, and an equivocal attitude on the part of Baldwin, the Chamberlain-Simon line carried the day and an election was called for mid-November.[30] Joint policy discussions between Liberal National headquarters and the Conservative Research Department had in fact been going on since the spring. The Liberal Nationals had entered these negotiations warily, worried that once the Tories had a programme worked out they would 'force [it] down the throats of their Liberal National and National Labour allies at the point of the pistol'. Gradually, however, such fears were assuaged.[31] The Conservative leadership was still keen to keep its Liberal National allies on board. The 'Liberal vote' remained a critical factor in the government's calculations. By late October Simon recorded that Baldwin, MacDonald and himself were 'busy on the National Government manifesto'.[32]

With hindsight and the benefit of modern psephological analysis another victory for the National Government appears to have been all but inevitable. The size of its majority deriving from its victory in 1931 was such as to render a Labour triumph virtually impossible. The government had defended 48 seats at by-elections during the course of the parliament, of which only nine were lost, and there was no extended period during which the swing to the opposition was sufficiently strong to imply a Labour victory at the next general election. Some of these nine losses, moreover, should have occasioned no surprise. The exceptional circumstances of 1931 had seen the government successful in many Labour strongholds which were always likely to revert to their natural political allegiance in the course of time. It is striking that in only two of the nine seats lost by the government was Labour victorious in constituencies which it had not also won in 1929 – a year in which Labour had done well, but not well enough to secure an overall parliamentary majority. Contemporary Conservative strategists failed, however, to interpret the situation this rationally. By early 1935 the tally of by-election losses had been sufficient to reduce Tory headquarters to a state of near panic. One veteran observer 'never knew our Central Office people so rattled as they were in February. They looked on no seat as safe.'[33] Such thinking inevitably emphasised the continuing importance of association with the Liberal Nationals in order to attract votes to which mere Conservatives unaided could not hope to aspire. Orthodox Liberals, of course, had a vested interest in denying the truth of such a proposition. Following a by-election in Lambeth, Norwood in March 1935, Baldwin got hold of a report from Lloyd George claiming that National Government candidates were now failing to attract any Liberal support. But the Tories' Principal Agent, Robert Topping, produced contrary evidence to suggest that one in three of those who had voted Liberal in 1929 were still supporting the government.[34] The important thing was 'to gather to the help of the Tories a large voting strength of Liberals and unattached folk who like [Baldwin's] sober and sincere accents, and who are afraid of the menace to small owners and investors associated with Socialism'.[35] Should the 'Liberal vote' be lost, however, then it was believed that the consequences for the government might be catastrophic. As the Conservatives' Chief Publicity Officer explained a few months before the General Election: 'Even if the Socialist party did not obtain the support of a largely increased section of the electorate we could still lose the next election or at any rate arrive at a stale-mate position if the bulk of the Liberal vote went over to them.'[36]

The General Election of 1935 offered the first real test of the Liberal Nationals' credibility as a national political party. Few of those voters who had offered their support in 1931 had done so in the knowledge or even expectation that they were backing a new force in British politics. The position should now have been much clearer though, as will be seen, lines of distinction remained blurred in some constituencies. Equally, the General Election afforded the orthodox Liberal party the chance to reassert its claim to be the one and only representative of true Liberalism. Yet, as had been the case during the intervening years, the Samuelites remained curiously reluctant to take up this challenge. There were some justifications for this cautious approach. It allowed Liberals to keep up the pretence that the split of 1931–32, like many previous fissures in the party's history, was no more than a passing family spat and that the Liberal Nationals would one day return, repentant, to the fold. As the *Liberal Magazine* put it in January 1934, 'with one or two exceptions the Liberal Nationals are bound in the course of time to reunite with the normal Liberal Party'.[37] Furthermore, clashes between the two groups would inevitably split the Liberal vote to the advantage of neither. The result would probably be a further erosion of Liberal strength in the House of Commons. Finally, if Liberals challenged Liberal Nationals but failed to defeat them, the claims of the mainstream party would be discredited and the effect would be worse than if Liberal Nationals had been left undisturbed in their constituencies.

But the policy of peaceful co-existence with the Liberal Nationals also had its downside. Writing as early as November 1932 Archibald Sinclair, the Liberals' former chief whip and future leader, had drawn attention to his party's need to stress its claim to be *the* Liberal party rather than merely one representation of the Liberal creed. 'If you will forgive me for saying so', he reminded his leader, 'we don't want to be called Samuelite Liberals as opposed to Simonite Liberals, we want to emphasise the fact that we are the Liberal Party.'[38] There was a danger that leaving Liberal Nationals in place and unchallenged in constituencies where a significant Liberal tradition persisted could only encourage a perception that the breakaway group was indeed the authentic voice of the Liberal creed, or at least an acceptable version of it. This, of course, was an image which the Liberal Nationals themselves were understandably keen to foster. 'It must be noted', their house journal later suggested, 'that the Liberal Nationals had not split off from the rest of the Liberal Party. The Party as a whole formed part of the First National Government [August – November 1931] and the small section which now forms the Opposition Liberal Group subsequently split off from the Party.'[39]

Overall, it was the arguments against confrontation which prevailed. Though the ultimate decision on whether to field a candidate rested with each local party association, Liberal headquarters gave no encouragement to oppose sitting Simonite MPs. The party was in any case in no condition to fight on a broad front. Its position in Scotland, where the Liberal Nationals had succeeded in capturing control of the Scottish Liberal Federation during the crucial six months between April and October 1935, was particularly weak. Samuel had spoken optimistically in 1933 of fielding at least 400 candidates to give the electorate a genuine opportunity to return a Liberal government. But with local organisation often crumbling there was no realistic prospect of this happening. When the election came, only 161 Samuelites entered the fray. As a result, the 1935 General Election witnessed just two inter-Liberal contests, in the North Wales seat of Denbighshire West and the two-member constituency of Oldham in Lancashire. Differentiating between Liberals and Liberal Nationals was made no easier by the fact that from late May to the election in November the Samuelite Liberals offered broad support for the government's defence policy. This made good sense in the context of publicly admitted German rearmament and served to distance the Liberals from the Labour party but, with the election campaign focussing heavily on foreign and defence policy, it made it no easier for the voter to distinguish one version of the Liberal creed from another.

In the event Liberal National candidates contested 44 seats. Nowhere were they opposed by Conservatives. Indeed, Liberal Nationals and Tories worked much more closely together than had been the case in 1931. A letter of support from Runciman to all Conservative candidates had in fact been drafted by Sir Joseph Ball of the Conservative Research Department.[40] As befitted the leader of a national political party, Simon embarked on an extensive speaking tour which took him from Peterborough to Aberdeen and from Manchester to Devizes. Meanwhile, Lady Simon played a prominent role in her husband's own constituency of Spen Valley, where she addressed over 40 women's meetings. Whatever his thoughts about the pressing needs of national defence, Simon chose to focus his own campaign on domestic issues, stressing once again the dangers of socialism. In a radio broadcast he appealed to Liberals to recognise that their political beliefs were broader than the opposition Liberal party and argued that all Liberals could safely place their trust in Baldwin.[41] Simon presented the distinction between the two Liberal groups in terms of their contrasting influence:

A handful of Liberals in opposition, however able and sincere, sniping here, censuring there, with intermittent intervals of pontifical approval, can never influence the course of policy. Inside a government, with responsibility to be shared, they may be a real co-operative element and Liberals in the country can share in that responsibility.[42]

Speaking at Manchester's Reform Club on 7 November – a venue whose significance prompted a formal protest from the Manchester Liberal Federation[43] – Simon insisted upon his own unchanging Liberalism. Indeed, should the government in future ever pursue an illiberal policy, he pledged himself to oppose it.[44] It was a message reiterated by many other Liberal National candidates. 'I stood as a Liberal', insisted Clement Davies in Montgomeryshire. 'I was nominated by the Liberals as a Liberal. I remain a Liberal.'[45]

The contests in Denbighshire West (Denbigh) and Oldham were of particular interest. Henry Morris-Jones, the member for Denbigh, had been only partially successful in carrying the local Liberal party with him in his transition to Liberal Nationalism since 1931. A number of local activists, particularly in the Colwyn Bay area, had refused to accept the MP's change of allegiance. Having survived a number of hostile votes within the local party organisation, Morris-Jones knew that he could take nothing for granted when the annual meeting of the West Denbighshire Liberal Association took place in October 1935. After a 'boisterous' meeting lasting for two hours, local Liberals secured the adoption of J.C. Davies, Director of Education for Denbighshire and a former MP for the division, in opposition to the sitting member.[46] This decision compelled Morris-Jones to come out openly as the Liberal National candidate and to drop the pretence that he was the constituency's Liberal nominee, although he could still count on the backing of most of the key officers of the West Denbighshire Liberal Association.

In the course of the campaign both Morris-Jones and Davies sought to lay claim to the mantle of true Liberalism. Taking his case to his critics' stronghold in Colwyn Bay, the former explained his position on what remained the central point of division between the two Liberal factions. He was, he stressed, as much a free trader as anyone present at his meeting and he wanted to see all tariff barriers removed. But the realities of the international situation could not be ignored. In a world which had largely abandoned free trade, it made no sense for Britain alone to persist with it. Morris-Jones, moreover, could claim indirect backing from an unlikely quarter. In launching his so-called 'New Deal' proposals, David Lloyd George had called for 'the implementation of a policy of Protection, the use of tariffs "ruthlessly and to the full" to effect the reduction, and ultimately the elimination, of tariffs in the USA'.[47] Morris-Jones, of course, was speaking in a part of the country where the former Prime Minister's influence remained at its strongest. It would have taken a bold man indeed to suggest that Lloyd George's apparent conversion to the policy of protection deprived him of his Liberal credentials. Morris-Jones was keen to jump on to a parallel bandwagon. One of the constituency's former Liberal MPs, Lord Clwyd, added his weight to the sitting member's campaign. Under existing international conditions, explained Clwyd, he was in favour of a National Government and his desire was to strengthen the influence of Liberalism in the interests of peace. 'I am, therefore, a supporter of your candidature.'[48] In response, Davies's campaign centred around his claim that he was the only true Liberal – without prefix or suffix – in the field. He presented the contest as one between Liberalism and Toryism masquerading as Liberalism. But if this was meant to clarify the issue for the electors, Davies tended to undermine his own efforts by also following Lloyd George's lead on the issue of tariffs. 'I am and always have been', he stressed, 'a free trader, but I quite recognise that under present circumstances free trade is not practical politics.'[49]

As a two-member constituency Oldham offered obvious scope for Conservatives and Liberal Nationals to demonstrate the reality of their political partnership. Recent electoral history, notwithstanding the unique circumstances of 1931, suggested that this was not natural Conservative territory. As a result, although two Conservative MPs had been comfortably returned in 1931, the local Tory association decided in June 1935 to put forward just one candidate at the next election and to throw its weight behind a Liberal National for the second seat, 'both being supporters of the National Government'.[50] The credibility of the Liberal Nationals' challenge and, in particular, of their claim to represent the authentic voice of Liberalism in Oldham, was boosted by the selection of J.S. Dodd as their candidate, for Dodd had unsuccessfully contested the seat for the mainstream party in the General Election of 1929. By the end of October, however, W. Gretton Ward had been chosen as the Liberal candidate for the constituency, satisfying the call of the *Oldham Chronicle* that the 'rightful heirs of the Oldham radical tradition' should not allow the contest to go by default.[51] But the fact that the Liberal party only succeeded in putting one candidate into the field in this two-member constituency raised interesting questions about how Liberal voters would use their second votes.

Dodd and Gretton Ward, together with their respective followers, presented the electorate's choice in starkly differing terms. The former argued that it would be 'supreme folly' to split the anti-socialist vote as, he claimed, had happened when he had contested the seat in 1929. The real struggle was between 'socialist' and 'anti-socialist' forces and 'the sooner this is recognised also by those [Liberal voters] who supported him six years ago, the better it will be for the country'.[52] But Dodd was also insistent that he remained as much a Liberal as he had ever been. 'We have not changed our opinions in the slightest degree', he insisted. 'I am still just the same Liberal I was in 1929 when 20,000 people voted for me. I had not changed my opinions by 1931 and I have not changed them by 1935.' The first plank of Liberal politics, he claimed, was personal liberty. This was the absolute and direct antithesis of socialism, so a Liberal must be an anti-socialist before he was anything else. And, in the circumstances of the time, the only guaranteed way to thwart the socialists was to support the National Government.[53] By contrast Gretton Ward, like Davies in Denbigh, strove to present himself as the only real Liberal in the contest and he revealed that he had received 'one or two rather tempting offers if only [he] would join a certain other party'.[54] Ward claimed that the Liberal National candidate was living a lie. He had fatally entangled himself with the Conservatives and, if elected, would be obliged to support measures which no true Liberal could honestly endorse. Indeed, the National Government itself was a deception. It was a Conservative government and, if re-elected, the least Liberal elements within it would dominate its policies and direction even more than had been the case so far.[55]

Such Liberal interventions did not, of course, complicate the campaigns of the remaining Liberal National candidates, enabling them in many cases to draw a continuing veneer of ambiguity over their political affiliation. In Huddersfield William Mabane had succeeded, with only a few voices of protest, in carrying the local Liberal party with him as he moved into the Liberal National camp. Now, insisting that he remained a supporter of the National Government, he was re-adopted with just two dissentients as the 'Liberal' candidate for the constituency by a body still calling itself the Huddersfield Liberal Association.[56] Thereafter, the local Conservatives agreed not to field a candidate of their own and to throw the full weight of their party organisation into Mabane's re-election campaign. In the industrial seat of Walsall in the West Midlands the path of Joseph Leckie was even smoother. With the full backing of his local constituency party, Leckie's defection to the Liberal Nationals probably went unnoticed by the majority of those who had supported him in 1931. In essence the MP behaved as a Liberal National at Westminster while posing as a Liberal in his constituency. The Walsall Liberal Association remained affiliated to, and continued to send delegates to meetings of, the National Liberal Federation, the leading organisational body of the mainstream party. Leckie's re-adoption for the General Election of 1935 was achieved without difficulty. He addressed the Walsall Unionist Association's annual meeting in March and warned that the only alternative to the National Government's continuation was a Socialist administration which would herald disaster. By October a provisional agreement was in place to renew the Conservative co-operation which had been offered in 1931. The local Liberal party chairman argued that Leckie had fulfilled all the promises he had made four years earlier and a motion to support him at the forthcoming election was passed unanimously by the Walsall Liberal Association's General Committee.[57] In the campaign itself W. Graham, the Labour candidate, did his best to convince voters that their MP had betrayed true Liberalism. 'What could be more humiliating', he enquired, 'than for the once great Liberal Party in this borough to see its representative slink into Parliament with the support and to do the bidding of the most reactionary Tory caucus of all time? What remained of the Liberal Party must not allow itself to be fooled again, as in 1931.'[58] But no prominent Liberal came to the constituency to confirm this message, while others took a different line. Indeed, Leckie received valuable backing from William Brown, who had himself been the town's Liberal candidate between 1913 and 1918.[59]

In the rural constituency of Eddisbury in Cheshire the Liberal National MP, Richard Russell, had had only marginally more difficulty in sustaining his position. He was, on the surface, an archetypal Liberal of the Gladstonian tradition – a Methodist lay preacher, staunch opponent of gambling and committed advocate of free trade. The Liberal association in the constituency remained affiliated to the Lancashire, Cheshire and North-Western Federation of the mainstream Liberal party, even though it was clear by 1932 at the latest that the MP himself had thrown in his lot with the Simonite grouping. Over the intervening years there had been repeated rumours that discontented local Liberals would try to organise a new association, loyal to the Samuelite party, but this had never come about, largely because of fear of exacerbating existing divisions within the constituency. 'There was undoubtedly a strong anti-Russell feeling in the division but leaders who ought to be prepared to act as Officers were not forthcoming.'[60] Not surprisingly, there was no sign of a challenge to the sitting MP from the orthodox Liberal party as the General Election of 1935 drew near.

No doubt discerning voters in constituencies such as Huddersfield, Walsall and Eddisbury were aware that something significant had happened to the nature of their parliamentary representation. Yet the fact remained that they, along with those of a more limited perception, had only one option open to them if they wished to record a vote for Liberalism of any description when the country went to the polls. In a handful of other seats the position was even more ambiguous. The designation of a few Liberal candidates clearly remained flexible. Henry Fildes, Liberal MP for Stockport 1920–23, had been nominated again for the seat in 1931, despite an equivocal attitude towards free trade and the fact that he would not give a direct answer to the allegation that he was really a supporter of Sir John Simon.[61] In the event he had dropped out of the contest before polling day. Yet in 1935 the Stockport Liberal Association was still keen to secure him as their candidate. Fildes, however, preferred to stand in Dumfriesshire for the Liberal Nationals.[62] In Bristol North Robert Bernays stood, with the backing of his local association, as an independent Liberal supporting the National Government. He had remained on the government benches when the Samuelites had gone into opposition in November 1933, but had so far resisted the advances of the Liberal Nationals, largely because of a personal antipathy towards Simon whose foreign policy he had frequently criticised in the House of Commons. As he explained to Baldwin, he could not call himself a Liberal National because to do so 'would involve accepting the leadership of Sir John Simon and, by implication, supporting the manner in which he handled foreign affairs which in fact I deplored'.[63] The Conservatives, who had not contested the seat since 1923, could see no purpose in splitting the anti-socialist vote on this occasion, so Bernays was allowed a straight fight against his Labour opponent.

A somewhat similar situation developed in Wrexham. Here the sitting Liberal MP, Aled Roberts, had followed the lead of Herbert Samuel and crossed the floor of the Commons in the autumn of 1933. But the long-term power broker of local Liberal politics, Alderman Edward Hughes, well understood that the party's precarious hold on the constituency was entirely a function of Conservative support. Since the 1920s, long before the Liberal Nationals themselves had come into existence, he had regarded Labour as the ultimate enemy and had consistently espoused what became the Liberal National analysis of three-party politics – that Liberals in Wrexham could only prevail in electoral partnership with the Tories. With the approach of another general election and amid fears that this semi-industrial seat suffering from high unemployment would revert to Labour control, Hughes therefore strove to bring Roberts round to his way of thinking. 'If I were in your shoes', he argued, 'I would be prepared to take certain risks. I would state frankly that I was a convinced Free Trader but that I realised that tariffs had become an accomplished fact and that the only thing to do – while they so remained – was to fight for a universal lowering of tariff walls and to use our tariffs as a weapon in that direction.' The MP's precise party affiliation would, Hughes admitted, be a problem, but 'I have no confidence in the Samuelite label'.[64] Though no Liberal National organisation yet existed in the constituency, it was clear that Roberts was being steered towards that party's stance. In the meantime, following negotiations with the leaders of the local Tory party, Hughes was able to repeat what he had previously achieved in 1924 and secure the withdrawal of the Conservative candidate.

YEARS OF CONSOLIDATION, 1935–39   95

*   *   *

Polling took place on 14 November. Granted the size of the National Government's majority in 1931, it was inevitable that it would lose some ground to Labour. But, with an overall majority of 255 seats in the new House of Commons, its position remained secure. Simon, in what would prove to be his last Commons election, scraped home in Spen Valley by a mere 642 votes against his Labour opponent. His band of Liberal National followers returned 32 members, but eight seats held by the Simonites at the dissolution were lost to Labour in constituencies as varied as Shoreditch and the Western Isles. Among successful Liberal Nationals, Richard Russell was returned unopposed in Eddisbury, Leckie defied national trends and increased his majority in Walsall, while Mabane emerged with a considerably reduced but still very comfortable majority of over 13,000 in Huddersfield. Meanwhile, in Bristol North, Bernays, still insisting upon his independence but already in communication with the Simonite leadership, was also returned on a reduced majority. By contrast, Aled Roberts lost his seat in Wrexham. Though no Tory stood against him, the Chairman of the Wrexham Conservative party advised Conservative voters to abstain rather than support the Liberal MP. Labour re-captured the seat with a majority of over 5,000.

It was the first time since the Coupon Election at the end of the War that a government had appealed to the country and been confirmed in power. This Simon attributed to the reassuring personality of the Prime Minister, the success of the government both domestically and internationally (an assessment of his own performance at the Foreign Office which would not have secured universal endorsement), the divisive policies of the opposition and the fact that the concept of a national administration – 'the way of co-operation rather than of conflict' – appealed to the outlook of the ordinary voter.[65] He also took comfort from the fact that proportionately his group had retained its strength better than either of the other components of the National Government.[66] In fact the situation was more complex. While the tally of Liberal National seats had held up well, the swing to the opposition in Labour-Liberal National contests was almost universally stronger than in seats where Labour opposed the Conservatives. At 16 per cent, the swing away from the Liberal Nationals in London seats was particularly high.

But perhaps of greater importance than the performance of the Liberal Nationals was the continued erosion of the strength of the mainstream Liberal party. The Samuelites were reduced to just 21 MPs, with Samuel himself at Darwen among the defeated along with Isaac Foot in Bodmin and Walter Rea in Dewsbury. In Montgomeryshire one independent Liberal wrote of the 'pent-up disappointment of genuine Liberals' who had viewed 'with dismay and anger the so-called "Liberals" of the Simonite group consistently voting with the Tory majority' and thereby helping to keep in power a government with just the 'thin veneer of "National" hypocrisy'.[67] But while Liberals failed to take up the Liberal National challenge it was difficult to see how this situation was going to be remedied.

In the two constituencies where Liberal Nationals and Liberals did clash it was the former who came out on top. A lively contest in Denbigh turned 'very bitter' in its last days and there was talk of a remarkable late swing to the independent Liberal candidate.[68] In the event, however, Morris-Jones held on. Polling more than 17,000 votes, he had a majority in excess of 5,000 over his opponent. The MP estimated that he had captured something over 7,000 Liberal votes.[69] The impact of such figures was, Morris-Jones concluded, decisive in what was 'really a Liberal seat', one which 'would – had it not been divided – be the last to fall in the Liberal decline which has come and is coming more'.[70] *The Times* made special mention of Morris-Jones' triumph and, somewhat misleadingly, hailed him as 'the only Government Liberal who fought a Liberal'.[71] Both Oldham seats were held by the National Government. The Conservative candidate, H.W. Kerr, came top of the poll with over 36,000 votes. Dodd, for the Liberal Nationals, was in second place, 2,000 votes behind and narrowly holding off the challenge of the first of the two Labour candidates. The Liberal, Gretton Ward, with just over 8,500 votes was bottom of the poll and lost his deposit. The vast majority of those Oldham electors who had voted Conservative had also supported the Liberal National. But the most interesting feature of the result was in the distribution of Liberal second votes. It was an indication of the confusion now lying at the heart of British Liberalism that these were well spread out between all the other candidates. Some 3,000 seem to have followed the advice of Lloyd George's Council of Action and supported a Labour candidate; others used only one of their votes. But enough – 1,138 – went to Dodd to ensure his return to Westminister.[72] What can only be guessed is the number of one-time Liberal supporters who had accepted the full logic of the Liberal National case and divided their votes between Dodd and his Tory partner, Kerr.

Overall, it was a remarkable achievement by the National Government. For the last time in the twentieth century the winning side had secured more than 50 per cent of the popular vote. Of course, within the sea of almost 400 successful Conservative candidates, the contingent of Liberal National MPs in the new House seems of only limited significance. Furthermore, it is easy to point to the artificiality of even this level of Liberal National representation. It is an open question how many of them could have held on to their seats in the face of a Tory challenge. But such observations largely miss the point. Perhaps as many as 150 of the Conservatives elected in 1931 had owed their success to their 'National' credentials. The survival of many of them in 1935 owed much to Baldwin's ability to convince the country that his version of Liberal Toryism was now firmly entrenched in the vital middle ground of British politics. In this, the Conservatives' on-going partnership with the Liberal National wing of British Liberalism was of considerable importance, even in constituencies where no Liberal National candidate was standing. The Labour party had secured a slightly higher percentage of the popular vote in 1935 than in 1929, but captured 134 fewer seats, largely because of the capacity of 'National' candidates to monopolise the anti-socialist vote, instead of dividing it, as in 1929, between Conservatives and Liberals. The 1935 result suggested that the National Government was still managing to attract a substantial proportion of the 'Liberal vote'.

* * *

The very fact that the Liberal Nationals had fought, and survived, a second general election did much to confirm their claim to be a genuine force in British politics. Nonetheless, the executive of the National Liberal Federation had taken advantage of the election campaign to reiterate Samuel's charge that such pretensions were illusory. It pointed out that not one of the national or district representative bodies of the Liberal party supported the Simonites. 'In spite of repeated attempts, Sir John Simon and his friends have always conspicuously failed to obtain any serious support for their proposals to establish either district or national organisations for their followers. They have never ventured to hold a national conference.'[73] There were, however, signs that this situation was changing. As Simon confided to his diary, 'I have been very busy with the Liberal National organisation, which is now greatly strengthened both as regards personnel and funds'.[74] With the election out of the way such efforts were intensified. The first issue of the *Liberal National Magazine* was published in March 1936 as a means of propagating the party's ideas and policies. Its aim was 'to help in every possible way those who are working for the Party; and to do all it can to stimulate the effects of their efforts among the public'.[75] A second periodical entitled *The Liberal* began publication in June. Its title may have been presumptuous, but its slogan, 'Be an Effective Liberal and join the Liberal National Organisation', was not without resonance at a time when the mainstream party seemed to have been reduced to impotence. By this time England had been divided up for organisational purposes into nine areas, each with its own local headquarters. A Liberal National Council had been formed in South Wales and one in North Wales was in the process of being established. A Scottish National Council, comprising two district councils with offices in Glasgow and Edinburgh respectively, had already been set up.[76] The *Liberal National Magazine* carried monthly reports of the political and social activities of these regional bodies.

The holding of a successful first National Convention in June 1936, attended by over 700 delegates, marked the culmination of a period of intense organisational activity. 'Conference a great success in numbers and quality', noted Henry Morris-Jones.[77] Then, at the end of the convention, around 150 women attended the first meeting of the Women's Division of the Liberal National Council. The following year saw the establishment of a Liberal National League of Youth. The scope of their organisation, suggested *The Times*, indicated that the Liberal Nationals were a 'lively political force'.[78] By the end of 1936 the Liberal National Organisation had had to take over additional office space in numbers 3, 5 and 7 Old Queen Street. 'We shall then be in a better position to deal with the rapidly expanding work arising out of the development of our organisation throughout the country.'[79]

Addressing the convention in June, Lord Hutchison justified what was being done. In many of the 'opposition Liberal' organisations Liberal Nationals were treated as heretics and had in some cases been 'excommunicated from the community'. A new organisation was therefore a necessity to accommodate those Liberals who took the view that the only alternative to a socialist regime was a National Government. A succession of speakers insisted that the Liberal Nationals were the true heirs of the Liberal tradition of their forefathers. Simon even quoted Asquith's words to support his case. 'Liberalism is flexible', the great leader had declared back in 1920, 'adaptable, and brings principles which are immortal and eternal to the ever-shifting growing requirements of a progressive society such as our own.' These thoughts, suggested Simon, could be the motto of the new party. If other Liberals agreed with this analysis, added Hutchison, 'then ... come along, our organisation will open its door and will welcome you all'.[80]

There were some signs that this was happening. It was a brave Liberal who could discern much future for the mainstream party, now led by Sir Archibald Sinclair. An exercise in rebranding which saw the National Liberal Federation replaced in June 1936 by the Liberal Party Organisation did little to conceal the party's parlous condition. Facing the prospect not just of continuing decline but of disappearing altogether, it was hardly surprising that many Liberals began to take the Liberal National option more seriously. Among a number of prominent defections that of Robert Bernays, MP for Bristol North, finally announced in September 1936, was the most significant. Some well-known Liberals considered adopting a Liberal National strategy, even if they stopped short of advocating joining up with their former colleagues. According to Lord Lothian, 'it may prove to be the best, perhaps the only course, for Liberals to join one or other of the two main parties and liberalise from within'.[81]

Soon after the General Election, the Liberal party experienced renewed humiliation at a by-election in Ross and Cromarty in the Scottish Highlands. Just 4 per cent of the poll was secured in a seat with a strong Liberal tradition. Within a few months the defeated Liberal candidate, Dr Russell Thomas, had decided to join the Liberal Nationals. He was disturbed by his former party's tendency to 'flirt with the Parties of the extreme Left' in a way that was 'antagonistic to what is best in Liberalism'. Now that earlier disputes over free trade had largely subsided, Thomas also gave voice to a new division in the ranks of Liberalism, a division which would serve as an increasingly powerful recruiting agent for the Liberal Nationals as the decade progressed:

> I feel that their [the Sinclairites'] blind devotion to what is called 'collective security' with a tendency to ignore the facts of the European situation, and to hinder the rearmament of our country, shows a lack of realism I can no longer support. Nor can I uphold a policy which may embroil us in war, unprepared as we should be, with, paradoxically, peace as the new *casus belli*.[82]

In Wrexham the result of the General Election convinced Edward Hughes that the time had now come to embrace the Liberal National cause without reservation. At a well attended meeting at the Queen's Hotel, Chester, in June 1936, at which the principal guest was the Liberal National cabinet minister, Leslie Hore-Belisha, the ground was prepared for a new divisional association in Wrexham. One speaker explained the situation as he saw it:

'In East Denbighshire Mr Aled Roberts had unfortunately not felt able to come forward as a Liberal National, and the seat was lost ... but he thought it could be won again'.[83] A local Liberal National association was duly set up on 14 October with Hughes as chairman.

If, however, Liberal Nationalism were to expand significantly beyond the constituencies of those MPs who had defected back in 1931, the experience of Wrexham would need to be repeated many times across the country. Such an expansion was clearly now the goal of the party leadership. Hore-Belisha used the pages of the *Liberal National Magazine* to explain the party's ambitions:

The circumstances in which the Liberal National Party came into being dictated that, although they were a majority of the Liberal members, they were deprived of intimate contact with a widespread, far-flung and long established apparatus of organisation. Consequently they had not the means of acting as the representatives of a vast and vocal electoral opinion, expressed through the usual conferences. Liberal National members had associations in their own constituencies but not in other constituencies. There was therefore no system of recruitment, and it is not surprising that Liberals in many constituencies felt themselves without the opportunities of active and corporate political life. *These deficiencies we propose to remedy*.[84]

From the spring of 1936 there was considerable evidence of Liberal National growth and development in many parts of the country. In May, for example, a Liberal National association was set up in Yorkshire. It was reported that an active branch association already existed in Sheffield and that it was hoped that this would expand to embrace towns in South Yorkshire and Derbyshire, including Chesterfield.[85] Often the task was eased by the complete or partial collapse of the local infrastructure of the mainstream Liberal party. Liberal Nationals found themselves stepping into an organisational void in which local Liberals were often prepared to support a Liberal candidate of any description. According to a report from the Liberal Nationals' Northern Area invitations were being received from local associations in constituencies, 'which have come to be considered derelict from the Liberal standpoint', to assist them in re-organising their forces.[86] It seemed to cause little local disquiet when the Liberal National Association in Asquith's old seat of East Fife celebrated the jubilee of the former Liberal leader's connection with the constituency. 'One of the most remarkable features', noted James Henderson Stewart, the local Liberal National MP, 'is that it is the old Asquithian Liberals, many of whom were present at the ceremony ..., who are the strongest in their support of the principle of National Government at this time.'[87] It was reported from Llanelly, where Liberals had been the main challengers to Labour throughout the 1920s, that a well attended meeting of the constituency Liberal association had agreed, with just two dissentients, to support a Liberal National candidate at the forthcoming by-election in March.[88] The situation in many West Midlands seats was very similar:

> It is no exaggeration to say that in nine-tenths of the West Midlands constituencies Liberals, denied self-expression in the polling booth, met the socialist menace by giving support to the Government candidate last November. This is satisfactory as far as it goes, but Liberals everywhere are looking for a means of crystallising their strength, and making it effective in public affairs.

Only the Liberal Nationals, it was argued, now had the potential to keep Liberalism itself alive and effective in conditions which would otherwise threaten its extinction:

> Twelve months ago it might have been difficult to bring this fact home to the average Liberal in constituencies which are sometimes considered derelict from the Liberal standpoint, but, now the atmosphere has cleared, we find over and over again that we are preaching to the converted.[89]

Speaking in Sheffield, Simon was able to declare that he and his party had now got the organisation 'necessary if they were going to build up the Liberal opinion of the country in support of broad national purposes as they all meant to do'.[90] A 'great power' was forming, confirmed Hore-Belisha with forgivable exaggeration.[91]

Securing a new batch of local Liberal National constituency organisations was, of course, only half the battle. Their impact would be limited unless the Conservatives allowed Liberal Nationals a more generous share in the representation of the National banner than had been the case in the General Elections of 1931 and 1935. This would not be easy to secure. It would mean existing Conservative organisations having to play second fiddle to newly constituted Liberal National bodies, with Tory headquarters always able to take cover behind the autonomy of its local associations in the question of candidate selection. In the wake of the 1935 General Election, therefore, leading Liberal Nationals were understandably keen to maximise estimates of the size and importance of the vote they had delivered on behalf of the National Government. The actual figure secured by Liberal National candidates was around 860,000, but many of these were undoubtedly Conservatives voting for a Liberal National in the absence of a Tory alternative. According to Hore-Belisha and Simon, however, the Liberal National partnership was delivering something like three million extra votes to the National Government's cause. The calculations used to reach this figure were simplistic, but not entirely devoid of merit:

> The National Government in 1935 polled three million votes more than the Conservative Government in 1929. The Opposition Liberal Party polled four million votes fewer than the Liberal Party in 1929. It is not an exaggerated inference therefore that the three million additional votes polled for the National Government were Liberal votes ... Indeed, without these Liberal votes there would not be a National Government today.[92]

But when Hutchison suggested that the true figure might be as high as four million, Sinclair could not resist the challenge. Addressing the Home Counties Liberal Federation, he ridiculed these Liberal National claims:

> To arrive at the four million you first take the number of votes cast for Simonites last November (ignoring the fact that probably at least half of these were Tory votes). This gives a figure of 880,000. You divide this by 44, the number of Simonite candidates, and get 20,000 as the average number of votes each candidate polls. You then assume that if Simonites had contested 600 constituencies instead of only 44, they would have obtained 20,000 votes in each constituency, a total of 12,000,000. But you then remember that some of these would have been the votes of your Tory and National Labour allies, so to be on the safe side you divide by three and behold the Liberal National vote is four million.[93]

At the end of the day, however, it was not the independent Liberals but the Conservative party which needed to be impressed by the Liberal Nationals' creative arithmetic. Worryingly, there were indications that the

Tory leadership were still not thinking of their electoral allies as a permanent feature on the political landscape. Addressing a private meeting of Conservative MPs in May 1936, Baldwin expressed the opinion that the example of the Liberal Unionists in an earlier generation would be repeated and that the Liberal Nationals would one day be absorbed by the Tories.[94] When Baldwin's words entered the public domain, his prophecy 'agitated every honest Liberal National heart'.[95] The best the *Liberal National Magazine* could do was to point out that no reporters had been present at the Conservative leader's meeting and that he might therefore never have used such tactless words. Indeed,

> it is difficult to believe that Mr Baldwin can have advocated such a step in view of the fact that he is also reported ... to have pointed to the necessity of the continuation of National Government, which would clearly cease to exist were the Liberal Nationals to be absorbed in the Conservative Party.[96]

Perhaps the most forceful statement of the Liberal National case was made by one who had not yet announced his conversion to the party's ranks. Robert Bernays, the independent Liberal member for Bristol North, wrote to *The Times* on 20 May 1936 to support the recent call of Lord De La Warr, a junior government minister representing the National Labour party, for a 'strong centre group'. Bernays declared that, ever since declining to follow Samuel on to the opposition benches in 1933, he had felt the need for some definite and coherent organisation, determined to work within the ranks of the government's supporters for a searching programme of social reform and the maintenance of the greatest possible measure of collective security. Such policies, he believed, already enjoyed substantial backing. 'But we have neither organisation nor leadership and so, working in isolation as we do, we are not able to exercise our rightful influence in shaping the programme and policy of the Government.'

Bernays was ready to look beyond the immediate situation. Baldwin, notwithstanding his unguarded reference to the fate of the Liberal Unionists, had so far behaved honourably towards the government's non-Conservative supporters. But he was evidently nearing the end of his political career. Unwell for much of 1936, the Prime Minister was unlikely to remain in office after the forthcoming royal coronation. His resignation, argued Bernays, was bound to endanger the 'liberalizing influences in the Government'. Though the succession of Neville Chamberlain was by now widely anticipated, Bernays claimed that it was impossible to foresee with any certainty who would take over in Downing Street, 'or to what wing of the National Government his successor will incline'. In such circumstances it was vital that the progressive forces supporting the government should do everything in their power to maintain as wide and as united a front as possible to guard against all eventualities. Bernays called for much closer co-operation between the 'left-wing forces of the National Government' than had been seen hitherto. This would involve weekly meetings of the Liberal National and National Labour groups to work out a joint line and an agreed speaker on all the important issues of government business. 'A really powerful group consulting together, acting together, sitting together, bringing their influence to bear upon debates with fire and conviction, would revolutionize the viewpoint of our Conservative colleagues' and perhaps in time even attract the adherence of left-wing Tories and independent Liberals. But if such steps were not taken, the grip of the 'hard-shelled Tories' would progressively tighten and lead to a government stripped of the remaining elements which gave it the right to call itself 'National'.[97] Behind the scenes Simon urged Chamberlain to make a public declaration of his own commitment to preserving the broad basis of the government. Simon professed not to doubt that Chamberlain was fully signed up to the National project, 'but in view of the possibility of a change at the top, I find a certain anxiety in some Liberal quarters lest this may be accompanied by a return to strictly party government'.[98]

The Liberal Nationals' difficulties were well illustrated with the death in October 1936 of Sir Godfrey Collins, Secretary of State for Scotland and one of the party's four representatives in the cabinet. Collins was replaced by the Conservative, Walter Elliot. Though the Minister of Transport, Leslie Hore-Belisha, was elevated to the cabinet, Liberal Nationals felt that they were due at least an additional under-secretaryship. Simon's failure to secure this renewed suspicions of his inability to stand up for his colleagues. Insult was added to injury when the party failed to hold on to Collins' seat in Greenock. Indeed, there was some question as to whether the Liberal National candidate at the by-election was a Liberal National at all. Vivian Cornelius had stood previously as a Conservative and was to do so again. On this occasion his candidature was approved by the Greenock Unionist Association – two earlier Liberal nominations having already been rejected – before being submitted to the Liberal Nationals. Yet not even Simon's endorsement of his 'progressive outlook' could save Cornelius from going down to defeat at the hands of his Labour opponent.[99]

The Liberal National leader did his best to reassure his party that he had received promises from both Baldwin and Chamberlain that the National character of the government would be confirmed and that the Liberal National quota of posts would not be whittled away. These assurances were 'explicit and on record'.[100] But Liberal Nationals would have been less content had they known of Chamberlain's private thoughts on the matter:

> If [Baldwin] seeks to buy off Simon's claims for Liberal advancement by promises to be fulfilled by his successor, he will find an insuperable obstacle. I may or may not succeed him, but in any case I am not going to agree now to anything that would hamper my freedom of action hereafter.[101]

In the event Baldwin masterfully overcame the constitutional crisis occasioned by the abdication of Edward VIII in December before presiding over the coronation of the latter's successor as George VI the following May. This enabled him, unusually among Prime Ministers of the twentieth century, to take his leave of the political stage at a moment of his own choosing. The succession of Neville Chamberlain was never seriously questioned. His closest cabinet colleague, Samuel Hoare, urged the Prime Minister-designate to make his government as little like that of his predecessor as possible. 'Keep the National character, of course', conceded Hoare, 'but remember, as I know you will, the solid fact that so far as the House of Commons is concerned you depend on the Conservatives ... This being so, I should be inclined to bring in one or two of the right.'[102] Chamberlain was certainly a more abrasive and less consensual figure than Baldwin. Yet fundamentally both men belonged to the same moderate wing of the Conservative party and Chamberlain proved as committed to the concept of National government as his predecessor had been. The new cabinet of 21 contained four Liberal Nationals. Simon moved from the Home Office to the Exchequer; Hore-Belisha was promoted from Transport to the War Office; Leslie Burgin entered the cabinet to replace Hore-Belisha at Transport; and Ernest Brown retained his post at the Ministry of Labour. The one casualty was the elderly Walter Runciman, eased out reluctantly from the Board of Trade which he had occupied since November 1931, and declining to accept the lesser post of Lord Privy Seal.[103] Simon expressed dismay at Runciman's fate, but any regrets could only have been based upon clinical calculations of his party's strength, for the two men had always disliked one another.[104]

With Chamberlain also bringing De La Warr from the National Labour group into the cabinet, the new appointments caused some disquiet on the Conservative benches where the feeling existed that the two minority parties were already in receipt of office and preferment out of proportion to their influence and value. The reshuffle, thought Amery, was dominated by no other consideration than giving the appropriate number of places to the representatives 'of the so-called Parties'. 'N[eville]'s idea', he added, 'is that he wants to impress on the public that he is not swinging to the Right and then pursue his own policy.'[105] Among new junior appointments, one Liberal National gain caused some consternation among the party's own membership. Robert Bernays, only recently recruited from the orthodox Liberals, was preferred over William Mabane, the MP for Huddersfield who had adhered to the Liberal Nationals since 1931, for an under-secretaryship at the Ministry of Health. Such 'queue-jumping' was bound to 'create much dissatisfaction in the Party', especially in view of Simon's admission that 'the Tories think so highly of [Bernays]'.[106]

But the most striking of the Liberal National appointments was that of Simon himself. At the Home Office the Liberal National leader had done much to refurbish his reputation, particularly among his Conservative colleagues, after the difficulties he had experienced in three and a half years as Foreign Secretary. It was a department in which he was fully at home, having served there in Asquith's wartime coalition in 1915. It also gave scope for his innate liberalism. Though there were only limited legislative achievements, Simon's Factories Act of 1937 was a welcome and overdue measure of reform, improving safety provisions, fixing a shorter working week for women and young people and ensuring proper lighting and better welfare regulations. 'At the Home Office', predicted the *Manchester Guardian* at the time of his appointment, 'one would expect to find him a humanitarian and, in a department powerful for either good or evil, a guardian of personal freedom.'[107] But Simon found it necessary to limit that freedom in order to confront the excesses of the British Union of Fascists. He handled the situation wisely and his Public Order Act was passed to general approval, taking much of the steam out of Oswald Mosley's movement. Of one Commons performance the political correspondent of the *Spectator* was particularly appreciative:

> I cannot recall ever having witnessed a more skilful performance than Sir John Simon's conduct on Monday of the Committee stage of the Public Order Bill. Always urbane, never at a loss for the right

argument, ready to meet points when they were sound, never wavering on essentials, he disarmed his opponents, encouraged his friends and succeeded through a gruelling Parliamentary day in avoiding a division on any of the questions that seemed likely at one time to raise controversial issues.[108]

Simon's most valuable contribution at the Home Office probably came in relation to the Abdication Crisis at the end of 1936. Primary credit must be given to Baldwin, but there were legal and constitutional aspects for which the Prime Minister was not ideally equipped and, according to the Cabinet Secretary, it was Simon as Home Secretary who had 'become a very great strength to the Cabinet' and 'who steered us through the Duke of Windsor crisis and its many pitfalls'.[109] Morris-Jones, generally sparing in his compliments as far as his party leader was concerned, was forced to concede that the Home Secretary had shown himself to be the 'ablest legal mind we have, an honourable man and a great patriot'.[110] It was some testimony to the restoration of Simon's political standing that, as Baldwin's premiership drew to a close, the talk was not, as it had been in 1935, of whether the Home Secretary would survive the ensuing reshuffle, but of which great office he would occupy next. Chamberlain had certainly revised the somewhat jaundiced opinion he had held of Simon earlier in the decade. Discussing the forthcoming changes with Baldwin in mid-January 1937, he revealed that he now favoured Simon rather than Hoare for the post of Chancellor. It would, responded the out-going premier, be 'most valuable' to have the Liberal National leader fully satisfied.[111] Simon's satisfaction was beyond question. His new post brought him, as he took pleasure in pointing out, to the 'next post to PM'.[112]

The consolidation of the Liberal Nationals' strength within the cabinet did not, of course, resolve the on-going question of their limited parliamentary representation. Indeed, it made it ever more anomalous. Bernays took up this issue again in January 1937. It was vital, he stressed, to preserve a separate Liberal National identity, otherwise the National Government would become 'a fraud on the electorate'. In this task the Conservatives must play their part:

> If the Liberal Nationals are to continue as allies they must be given opportunities for growth and expansion. There must be a more reasonable distribution of seats ... I realise the difficulty of persuading local Conservative associations to make any sacrifice in

Party representation, but a plain and unequivocal recommendation by the Leader of the Conservative Party, on occasion, when the Liberal Nationals have obvious claims to the seat, would be unlikely to be ignored.

But Bernays went further and seemed to envisage a degree of independence within the National Government alliance to which the Liberal Nationals had not as yet aspired. The group should become 'a vital Left Wing of the National Government'. The country, he claimed, was essentially 'Liberal' and the task of the Liberal Nationals ought to be to work for the progressive Liberalisation of government policy. They must convey to both the government and the country that they were not just the patient oxen of the Conservative party and that there might be moments when they would feel it their duty to retire to an independent position. This display of autonomy would assist the government as a whole by attracting additional non-Conservative voters to the National cause:

> It too often happens that on such essentially Liberal questions as the struggle for freer trade, the strengthening of collective security, the need for economy in financial administration, or the threat to personal liberty, the voices that ought to be raised from the Government Liberal Benches are hesitant. Such a position may satisfy the Conservative Whips but it must inevitably be damaging to the Liberal National cause in the country.[113]

William Mabane picked up Bernays' point about parliamentary representation a few weeks later. Writing in the *Liberal National Magazine*, the MP for Huddersfield argued that co-operation could only be real if, in appropriate constituencies, the banner of the National Government was carried by Liberals and not by Conservatives. So far, however, the progress made in this direction had not been satisfactory. 'Conservatives are apt to agree with the notion in principle and then suggest that the sacrifice should be made in any constituency but their own.'[114]

Over the 1935 parliament as a whole there were some superficial signs that the Conservative-Liberal National parliamentary imbalance was being addressed. A National Co-ordinating Committee had been established in March 1933, having among its aims to preserve the identity of the two junior parties in the National Government by finding more opportunities for their candidates or, as many Tories saw it, to give away seats to the

Liberal National and National Labour parties.[115] Announcements were made that Liberal National candidates had been selected to fight a number of constituencies at the next general election, none of which had been contested by the party in 1935. These included the Clayton division of Manchester, Chesterfield, Dewsbury, Doncaster, Gower, Hackney South, Hanley, Motherwell, Sheffield Hillsborough, South Shields and Swansea East. It was an exercise which rank and file Conservatives looked upon with contempt. After the selection of a Liberal National in South Shields, the neighbouring Tory MP, Cuthbert Headlam, recorded:

> The man Pilkington made a Conservative speech, assured us that he was an out and out supporter of the Nat Govt, supported Neville's foreign policy, etc. etc. He lead us to understand that he was a man of unimpeachable honour, honest God-fearing etc, – of course I did not like him or his manner of speech – he smelt of 'Liberalism' and the lower middle class and chapel – but the South Shields people appeared to be quite satisfied with him and no doubt he is good enough for them.[116]

But in any case the extent of Conservative sacrifice involved was extremely limited. Both Dewsbury and South Shields had been contested by the National Labour party in 1935; in Gower the government candidate had been described as 'National' without further qualification; in Swansea East the Labour member had been returned unopposed. Only in seven constituencies had the previous government candidate been a Conservative and in none of the seats listed had the government candidate been victorious. Granted the strong National performance in 1935, it would have needed an unlikely anti-Labour swing at the next electoral contest for this crop of Liberal National nominations to result in any additional parliamentary strength.

In more promising constituencies the Liberal Nationals had a harder fight on their hands to assert themselves. In the broader interests of the National Government the party probably had no alternative but to stand down in Ross and Cromarty when the sitting Liberal National MP, Sir Ian Macpherson, was elevated to the peerage as Lord Strathcarron at the beginning of 1936. The National Labour minister, Malcolm MacDonald, son of the former Prime Minister, had lost his seat at the General Election and now slipped gratefully into the vacancy created by Macpherson's ennoblement. But a vacancy in the Conservative-controlled two-member constituency of Preston seemed to offer obvious scope for a division of the electoral spoils, especially as a Liberal had won one of the Preston seats in each of the General Elections of 1922, 1923 and 1929. Without consulting the local Tories, the newly formed Preston Liberal National Association invited Sir John Barlow, a member of a prominent local family and himself engaged in the cotton industry upon which Preston was heavily dependent, to address them with a view to his adoption as their candidate. Preston Conservatives, however, refused to co-operate and brought forward their own nominee, Captain Edward Cobb. Barlow was left with little choice but to withdraw. Relations between the two local parties rapidly deteriorated with the Liberal Nationals warning that the seat might well be lost. Eventually they decided not to take any part in the by-election and announced that the only advice they were prepared to give to the Liberals of Preston was to act according to their own judgement.[117] As one activist put it, 'the Liberal Nationals have given unstinted support to the Government and many of them think that they should have more consideration in the matter of seats. Where there is a double-membered constituency like Preston, surely it would be a graceful and politic act to allow one nomination to come from the Liberal supporters of the Government.'[118] Yet it was a sign of the essential reality of power in the Conservative-Liberal National relationship that Simon ended up writing a letter of support to the Conservative candidate, Cobb.

Even in seats held by Liberal National MPs, the party's continued tenure could not be taken for granted. The death of the Liberal National member for Walsall, Joseph Leckie, necessitated a by-election in November 1938. The Walsall Liberal Association quickly agreed to support a Liberal National candidate, but finding a suitable local man proved no easy task, especially when the association's chairman refused to accept the nomination. In this situation leading Walsall Conservatives began to press for the adoption of a Tory candidate amid suggestions that a tacit agreement had been reached back in 1931 that the seat would revert to the Conservatives once Leckie ceased to be the MP. On this occasion it was only the intervention of Conservative party headquarters in London which reasserted the principle that Walsall should still be regarded as a Liberal National seat.[119] Eventually, Sir George Schuster, a distinguished public servant and colonial administrator, agreed to stand as the Liberal National candidate, even though he had had no previous association with the party.

A similar, but even more difficult situation arose in East Norfolk. A vacancy occurred at the end of 1938 following the succession to the peerage of the sitting Liberal National MP, Viscount Elmley, as Earl Beauchamp. A joint meeting of the East Norfolk Liberal and Conservative Associations on the last day of the year decided by 95 votes to 51 to adopt a young London solicitor, Frank Medlicott, as Liberal National candidate for the impending by-election. Before the joint meeting, however, a separate meeting of the Conservative Association had rejected Medlicott by 89 votes to 83 and, on a show of hands, decided to instruct Tory branches in the division to support J.F. Wright, a so-called Conservative and agricultural candidate. Wright had the backing of a body described as the East Norfolk National Conservative and Agricultural Association which had been formed less than a fortnight earlier. The ostensible reason for this decision was that a 'Liberal caucus in a purely agricultural constituency is giving the official National "ticket" to a solicitor from London who, it is said, "does not know a cow from a rabbit"!'[120] Before long, however, rumours abounded that questions of party rather than policy lay behind the opposition to Medlicott. It emerged that, before Medlicott's selection, E.W. Langford, a former President of the National Farmers' Union, had been prepared to stand as the Liberal National candidate but had failed to secure the backing of the Norfolk branch of the NFU. Its executive, 'by the terms of its resolution, made it clear that it would not support him because he is a Liberal National'.[121]

Speaking on Medlicott's behalf Geoffrey Shakespeare described a rebellion on the part of a small minority of Conservatives in East Norfolk, designed to secure a return to party politics under the guise of helping agriculture, and indicated that considerable intimidation had been employed to prevent loyal Conservatives from outside the constituency coming in to help the Liberal National candidate.[122] Broadening the issue, Shakespeare pointed out that there were currently 'well over 100' Conservative MPs who owed their positions to Liberal National support. 'If a loyal Liberal National candidate was to be thrown over in favour of a minority candidate like Mr Wright, an open opponent of part of Mr Chamberlain's domestic policy, how could the national unity be maintained?'[123] In the end it took a letter to Wright from the Prime Minister himself, together with two meetings between the chairman of Wright's National Conservative and Agricultural Association and David Margesson, the government's chief whip, before Medlicott was allowed a free run against his Labour opponent. Even then, considerable bitterness persisted. One of Wright's leading supporters suggested that the constituency would now be saddled with Medlicott for the foreseeable future with the result that rural and agricultural East

Norfolk would, in effect, be unrepresented.[124] *The Times* commented on the broader picture:

> In every association between parties the numerically weaker allies have always the more difficult tasks. Their strength is hard to ascertain. Their prominence in the Government arouses jealousy, not indeed among their colleagues, but among partisan stalwarts, of whom, even in days when the traditional party divisions are obsolete, there are still many survivors. Short-sighted persons show a vivid understanding of the help which Conservatives render to their allies and total oblivion of the help which their allies may well render to them. But the continuance of loyal co-operation ... is essential to a Government whose great strength both at home and abroad is that it can claim to speak for more than one party.[125]

If the Liberal Nationals' relationship with the Conservatives remained unresolved in the late 1930s, that between the severed wings of the Liberal party showed signs of greater clarification. The new leader of the orthodox party could take little credit for this development. Convinced that the Liberal Nationals had no other option in the long term, Archibald Sinclair believed that the vast majority of them would one day return to the fold.[126] In any case, he regarded the reunion of the old Liberal party as a far more attractive option than the idea of a Liberal-Labour alliance being canvassed by some of his more left-wing supporters. As late as 1937 Sinclair seemed to rule out endorsing direct electoral challenges in Liberal National constituencies: 'We at headquarters cannot – at any rate yet – countenance attacks upon seats held by Liberal National members of Parliament. They have not yet done it to us openly, and we should have to consider very carefully before we took the initiative against them.'[127] In line with the leader's thinking, the annual *Liberal Year Book* continued throughout the decade to list Liberal National bodies among the Liberal party's principal organisations, as if refusing to acknowledge that two separate parties now existed.

Other Liberals, however, were more ready to accept reality and thereby to try to regain the initiative in Liberal politics. An important step was taken with a motion moved at the National Liberal Federation in June 1936 by the Oldham Liberal Association, still smarting from its experience at the polls the previous November. The motion, incorporated in the Liberal party's new constitution, said that no constituency Liberal association should be entitled to affiliate or adhere to any other political organisation, the object of which was to secure representation for its members in parliament. It was clearly designed to smoke out those local organisations which had maintained the semblance of continuing to belong to the Liberal party, while in practice giving support to an MP who had defected to the Liberal Nationals. The result was an increasing trend to re-establish Liberal associations in constituencies where for several years Simonite organisations had been able to claim that they were the only representatives of organised Liberalism.

One of the first to be affected was Walter Runciman's seat of St Ives in Cornwall. Feelings ran high as a result of Runciman's decision during the 1935 General Election to speak on behalf of John Rathbone, the victorious Conservative candidate in neighbouring Bodmin, thus helping to secure the defeat of the local Liberal grandee, Isaac Foot. Foot was then instrumental in the creation of an independent Liberal association in St Ives, spurred on by knowledge of the failing health of Runciman's father, whose demise might soon catapult the sitting member into the House of Lords and precipitate a by-election. The potential for an escalation of inter-Liberal conflict was evident. Learning of the growing opposition within his constituency, Runciman shared his thoughts with Lord Hutchison at Liberal National headquarters: 'the moment has arrived for the Samuelites to be reminded that if I am attacked in St Ives we cannot leave Dingle Foot [Isaac's eldest son] to sit uncontested at Dundee. I hate the idea of reprisals, but I fear it is inevitable.'[128] In fact Dingle Foot took the initiative himself by coming to speak against Runciman in St Ives. According to the local Liberal National agent he had thereby broken a tacit understanding, observed by all types of Liberal MP for the past five years, and created a precedent 'which he may sincerely regret'. He was 'the first Liberal Member of the House of Commons to speak in another Liberal Member's constituency at a meeting called to oppose the sitting Member'.[129]

In the event, Runciman moved to the Lords with a viscountcy after being dropped from the cabinet in May 1937. The resulting by-election, a straight fight between Alec Beechman for the Liberal Nationals and Isaac Foot for the Liberals, served as a defining moment in the relationship between the two parties. Both men could claim impeccable Liberal credentials. Foot, an unyielding opponent of protective tariffs, had been elected to parliament at his fifth attempt as member for Bodmin in 1922. Losing his seat in the Liberal disaster of 1924, he returned to parliament in 1929 and continued to represent Bodmin until defeated in 1935. Beechman won the Military Cross and received nine wounds in 15 minutes at Passchendaele. After the war he went up to Oxford where he was the first post-war undergraduate president of the Oxford Liberal Club, before being nominated as Liberal candidate for Oldham in 1931. Though Foot's Liberalism was deeply rooted in Cornish Methodism, it was by no means clear that his commitment to free trade was still the asset it had once been. Cornish market gardeners had prospered under safeguarding duties, while local quarrymen had also seen the benefits of a tariff on imported stone. But for most electors the main issue seemed to be support for or opposition to the National Government. In a close contest Beechman retained the seat for the Liberal Nationals by just 210 votes. Significantly, it was widely remarked that the seat could not have been held by a Conservative and that Foot's challenge could not have been resisted except by a Simonite 'on a very advanced programme'.[130]

The revival of independent Liberalism in Huddersfield was rather less dramatic. The sitting Liberal National MP, William Mabane, had for several years skilfully muddied the waters as far as his precise party affiliation was concerned, even persuading the local Liberal association to maintain its subscription to the Liberal Party Organisation. But discontent had been mounting for some time and came to a head when, at a meeting of the Yorkshire Liberal Nationals in February 1939, Mabane proposed the creation of a Liberal National association in every constituency in the county. This was bound to mean that several existing Liberal associations, loyal to the mainstream party, would now be challenged by rival organisations. Such a clear display of Mabane's loyalties was hard to ignore and, when the following month he came to address the annual meeting of what still called itself the Huddersfield Liberal Association, he was roundly condemned by Ernest Woodhead, himself a former Liberal candidate for Huddersfield, in the course of what was supposed to be a vote of thanks to the MP. A meeting of independent Liberals was arranged for early April where Ashley Mitchell, a veteran of four electoral campaigns in the Liberal interest, declared that the present situation in which there was 'no Liberalism in Huddersfield at all' could be tolerated no longer. With support offered from party headquarters in London, it was agreed with just one contrary vote to create the Huddersfield Borough Liberal Association – the Liberal Nationals would not relinquish the title 'Huddersfield Liberal Association' – and to affiliate the new body to the Liberal Party Organisation. Under the headline 'Liberalism Resurgans' the *Huddersfield*

Daily Examiner enthused at the 'sense of a spring released, of Liberalism, stifled and repressed, rejoicing to find expression'.[131]

In many other constituencies, however, it proved harder to re-establish an orthodox Liberal identity after several years of inactivity. In Huntingdonshire, held by the Liberal National MP, Dr Sidney Peters, a Liberal association was revived with new rules in August 1936 and immediately affiliated to the Liberal Party Organisation. Two years later, however, the majority of local branches were still 'not functioning very well'. The constituency party secretary had repeatedly urged 'old friends' to get moving, but the inevitable reply was that, until there was an independent candidate in the field, they did not see any prospect of holding gatherings of any sort.[132] The position had not improved by 1939, with the secretary reporting that the association was 'still in a state of "suspended animation"'. The President explained that 'there was no doubt their inactivity lay in the fact of the divided Liberalism that was unfortunately in existence not only in this county but elsewhere ... there was no doubt it was the reason for Liberalism being so weak'.[133] In Montgomeryshire it was suggested that the position of the sitting Liberal National MP, Clement Davies, was 'anything but secure'.[134] Yet in the summer of 1938, when the Liberal branch associations in the county were canvassed as to whether they would prefer to affiliate to the Liberal Party Organisation or to the Liberal National Organisation, it was reported that the majority did not reply, 'as they were really indifferent and had not functioned for several years being really unorganised'.[135]

In Simon's seat of Spen Valley the Liberal party's 1936 resolution to exclude from membership associations affiliated to the Liberal National Council at least helped to clarify the situation. The Spen Valley Liberal Association now formally affiliated to the Yorkshire Liberal National Area Council and to the Liberal National Council in London.[136] But there were no corresponding signs of a revival of independent Liberalism in the constituency and it was admitted that many disgruntled Liberals had already been driven into the 'Socialist fold'. The best advice on offer to 'all Liberal-minded people who wish to help promote real Liberal ideals' was that they should send whatever subscription they could afford and appeal for personal membership of the Liberal Party Organisation.[137] Similarly, suggestions of a Liberal revival in Southampton proved exaggerated. Writing in the December 1936 issue of the *Westminster Newsletter*, Ramsay Muir reported that orthodox Liberals had won back control over the Southampton Liberal Association. In fact, a sparsely attended meeting had decided by a majority of just one not to affiliate to the Liberal National Organisation. Hearing this news, the sitting Liberal National MP, Sir Charles Barrie, summoned another meeting at which he won a vote of confidence from about 70 of the 80 members present. Then, early in the New Year, the association duly voted to affiliate to the Liberal National Organisation.[138] Two years later the local Liberal National secretary was noting a 'wonderful advance' in the membership of the various ward committees.[139]

In some instances local Liberals still seemed to look upon the Liberal Nationals as temporarily estranged colleagues rather than as potentially deadly rivals. When in March 1938 a proposal was brought before the General Council of the Manchester Liberal Federation to omit the name of a known supporter of the National Government from the federation's list of vice-presidents, the president drew a persuasive, but misleading, parallel with earlier times:

> Those who remembered the difficult times between 1918 and 1922 would remember the prominent and noble part played by the Manchester Liberal Federation in bridging the difficulties between one section of Liberals and another. The toleration displayed at that time largely led to the reunion of the Party with an increase in its House of Commons membership. The President thought it would be a great mistake if the Federation took any action which would make it more difficult for any section of the Party to return in the future.[140]

By a substantial majority vote the Liberal National vice-president was allowed to retain his post. Elsewhere, any hope of clarifying the distinction between the two Liberal parties was compromised by the growing tendency of Liberal councillors to join forces with the Tories in anti-socialist municipal alliances. When orthodox Liberals behaved in this way in local government, their protests at the Liberal Nationals for acting similarly on the national stage carried little conviction. More importantly, it was scarcely surprising if the average Liberal voter remained confused.

By the second half of the decade contrasting attitudes towards the National Government's foreign policy were serving to consolidate the distinction between Liberals and Liberal Nationals. The closing of ranks in this matter in the early months of 1935 did not long survive the General Election in November. The government's apparently cynical abandonment of the League of Nations at the time of the Hoare-Laval crisis in December was bound to result in renewed lines of division. The clear opposition to appeasement demonstrated by leading Liberals, including Sinclair himself, has subsequently attracted understandable commendation.[141] At the time, however, Sinclair's stance served as a catalyst for further defections to Liberal Nationalism. In Wrexham Edward Hughes, soon to set up a local Liberal National association, was brutally frank in his readiness to sacrifice Abyssinia in order to avoid war. 'Things are looking black this morning', he wrote as the crisis approached its conclusion. 'I hope the Government will steer clear of a War this week and not involve this country in complications in the interests of a lot of Niggers in Abyssinia.'[142]

By 1938 Chamberlain's increasingly personal diplomacy, culminating at the Munich Conference in September in the sacrifice of the Czechoslovakian Sudetenland in a vain attempt to satisfy Hitler's appetite for territory and aggrandisement, was polarising opinion across the country as a whole. But not all Liberals rallied behind the party's official stance. Well known figures such as the journalist J.A. Spender and even the party's former leader Lord Samuel openly backed the Prime Minister. Trying, unsuccessfully, to attract a new recruit, Simon wrote to Spender, justifying the government's position in explicitly 'Liberal' terms:

> I am very greatly distressed at the line taken, and still more by the general attitude shown by the Opposition Liberal rump in the Commons. Anyone would think they had never heard of Asquith, and they apparently are quite ignorant of the circumstances in which Czecho-Slovakia was created – as part of a French plan to keep Germany under control ... I am always repeating to myself Asquith's watchword of 'Patience' and indeed the most remarkable personal aspect of this whole business has been the quite amazing patience and self control which Chamberlain has shown.[143]

Chamberlain even offered Samuel a seat in the cabinet. This advance was also resisted, but the Liberal Nationals did derive some advantage from Munich when Runciman was recalled to the government, at the expense of the Tory Lord Hailsham, as a reward for his efforts to find a peaceful solution to the Czech crisis.

If Spender and Samuel managed to remain within the ranks of the mainstream party, Munich did prompt one high-profile defection to the Liberal Nationals. In Bradford South the sitting Liberal MP, Herbert Holdsworth, had become increasingly critical of his party's stance on issues of foreign policy. In the wake of the Munich settlement, he took the plunge, justifying his action in an open letter to Sinclair:

> The Prime Minister needs the goodwill of all if he is to succeed and I am forced to the conclusion that it is my duty to offer him my support in his efforts to attain 'Peace for our time'. With this purpose in mind I intend to apply for the Liberal National Whip ... I supported the actions of the Prime Minister in the agreement reached at Munich. I am convinced that the alternative to that agreement was war. You obviously believe otherwise.[144]

Holdsworth was unable to take his constituency party with him. The South Bradford Liberal Association remained under the control of the Sinclairite party, but many prominent activists put loyalty to their MP before commitment to the party in whose interest he had twice been elected. Furthermore, the *Bradford Telegraph and Argus* urged caution upon those Liberals who now wished to challenge the sitting MP at the next election. They

> will now have to make up their minds as to whether they will oppose a man who is still a Liberal and by so doing let in a candidate who is not a Liberal and who is opposed to the fundamental beliefs of Liberalism. For although Mr Holdsworth finds himself at variance with certain of those who were his Liberal supporters, he still professes belief in Liberalism.[145]

Even where support for appeasement did not provoke further defections to the Liberal Nationals, it could still have the effect of weakening efforts to revive independent Liberalism. By the end of 1938 the former MP and now President of the Montgomeryshire Liberal Association, Lord Davies of Llandinam, was leading the opposition to the sitting Liberal National member, Clement Davies or, in the MP's words, 'playing dirty and holding the Liberal Caucus while I was away in Africa'.[146] Lord Davies was keen to bring matters to a head in advance of the General Election which, it was widely anticipated, Chamberlain might now call to cash in on the wave of emotional relief which swept the country in the wake of Munich. But when it was decided to seek clarification of the MP's views, not all members of the Montgomeryshire Executive were ready to agree. According to one, 'it was everyone's duty to support the present Government in their policy of Appeasement'.[147]

The Liberal Nationals' relationships with the Tories on the one hand and with the orthodox Liberals on the other figured prominently at their national gatherings in the last years of the decade. The party's annual conference in 1937 at the Central Hall, Westminster, saw Simon claim that a new Liberal party had been created on the ruins of the old, while Lady Runciman, chairman of the Women's Division, pointed to the extraordinary 'Liberalization' of the Conservative party.[148] But Runciman himself, now elected President of the Liberal National Council, reminded delegates that Liberal Nationals were determined to retain their distinctive identity and not be swallowed up inside Conservatism. On the following day a resolution was adopted stating that the number of Liberal National MPs was in no way proportionate to the volume of the government's Liberal supporters throughout the country. Edgar Granville, MP for the Eye division of Suffolk, regarded the resolution as 'most constructive and most helpful'. The future of the party depended, he said, on preserving its identity on conditions of equal partnership in the government. He understood that it had around 50 candidates selected for the next election, but suggested that the figure ought to be 150, a call backed by James Henderson Stewart, MP for East Fife.[149]

Speaking at the Scottish Liberal National Association's conference in the autumn, Simon insisted that the old political battles were a thing of the past. The contests of the future would not be between old-style Conservatism, which had been completely transformed over the previous 20 years, and the old Liberalism, which remained stuck in its trenches, unable to move and forgetting that the very essence of Liberalism was that it was a movement.[150] He took up again the theme of the transformation of the Conservative party at the Liberal Nationals' annual conference in June 1938, their last before the war. Speaking with the authority of one who had sat in the great Asquith cabinet before 1914, Simon suggested that the National Government's achievements in terms of social reform did not suffer by comparison with those of the earlier administration. It was certainly a bold claim. But the National Government's record in slum clearance, raising the school-leaving age to 15, extending pension and unemployment provision, bringing the royalties from coal-mining into state ownership, and passing a Factory Act and a Holidays with Pay Act was certainly creditable in the economic circumstances of the 1930s. Simon teased his 'old Liberal friends' who had dissociated themselves from these achievements. Like those Englishmen who had missed the Battle of Agincourt, 'Liberals in England now abed must think themselves abashed'.[151]

*   *   *

By the coming of war in September 1939, therefore, the Liberal Nationals had become an established feature on the political landscape. Some doubts persisted. Henry Morris-Jones was worried about his dependence on Conservatives in Denbigh. Hore-Belisha, notwithstanding his public pronouncements, saw no long-term future for the party and spoke privately of the eventual need for fusion with the Conservatives. Certainly, Liberal Nationals had to be careful about straying too far from the Tory line. Almost unnoticed, a Liberal National policy statement published in January 1938 contained a commitment to provide pensions for spinsters at the age of 55. When a Labour spokesman drew attention to this point in the House of Commons, the Liberal National leadership had to back-pedal as elegantly as it could. 'Ministers forming part of the Government', explained Runciman and Hutchison, 'naturally endorse the policy adopted by the Government to which they belong, and no other.' But this did not prevent members of the party holding 'more advanced' views than those which the government with its wide-ranging responsibilities felt able to put forward.[152] Even more strikingly, Captain Frederick Boult, the prospective Liberal National candidate for Hanley in the Potteries, was asked to stand down after proposing a vote of thanks to Simon in which he allowed his enthusiasm to get the better of him and said he looked forward to his leader becoming Prime Minister. 'My language was too flowery', he later explained, 'and in addition I stated that I looked forward to seeing Sir John Simon in course of time Prime Minister. But I only meant when our present Prime Minister decides to lay down his burden.'[153]

Overall, however, the mood was one of optimism. In terms of Liberal politics the impetus was with the Liberal Nationals rather than with their rivals in the mainstream party. The attitude of local Conservative associations still posed a serious barrier to further significant expansion, but the fact remained that the party was now active in more constituencies than ever before, and it approached the next General Election, scheduled for 1940 at the latest, with some degree of confidence. By-election results suggested a third successive victory for the National Government in which the Liberal Nationals could at least expect to maintain their position. The threat of absorption into Conservatism, earlier hinted at by Baldwin, no longer appeared to be on the immediate political agenda. In April 1938 Neville Chamberlain made a public statement that he hoped to see the present association of parties continuing 'for the rest of our political lives for the benefit of the country and, I hope, the world'.[154] By contrast, the position of the Sinclair Liberals remained precarious. A mini-revival in the party's electoral fortunes in 1937 proved to be no more than a typical mid-term reaction against an incumbent government. Many of their remaining parliamentary seats were vulnerable to even a moderate swing of the political pendulum. It is thus at least a plausible proposition that, but for the advent of war, the Liberal Nationals might have succeeded in displacing their rivals as the leading exponents of the Liberal creed, a position many were in fact already claiming. Pointing to renewed signs of division among Sinclair's followers over the government's National Service Bill, the *Liberal National Magazine* in May 1939 confidently predicted that 'the small minority of Liberals still in opposition' would soon rejoin 'the main body ... under Sir John Simon's leadership'.[155] By this date the Liberal Nationals were increasingly inclined to refer to the orthodox party as the breakaway group, the band of Liberal MPs who had not stayed with the concept of National Government to which all had subscribed back in 1931.

In contrast to the increasingly moribund infrastructure of the orthodox party, the Liberal Nationals were quietly gaining in strength. Increasingly, the party was getting involved in local elections with activity reported in such constituencies as Luton, Norwich, Oldham, Plymouth and Pontefract. Negotiations were in progress in the early months of 1939 which, it was hoped, would result in an additional number of the party's candidates being adopted in Scotland. Outside parliament, attempts were being made to build for the future. It was reported that membership of the Liberal National League of Youth was increasing 'very rapidly' in the London area. 'Meetings of a political and social character are held weekly. Some of the branches have organised football teams, darts teams, keep fit classes and debating circles.'[156] A Liberal National Forum was established in the autumn of 1937 to provide opportunities for the discussion of topical issues by party supporters during the winter months. The first address was given by the novelist, C.S. Forester, on 'The Spanish Conflict and its Implications'. The Forum would survive, with an interval for the war, for the next three decades.

These domestic developments were, of course, played out against the background of an ever-worsening international scene. The Liberal Nationals remained throughout staunch defenders of the government's policy of appeasement. In time this would redound to their considerable disadvantage, as a simplistic analysis of the complex problems of the 1930s branded all supporters of the National Government in a blanket indictment as 'guilty men' for having brought the country to the very verge of military disaster.[157] When Chamberlain returned from Munich, rashly predicting 'peace for our time', Hutchison issued a statement on behalf of the Liberal National Organisation expressing 'grateful thanks' for the Prime Minister's 'untiring efforts for peace' and 'congratulations' on his 'marvellous achievement'.[158] In the parliamentary debate on the Prime Minister's agreement with Hitler over Czechoslovakia, William Mabane made one of the more effective defences of the government's actions.[159] Robert Bernays claimed to have gone through 'great mental agonies', but eventually pulled back from resigning his junior office.[160] Opinion in the party, as in the government as a whole, began slowly to change as evidence mounted of the full extent of Hitler's intentions and of the true nature of his regime. After Kristallnacht in November 1938, the *Liberal National Magazine* noted that the Führer's 'violent measures against all the Jews in Germany have shown that racial passion counts for more with him than British friendship'.[161]

When the war crisis arrived the following September, Simon played an important, if at the time largely unappreciated, role. Germany invaded Poland in the early hours of 1 September, apparently activating the British guarantee of Polish independence, but for the next two days Chamberlain appeared to hesitate. He was anxious to synchronise declarations of war with the French, but the suspicion was inevitably aroused that he was looking for a Munich-style solution to this latest act of Nazi aggression. By the evening of 2 September, something like half the cabinet was in a state of open revolt and looking to Simon to make their views known to Chamberlain. 'The language and feeling of some of my colleagues were so strong and deep', noted Simon, 'that I thought it right at once to inform the Prime Minister.'[162] Brushing aside the objections of the French ambassador, Simon insisted that, by the time parliament met at noon on the following day, it was imperative that Chamberlain should be in a position to make a definite announcement – either that Hitler had agreed to withdraw his forces or that a state of war existed. It was thus at the Chancellor's suggestion that the expiry of the British ultimatum to Germany was fixed for 11 a.m. 'So ended this remarkable day', recorded Simon, 'the last day of peace, possibly, that I shall ever see.'[163] In this last prediction he was unduly pessimistic. It was not, of course, a moment to consider the implications of the situation from a party point of view. But those implications were nonetheless real. Existing lines of political development were now diverted; the General Election anticipated for the autumn of 1939 or the spring of 1940 never took place; the Liberal Nationals' annual conference scheduled for Harrogate in September was cancelled; and the circumstances that had brought the party into being nearly a decade earlier soon receded into an earlier age.

4

The War Years and Beyond, 1939–47

It is now widely recognised that the Second World War was a period of crucial importance in the evolution of the modern British political structure. To all parties it posed searching challenges. By its end the party political landscape was scarcely recognisable as that which had characterised the 1920s and 1930s. The maintenance of party organisation, threatened in wartime by the cessation of routine political activity, understandably changed priorities, shortage of funds and enforced absence for military and other reasons, was a particular problem, especially for smaller parties. For them, the difference in terms of critical mass between an infrastructure that could survive and one that could not was narrower than was the case with the larger organisations of the major parties. The Liberal Nationals, like their Liberal cousins, were likely to suffer in this respect. But the war also posed a series of problems more specific to the Liberal Nationals which threatened their very survival. The National Government, to which they owed their existence, came to an end in May 1940 and, although they maintained their place in government under Winston Churchill, their influence within the all-party coalition that was then formed was inevitably diluted by the presence also of Labour and the mainstream Liberal party. In addition, over the course of the war the idea of the 'threat of socialism', upon which the party had based much of its electoral propaganda, lost a good deal of its appeal. An increasing number of voters came to see 'socialism', however they defined it, as the way ahead, the best means of tackling the enormous problems of postwar reconstruction that would accompany the ending of hostilities. Furthermore, the war also saw the first tranche of Liberal National leaders begin to abandon the political stage. Their replacements were, on the whole, men of lesser stature and influence.

The first casualty was Viscount Runciman. With the outbreak of hostilities Runciman readily gave up his position as Lord President of the Council. In practice this made little difference. He had been ill for much of the year since his return to the cabinet and in February Chamberlain had agreed to three months leave of absence, which had enabled him to embark on a cruise to Australia in a vain attempt to restore his health. Runciman stayed on in the largely honorific post of President of the Liberal National Council until March 1945. But in the Prime Minister's hastily constructed War Cabinet Liberal Nationals still occupied two out of nine positions, Simon at the Exchequer and Hore-Belisha at the all-important War Office. Beneath them Ernest Brown and Leslie Burgin retained their cabinet-rank posts at the ministries of Labour and Supply respectively.

But it was clear that discontent was brewing inside the parliamentary party. The Liberal Nationals' contingent of MPs suffered its first defection in December when Clement Davies, the member for Montgomeryshire, resigned the government whip. He wrote to Chamberlain complaining of the government's failure to take the necessary measures for the vigorous prosecution of the war. The government had not 'the resolution, policy or energy demanded by the Country and by the situation itself to meet this crisis'.[1] By this time Davies had already become chairman of an all-party group of the government's critics and would play a critical, if at the time largely unsung, role in the fall of Chamberlain the following May.[2] For the time being he sat as an independent, before rejoining the mainstream Liberals in February 1942. Then, early in the New Year of 1940, James Henderson Stewart, MP for East Fife, wrote to *The Times* to complain that the government was still a party government, dominated more than ever by the Conservatives. He drew attention to the way in which the Tories' backbench 1922 Committee was able to invite senior ministers to its meetings from which Liberal Nationals were excluded.[3] Less than a month later he made a speech in Edinburgh calling upon all Liberals to unite. When peace returned, he argued, only the intervention of a strong Liberal party could prevent a big swing to the left which might destroy the great achievements of earlier generations.[4]

Most of Davies's criticisms had been related to the government's failure to secure the effective co-ordination of economic policy, a matter which remained the departmental responsibility of the Liberal Nationals' leader, John Simon. The latter's position was under some threat throughout the period of the Phoney War. The absence of full-blown military operations inevitably directed attention away from the service ministries and towards those such as the Treasury which were expected to put Britain in a position to win the war when fighting began in earnest. Thus, Simon's conduct as Chancellor was scrutinised more closely than ever before; and perceptions were increasingly unfavourable. Even in the first month of the conflict R.A. Butler, junior minister at the Foreign Office, remarked that 'if any Department was losing the War, it was the Treasury'.[5]

Many of the Chancellor's priorities remained unchanged from the pre-war era. In particular, he was just as concerned that the country should husband its resources so as to be able to survive a long conflict. There were cogent arguments in favour of such an approach, but Simon's cautious line offered ammunition for critics who believed that more could and should be done in the short term. When Simon delivered his spring budget in April 1940 and confirmed income tax at 7s 6d (37½p) in the pound, the reaction was instructive. A *Punch* cartoon pictured a tax-payer declaring: 'I tell you income tax at 7 and 6 pence is outrageous – it should have been ten shillings at least!'[6] *The Times* picked up on a remark which the Chancellor made that 'most of the economic problems in conducting a war consist of a conflict of arguments'. These words, so typical of Simon's style, were, thought *The Times*, the strongest reason for putting economic policy in the hands of someone who could take decisions instead of stating a case, however admirably, on both sides.[7]

At some point the desire for a new face at the Exchequer reached 10 Downing Street. By late December secret soundings were being made regarding the possibility of an enabling bill to allow a peer to speak but not vote in the Commons, so that the distinguished economist and businessman, Lord Stamp, could succeed Simon. The latter might become Lord President in a cabinet reshuffle. This strange plan, which may have originated in the mind of the Governor of the Bank of England, Montagu Norman, has left little documentary evidence behind it, though John Colville, Chamberlain's private secretary, recalled Norman, 'wearing a black cloak and, with his short beard closely resembling Mephistopheles', arriving after dark for clandestine meetings with Horace Wilson to discuss details.[8] Chamberlain saw Stamp at the beginning of January 1940, but the latter was reluctant to take on the role mapped out for him and the whole plan fizzled out. As the Prime Minister explained, 'the reason why I abandoned the daring project of which I told you was because when I broached it to the individual for whom I had designed the hero's role he showed such a very unheroic trepidation at the prospect that I saw he would be hissed off the stage'.[9] So Simon remained at his post, apparently blissfully unaware of the plans for his removal.

Altogether more public was Chamberlain's controversial reshuffle in January 1940, as a result of which Hore-Belisha left the government, declining to accept appointment to the Board of Trade after being removed from the War Office. His sacking was accompanied by rumours – probably unfounded – that he was the victim of deep-seated anti-Semitism at the heart of the British establishment. More probably, Hore-Belisha paid the penalty for his abrasive personality and his inability to establish a viable working relationship with the leading figures in the Army hierarchy.[10] At all events, Hore-Belisha was deeply disappointed at the lack of support he received from his party leader. His dismissal brought to a head the growing feeling in Liberal National circles that Simon was more concerned with looking after his own position within the upper echelons of the National Government than with championing the interests of his party. As Henry Morris-Jones put it, 'Peace at any price for John. His Party does not count – except when he wants to make use of it.'[11] Though Simon wrote to express his regret at Hore-Belisha's departure, the latter felt that he had failed to speak up for a party colleague. As he explained: 'Simon, who was consulted by the PM, never said a word to me until after I had resigned, when he asked me to stay in the team'.[12]

Many Liberal National MPs, however, felt that the former war minister had been badly treated. According to Morris-Jones,

> I think he is a big man politically, a reformer full of zeal and character and like many a reformer has antagonised powerful interests. His chief weakness is the lack of a party to back him. But the 33 Lib Nat MPs if united and determined could reinstate him in high office ... Had we a strong leader we could do much but Simon is a clever piece of jelly and has no backbone.[13]

Within a week of Hore-Belisha's dismissal, approaches by Archibald Sinclair suggested that around eight Liberal National MPs might be ready to return to the Liberal fold.[14] The former war minister confided that it was his intention to devise a policy to appeal to all Liberals. 'He believed that the prevailing sentiment of the country was liberal and he could appeal to it. He hoped to advocate an advanced social policy.'[15] When, however, Hore-Belisha began criticising the government in the Commons, Simon responded by seeking and securing his removal from the chairmanship of the parliamentary group. His supporters had 'no time to prepare or rally his defence'.[16]

The government's troubles came to a head as a result of the collapse of the military campaign in Scandinavia. Speaking at the Caxton Hall on 3 May, John Simon insisted that the government was ready to answer its critics. 'You may dismiss from your minds the idea that this is going to be material for some exciting political controversy or combat.'[17] A week later, however, the National Government, formed in 1931, finally came to an end. In the decisive vote on the Norwegian Campaign on 8 May 1940, which helped precipitate the fall of Chamberlain's government, it is worth noting that four Liberal Nationals – Hore-Belisha, Henderson Stewart, Herbert Butcher and Frank Medlicott – voted against the government. When Churchill then replaced Chamberlain as Prime Minister, it was widely anticipated that it would now be the turn of Simon himself to face political oblivion in the resulting reconstruction of the government. Morris-Jones was 'much happier ... politically' than he had been for a long time 'with prospects of the old gang including Simon ... going'.[18] The Liberal National leader was closely associated with Chamberlain and widely regarded as among the most craven of the appeasers. It had become apparent that even Chamberlain, in the last days of his administration, had been ready to ditch his long-term colleague in a desperate effort to cling on to power himself. But while Churchill was probably keen to exclude Simon from the higher direction of the British war effort, he was very conscious that his, unlike Chamberlain's, was now to be a genuinely all-party government and, in any case, he was still keen to make use of the talents of one of the most distinguished lawyer-politicians of the age. Accordingly, Simon now found himself ennobled as Lord Chancellor – the Woolsack instead of the scrap-heap as Asquith's daughter put it.[19] Meanwhile no ministerial position was found for Hore-Belisha.

Simon's elevation to the upper chamber inevitably created a vacancy for the leadership of the Liberal National group in the House of Commons. Ernest Brown, now Secretary of State for Scotland, was the obvious successor in terms of seniority. But a group of Liberal National MPs, including Hore-Belisha, Henderson Stewart, Butcher, Morris-Jones and Murdoch Macdonald, who feared that Brown would be likely to follow Simon's course of unquestioning loyalty to the government, succeeded in blocking his appointment at party meetings in May and June. At the same time they engineered the appointment of the veteran George Lambert, whose parliamentary career went back to Victorian days, as temporary chairman.[20] Not until December was Brown finally elected to the party leadership, at which time Hore-Belisha was reinstated as chairman.[21] A group was clearly beginning to emerge within the Liberal National ranks which believed that the time had come for the party to reassert itself and put an end to what it regarded as the too quiescent attitude that had prevailed under Simon's direction. John Reith, the former head of the BBC and now a government minister, who had, somewhat reluctantly, been parachuted in to fill a Liberal National parliamentary vacancy in Southampton, noted considerable ill-feeling about Churchill's distribution of offices. The Prime Minister had seemed to be more generous to the Sinclair Liberals than he had been to the Liberal Nationals, 'bringing in Harcourt Johnstone for instance and putting Shakespeare out of Overseas Trade where he has only been for five weeks'.[22] As Morris-Jones explained:

> Winston so far has practically ignored Lib Nats which for 9 years have been a pivot of government. This is due to shocking bad leadership and timidity by Simon who has now finished his political career by going to the Lords as Lord Chancellor. 12 noon [Herbert] Butcher and I met H[ore]-B[elisha] at his house. H.B. full of fight and wants to revivify Lib Nat Party. Discussed further at lunch with Henderson Stewart, Murdoch Macdonald and Herbert Holdsworth.[23]

The Liberal National dissidents quickly developed into a sort of parliamentary 'awkward squad', moving an amendment to oppose the adjournment of parliament for even as little as a fortnight in the summer of 1940. By July, the so-called 'Silent Column Club' had been formed which was active in courting support in the press. There was a strong feeling that 'we could not win the war as things were now' and particular resentment at the way in which Churchill had retained a number of discredited appeasers inside his government.[24]

By the end of the year some of these concerns seemed to have been resolved. Terminal illness obliged Neville Chamberlain to give up the post of Lord President in October, while the sudden death of the British Ambassador to Washington, Lord Lothian, in December, afforded Churchill the opportunity to prise Lord Halifax from the Foreign Office to replace him. In turn, Halifax's place was taken by Anthony Eden. But the Liberal National critics were far from satisfied and still refused to give the government unconditional support. 'Our Party does not count in the H[ouse] or the country', complained Morris-Jones. 'A few of us are trying to revive it.'[25] Hore-Belisha, no doubt still smarting from Churchill's failure to make use of his ministerial talents, regarded 'the P.M. as a danger. He says he has no judgement and visualises a position when some calamity will arise as the result of his change of strategy.'[26] The British people had been inspired by their Prime Minister's oratory but 'the country would soon wake up and realise that speeches were not victories, and that we were drugged with Winston's oratory'.[27] For his part, Churchill viewed his critics with contempt. 'An opposition is being formed out of the left-outs of all Parties', he told his son, Randolph. 'L[loyd] G[eorge], Hore-Belisha, Shinwell, Winterton and some small fry, mostly National Liberals. They do their best to abuse us whenever the war news gives them an opportunity, but there is not the slightest sign that the House as a whole, or still less the country, will swerve from their purpose.'[28]

In May 1941, during a debate on the ill-fated invasion of Greece, Morris-Jones and Edgar Granville, Liberal National MP for Eye and formerly Simon's PPS, tabled an amendment to a motion of confidence in the government, which called for the appointment of a Minister of Production. Though this was not called by the Speaker, Granville used his speech during the debate to urge the creation of an Allied War Production Council. He argued that 'until we mobilise the full resources of the Empire and use them as a basis of total war we cannot achieve victory'.[29] But it was becoming difficult to mount a reasoned critique of the government's war effort without appearing to be lacking in patriotism. Churchill reacted angrily to Granville's intervention and there were calls in Eye for Granville to stand down and re-submit himself to his constituents in a by-election. The MP had to defend his actions to his local constituency association: 'I cannot but feel that it is unfortunate that normal friendly criticism should be referred to in this way'.[30]

As 1941 progressed, Morris-Jones and Granville began to distance themselves from their erstwhile mentor, Hore-Belisha. 'We may be suffering', noted Morris-Jones, 'from our supposed constant alliance with Hore-Belisha, who is unpopular in the House and [who] suffers from anti-Jewish bias and feeling.'[31] At the same time the position of the dissidents within the Liberal National party, which was after all still a component part of Churchill's coalition government, was becoming increasingly uncomfortable. In August Ernest Brown gave notice that he would be raising the question of the conduct of Morris-Jones and Granville at the next party meeting. 'He wants to deprive us of the inalienable right of every MP of fair criticism on questions of public policy', complained Morris-

Jones.[32] When the meeting took place on 6 August, it proved to be the occasion of further divisions in the party's ranks. To Morris-Jones's dismay, Hore-Belisha made no attempt to defend his two colleagues from the censure of the party hierarchy. 'HB has lost a good friend in Edgar and probably his most loyal and best friend in me.'[33]

Against this background it was scarcely surprising that the Liberal Nationals' annual conference in September, where the delegates numbered 'no more than 160', was a less than happy occasion.[34] Edgar Granville and Murdoch Macdonald were absent, pleading prior engagements in their constituencies. In an admittedly biased report drawn up for Lloyd George, A.J. Sylvester suggested that 'the conference of the Sinclair Liberals was a lively show in comparison with this, so you can tell how bad this one was. A third of the delegates present yesterday were asleep. They had nothing to say. The whole thing was run by the platform.'[35] Nonetheless, the proceedings were not without interest. In a statement on postwar policy the party insisted that finding a solution to the problem of unemployment, so as to give all able-bodied citizens the opportunity to work, must be regarded as one of the government's essential aims. Furthermore, pride was expressed in the fact that it was Liberal policy that had 'laid the foundation and built the first sections of Britain's great edifice of Social Services'. These services should now be co-ordinated and extended, for which purpose an expansive and liberal economic policy would have to be pursued. Leslie Burgin proposed a motion to the effect that the preservation and encouragement of private enterprise was an essential conception of the Liberal faith, while Hore-Belisha expressed the hope that the Atlantic Charter would be the prelude to common citizenship with the United States.[36]

In the meantime Morris-Jones and Granville determined to loosen the ties which bound them to the Liberal National party in order to distance themselves from the government's conduct of the war. The two men decided to cross the floor of the House of Commons 'to a position of more independence – Edgar below the gangway; me on the Front Opposition Bench largely amongst the Labour people'. Their purpose, as Morris-Jones explained, was two-fold:

1. To make an open clean cut from Hore-Belisha, who tars us with whatever we do willy nilly, and who has been a terrible disappointment to me after the self-sacrificing endeavours I have made for him.

2. In order to get a position of more independence and leave our Party guessing.³⁷

Morris-Jones secured the backing of the Denbigh Conservative Association for this initiative – 'provided that you whole heartedly support the Government in its efforts to win the war, I cannot see that constructive criticism without Party bias is out of place'³⁸ – though the attitude of the local Liberal Nationals was more cautious. In Eye it was the local Liberal party which gave Granville a unanimous vote of confidence.³⁹ Murdoch Macdonald, Liberal National MP for Inverness, soon indicated his support and, after talks with Clement Davies, T.L. Horabin, the left-wing Liberal MP for North Cornwall, and Frank Owen, future biographer of Lloyd George and former Liberal MP for Hereford, Morris-Jones was hopeful that 'a new democratic party' might emerge, incorporating perhaps Malcolm MacDonald and the remnants of the old National Labour party.⁴⁰

The entry of Japan into the war in December 1941 and the rapid subsequent collapse of Britain's far-eastern empire encouraged the rebels to greater boldness. Morris-Jones, Granville and Davies discussed the political situation together in mid-January 1942. 'Clem wants PM to go', recorded Morris-Jones. 'Says he is a danger.' Stafford Cripps, who had greatly enhanced his reputation as a result of his recent spell as Ambassador to Moscow, was seen as Churchill's most likely successor.⁴¹ Expressing such sentiments in public was, however, a very different matter and, in his Commons speech on a motion of confidence a week later, Morris-Jones went out of his way to praise the Prime Minister's personal contribution to the national war effort. But he drew a distinction between Churchill and the government which he led, with the composition of which the member for Denbigh remained dissatisfied, In like vein, Granville argued that, without the Prime Minister, the present government would not last three weeks. The public, he claimed, had confidence in Churchill, but no confidence that he had the right team around him to win the war, and he called upon the Prime Minister to offer Cripps a place in his government.

Thwarted by the Speaker in his attempt to move an amendment to the vote of confidence, urging 'the desirability of appointing to high office the most capable and active men irrespective of party',⁴² Morris-Jones nonetheless delivered a stinging critique of Churchill's attitude towards his administration. But striking the right balance between constructive criticism and inappropriate opposition was no easy task, and Morris-Jones rather spoilt the effect of his intervention by making the superficially logical but politically impossible suggestion that, with the entry of the Soviet Union and the United States into the war on Britain's side, the government should now consider reducing the size of the British army in order to use the resulting surplus manpower to safeguard the interests of the nation's agriculture. In the last resort, however, Morris-Jones

> would rather be a 'No' man occasionally and try to win the war than be a 'Yes' man and lose it. From that point of view I reserve the right as a Member of this House to make constructive criticism when I feel I can do so.[43]

In the event, Morris-Jones and Granville went into the government lobby on the motion of confidence, which was easily carried. But the two men, still nominally Liberal Nationals, had fallen foul of a party resolution requiring members to inform the party before tabling motions on matters of policy. In the context of their earlier behaviour, a showdown now appeared inevitable. Summoned to appear before a party meeting in February 1942 at which it was clearly intended 'to put us on the carpet', Morris-Jones and Granville decided upon their course of action.[44] In view of the 'constant attitude of repression and the attempt to fetter us', the two men determined that no useful purpose would be served by remaining within the Liberal National ranks. It was a serious and risky step to cut themselves adrift from their party and become 'independents'. On the other hand, 'the country is very restive, is very dissatisfied as we are with our present feeble war efforts, and is tired of Parties'. Furthermore, the rebels were now convinced that the Liberal National party itself had outlived its usefulness.[45]

The resignations were planned to create the maximum impact. A letter to Ernest Brown was composed in advance, with 40 copies made ready for distribution to the lobby correspondents of the British and imperial press and to the BBC. A well attended party meeting was held on 12 February. From the chair Brown – who was known to enjoy the sound of his own booming voice – began a somewhat long-winded critique of the conduct of the two MPs, when Morris-Jones interrupted him and declared:

> It is no use going into long past history. I cannot be bound by any letters which prohibit me exercising my full freedom of criticism especially in these desperately serious times. The idea is in any case

impracticable and moreover it is not enforced by any other Party in the House.

With that, he thanked his colleagues for their past kindness, and prepared to take his leave.

The next development had not, however, been anticipated. Hore-Belisha got to his feet and began to speak up for the two dissidents. Morris-Jones, realising that a long argument might now ensue resulting only in a 'mild reprimand', again interrupted the speaker and walked out. Within a couple of minutes he had been joined by Granville and the two men set about distributing their prepared statement to the representatives of the press. In this the rebels declared that

> for some time we have been convinced that something more than the present policy and the present Government was necessary to win the war. For a year we have taken the strongest action to plead for an Empire Cabinet and effective strategy, the reorganisation of production under a single Minister and a reconstruction of the present Government ... Our first loyalty must be to the winning of the war. There is no place today for party politics.

Inside the on-going meeting, however, Hore-Belisha chided the party for its 'impossible attitude in time of war' and announced that he too was resigning.[46]

Morris-Jones and Granville were less than pleased with Hore-Belisha's actions, not least because he, being better known than they to the general public as a former cabinet minister, tended to dominate some of the resulting headlines. The two men regarded his motives with suspicion:

> Leslie with his clever Jewish mind yesterday did some rapid calculations. Knew we were resigning at a good time on a good issue; decided to immediately jump on to our wagon and to become the conductor of it! This we have no intention of allowing if we can prevent it ...[47]

Within a month Murdoch Macdonald, referring to the 'grievous wrong' that had been done to his colleagues, announced that he too was resigning from the Liberal National parliamentary group, although he intended to continue to support the party in the country.[48]

The loss since the beginning of the war of Clement Davies, Hore-Belisha, Morris-Jones, Granville and Macdonald – about one sixth of the parliamentary party – was a serious matter. In short, the Liberal National group seemed on the verge of disintegration. Early in 1943 the Liberal Nationals lost the seemingly impregnable seat of Eddisbury in Cheshire to the newly formed Common Wealth party. In part, this reflected the wave of anti-government, or more particularly anti-Conservative, sentiment which found expression in a number of contested wartime by-elections, resulting in victories for, or at least strong performances by, independent, and usually left-wing, candidates. But in this instance it was also the result of a worrying collapse in the Liberal Nationals' constituency party organisation. This allowed the local branch of the National Farmers' Union to foist a Cheshire landowner on to the Eddisbury Liberal National Association as their candidate, even though the individual concerned had had no previous connection with the party and was, *prima facie*, a committed Conservative.[49]

In the event, the erosion of the Liberal Nationals' parliamentary base went no further before the end of the war. While Hore-Belisha edged his way towards the Conservatives, Edgar Granville was readmitted to the mainstream Liberal party. Murdoch Macdonald retained his somewhat ambiguous status and secured re-election in Inverness in the 1945 General Election, standing as an independent Liberal pledged to support Churchill. Morris-Jones, on the other hand, quickly came to regret his acts of rebellion. 'Independence' proved to be 'a sort of no-man's land' and he soon became uncomfortable in the political company he now kept. But his own political thinking was clearly evolving. At heart, he reflected, he was 'really a Tory or a Liberal Unionist'. He had 'no left sympathies whatsoever' and hoped that he would eventually find his way into his 'proper political home – a new Tory democratic party'.[50] As early as the end of 1942 Morris-Jones was giving serious thought to rejoining the ranks of the Liberal Nationals. Early the following year he reflected upon 'a year as an Independent and there is nothing in it. One must cooperate in a Party.'[51] Concluding that his political career had been 'much hampered through sticking to fallen stars', Morris-Jones was welcomed back into the Liberal National fold at the end of March.[52]

These developments took place against the background of a possible party political realignment with the war acting as the catalyst. One variation on this theme was the prospect that the two rival Liberal groups might come back together in order to meet the demands of the postwar era. Such an eventuality seemed well within the bounds of practical politics. Liberals and Liberal Nationals were after all working together inside the same government for the first time since 1932. Older members of both factions would remember that the Liberal party had emerged divided at the end of the First World War, ill-prepared to cope with the challenge posed by the Labour party in the early 1920s. Reunion had come only in 1923 by which time much damage had been done. As it happened, on the very day that Murdoch Macdonald's resignation was announced, the Sinclair Liberals were scheduled to debate the possibility of reunion at a meeting in London of the Council of the Liberal Party Organisation.[53] But the matter was bound to cause controversy. When Donald Johnson, a former and future parliamentary candidate, moved a resolution that the time was ripe for a reunion of the two parties, Lord Meston intervened to stress that this was 'really a family affair' and should be discussed inside the family first. Johnson withdrew his motion and the doyen of West Country Liberalism, Isaac Foot, sought and secured clarification that the 'family' in this instance was the Liberal parliamentary party.[54] Ten days later, Foot made it clear that, as far as he was concerned, reunion could only be on Liberal terms. Speaking to the Devon and Cornwall Liberal Federation at Liskeard, he stressed that there was only one Liberal party and that its door was open to those who wished to return to it. Foot mocked the Liberal National defectors such as Hore-Belisha who were now proclaiming the rights of the independent member. The very basis of the Simonite party had been the pledge to give absolute and unqualified support to the government of the day. The world's present troubles were, Foot argued, due in no small measure to the fact that for a decade there had been far too many 'yes-men' and 'rubber-stamp' MPs who had failed to exercise their right to independent criticism of the policies of the National Government.[55]

But the idea of reunion would not go away and, by the summer of 1943, a new impetus had been given to it by none other than the Prime Minister. In conversation with the Liberal economist and newspaper proprietor, Walter Layton, Churchill argued that the two wings of Liberalism should unite. 'He hoped that if they did so they would decide to work with the Government. He pressed [Layton] repeatedly to support this policy.'[56] After discussions inside the Liberal National parliamentary party, Brown seized the initiative in a speech to the party's Postwar Policy Committee on 13 July. Referring to a recent broadcast by Churchill in which the Prime Minister had stressed the continuing need, after the end of hostilities, for an all-party government to tackle the problems of postwar reconstruction, Brown said that the time was propitious for a frank statement to all who desired reunion of the two Liberal parties. Stressing his own Liberal credentials, he argued that agreement on policy would be the first prerequisite. Brown was ready to meet with Sinclair and his senior colleagues at any time to discuss the bases of a united Liberal policy. This would ensure that 'in the vast changes foreshadowed in the post-war world the authoritarians shall not overwhelm the men of freedom'.[57]

Brown's speech was clearly timed to ensure that the matter would be considered at the Liberal Party Conference meeting later that week. Here the Liberal chief whip, Percy Harris, responded enthusiastically. 'For God's sake let Liberals stand together. I am sick of differences. It is up to us to close our ranks and try to find a common platform.' His words reflected majority opinion at the conference, but it was also clear that moves towards reunion with the Liberal Nationals would run the risk of alienating the Liberals' radical left wing. In moving a motion in favour of greater state control, T.L. Horabin showed that a sizeable minority of Liberals no longer adhered to the classic tenets of economic liberalism so recently espoused by Brown. Supporting Horabin, Megan Lloyd George suggested that some of the speeches she had listened to at the Liberal assembly might have come from the 'dulcet siren tones of Mr Ernest Brown'. The Liberal Nationals had 'been living in a different world, a world in which it will be very difficult for Radicals to breathe freely. I am afraid that any marriage of convenience could only end once more in the Divorce Court.'[58]

In any case, it seems likely that Brown's initiative was largely tactical. The approach to the Sinclair Liberals was made 'knowing they could not accept our policy' and was designed simply 'to put ourselves right with our Liberal supporters in the country who might accuse us of maintaining divisions amongst Liberals'. It was even suggested that it had been 'decreed' by Churchill who regarded the fusion of the two Liberal factions as a significant first step towards the development of a broad anti-socialist front to resist the Labour party in the postwar era.[59] According to one estimate, not more than three Liberal National MPs genuinely desired reunion with the 'cranks and half baked Socialists' of the mainstream party.[60] For all that, Sinclair was prepared to enter negotiations, not least because they offered an opportunity to check the advance of the radical wing within his own party. In his speech to the Liberal Conference Sinclair did not rule out continuing Liberal participation in government after the end of the war for 'a period of reconstruction'. Equally significantly, he admitted, in a way that few Liberals had so far done, the damage that had been caused by the Liberal National schism:

Experience has shown that the existence alongside the Liberal Party of another party with a Liberal appellation confuses the electors. It gives Liberals an undeserved reputation for faction-fighting and heresy-hunting and plays into the hands of our opponents. Therefore I want to see the Liberal Party strong, united and reinforced by all men and women who subscribe to its principles, will support its policy and will resolutely maintain its identity and its independence.[61]

A first meeting between delegations from the two parties took place at London's St Ermin's Hotel on 3 August with Percy Harris in the chair. Two hours of 'extremely rambling discussion' revealed how difficult ultimate agreement would be. In an opening statement for the Liberal Nationals, Geoffrey Shakespeare stressed four points. There must be an agreed common policy in which the greatest emphasis should be placed on 'free enterprise'; the coalition government would need to continue after the war; a 'coupon' election of some kind was unavoidable, so there would need to be an agreement on the allocation of seats; and in no circumstances should Liberals ever again give support to a minority Labour government, although there would be no objection to supporting or taking part in a Conservative government on 'an agreed policy'. The Liberal Nationals said that they were willing to subscribe to a declaration that any reunited party should be 'free' and 'independent', but whether their understanding of these words was the same as that of the Liberals was another matter. Dingle Foot, who reported on the meeting to both Sinclair and Megan Lloyd George, sensed disunity among the Liberal National delegation with Shakespeare and Henderson Stewart representing the 'extreme pro-Tory point of view', while Lord Teviot, Sir Frederick Hamilton and Alec Beechman, the group's new chief whip, were 'more reasonable'. But the lack of progress was a source of comfort to Liberal left-wingers. 'So far, so good', concluded Foot. 'As far as I can gather nothing remotely resembling a basis of agreement ever looked like emerging from the discussion.'[62] From the Liberal right wing Violet Bonham Carter was equally dismissive. The Liberal Nationals 'have no policy, fear Labour and wld. sign on any "dotted line" which would enable them to keep safe seats under cover of a "Coupon"'.[63] Eventually proceedings were adjourned without a date being fixed for the next meeting.

A second meeting was in fact delayed until early November. By this time Brown had all but scuppered any prospect of a successful outcome by a renewed public declaration of the importance of the coalition continuing in being after the war. The problems of the peace, he asserted, would be of such magnitude that 'nothing less than a genuine attempt on the part of all concerned, and equal to everything they have done in the war, will suffice'. Brown specifically linked this point with the on-going talks on Liberal reunion. 'What the result of these conversations would be remained to be seen. It was his view, however, that the continuance of a National Government after the war was most vital.'64 Not surprisingly, Violet Bonham Carter felt 'even more defeatist' about the prospects for reunion than at the first meeting:

> Shakespeare and Hutch[ison] made it quite clear that they intend to pledge themselves to a post-war Coalition in advance. None of them is the least interested in 'politics' or ideas – and they all frankly admit that they 'lean to the right'.65

Desultory talks continued into 1944 but with little chance of a successful outcome. Both sides seemed reluctant to admit that the question of independence, which in practice meant the Liberal Nationals severing their links with the Conservative party, and therefore exposing themselves in many instances to electoral suicide, posed an insuperable hurdle. As the Executive of the Lancashire, Cheshire and North Western Liberal Federation appreciated, unity on the basis of compromising with the Tories was 'out of the question'.66 Finally, a resolution accepted by the Liberal parliamentary party in October 1944 forced both sides to face reality. This committed the Liberals at the next election to 'put forward, without any commitments to any other parties, the largest possible number of candidates in complete independence, presenting the party's independent programme'.67 The following month correspondence between Sinclair and Brown was published in the press which confirmed that attempts to reunite their two parties had ended in failure. Interestingly, Brown stressed that 'discussions on policy had gone a considerable way towards agreement'. He could not, however, resist the temptation to claim that the Liberal Nationals were the more legitimate heirs of the historic Liberal tradition. 'I must not overlook the fact that the tendency to seek association exclusively with Socialists, which has shown itself in your [Sinclair's] party, would be inconsistent with the forthright presentation of the case for liberty, in accordance with Liberal beliefs, upon which all Liberal Nationals are resolved.'68

This outcome to the talks on reunion greatly narrowed the options open to the Liberal Nationals. At a party dinner as early as November 1943 all had been agreed that 'our only hope was in alliance with Tories'.[69] This was even more the case a year later. Matters came to a head on 18 May 1945 when, with the war against Germany at an end, Churchill wrote to the leaders of the Labour, Liberal and Liberal National parties suggesting that they should either remain within the coalition until the end of the conflict in the Far East, and thereby postpone the calling of a general election, or else withdraw immediately so that an election could be held in July. The choice seemed at the time to be one of more importance than turned out to be the case. With even the knowledge of the existence of an atomic bomb restricted at this stage to a select few, and they having no certainty of its viability as an operational weapon, it was widely assumed that the struggle against Japan would continue for at least another 18 months and possibly two years. Almost no-one believed that an unconditional Japanese surrender lay only weeks away. In the event, both Attlee and Sinclair pressed for an autumn election, an option not put forward by the Prime Minister, and only Brown supported the idea of maintaining the coalition in being until victory over Japan had been secured.

As a result, Churchill was obliged, pending an election in July, to set up a caretaker administration, whose political complexion still purported to be 'national', but which in practice consisted only of Conservatives, Liberal Nationals and such independents as could be persuaded to take part.[70] Even the Liberal National component was relatively slender. The Earl of Rosebery, who had succeeded Runciman as party president and who proved, in this post, considerably more active and effective than his predecessor, was the sole Liberal National representative as Secretary of State for Scotland in a 16-strong cabinet. Rosebery had played little previous part in the political life of the country apart from a brief spell as a Liberal MP before the First World War, and was better known in horse-racing circles than in the corridors of Westminster. Among 24 junior ministers there were three Liberal Nationals – Brown, who moved to the Ministry of Aircraft Production, William Mabane, who became Minister of State at the Foreign Office, deputy to Anthony Eden, and, still ensconced on the woolsack, John Simon. The last named had proved himself more suited to the post of Lord Chancellor than he had been to any of the other great offices he had occupied in the course of his long career. But his exclusion from a cabinet of (almost) peacetime proportions was unique in the history of the Lord Chancellorship in the twentieth century. Violet

Bonham Carter was on sufficiently close and friendly terms with the Prime Minister to tease him about the government's composition:

And ranged behind you I see ... the Vermiform Appendix, the National Liberals – which I do not grudge you. (Dear Lord Moran [Churchill's personal physician] will tell you, if you ask him, that it is an anatomy which has outlived its usefulness in the higher forms of animal life – but that it still performs a vital though mysterious function in rabbits.)[71]

In the time available the caretaker government had little scope to do more than tread water in anticipation of the General Election which, despite widespread evidence to the contrary, it was generally assumed would be won by the Conservatives and their allies. The Liberal Nationals put forward 53 candidates, an increase of nine over the figure for the General Election of 1935 and largely an indication of the modest success the party had had in the last years of peace in securing the nomination of additional candidates. They fought in full alliance with the Conservatives, by whom they were nowhere opposed. Optimistically, Mabane promised that the Liberal Nationals could deliver 'the bulk of the Liberal vote'.[72] But, for the first time at a general election, Liberals and Liberal Nationals were in open conflict, the pretence that they remained the temporarily estranged partners of the same political movement now largely abandoned. Yet in most of the seats where the local party organisation had been surrendered into the hands of the Liberal Nationals, the Liberals found it difficult to recover lost ground and mount an effective challenge.[73] Not that the Liberal National infrastructure was itself in good order. The position in Bradford South was not untypical. When the sitting MP, Herbert Holdsworth, announced his decision not to seek re-election on the grounds of ill-health, local Liberal National officials seemed reluctant to carry on the fight. The constituency organisation had tended to atrophy during the years of war. 'There were financial responsibilities which at present were causing some anxiety' and 'the Ladies organisation had almost ceased to exist and it would be necessary to revive interest.' Holdsworth's own contention that 'if some enthusiasm could be raised, the Liberal National organisation in Bradford would again spring into activity' lacked conviction.[74] A similar situation existed in Wrexham, but at least here local officials displayed more energy and enthusiasm to repair the neglect of the past six years. 'During the war years we abandoned all our efforts', recalled the local party secretary. 'We had to do quite a lot of work building up the organisation ... In cooperation with our Conservative friends we had a complete organisation by early June.'[75]

Throughout the war the Liberal Nationals had done their best to sustain their Liberal credentials. The party's plans for postwar policy had been divided up for study by a number of committees. A key principle to emerge was that the growing wartime trend towards collectivism should be held in check. According to Mabane, the people would not accept 'a regime in which the State became the arbiter of the life and fortune of the individual. He would think a precise and logically ordered society a bad exchange for freedom.'[76] Brown confirmed that 'free enterprise and initiative' must be given 'full play in the broad sweep of all our national plans. We believe that complete State control of industry means the end of spiritual and civil liberty.'[77] A report entitled 'The State and Personal Liberty', published in May 1944, criticised the Labour party for seeing in the necessary controls of wartime 'a jumping-off point for the ordered, regulated State of their dreams'. 'It would be a mistake', the report added, 'alike in principle and in tactics for Liberals to minimize or slur over what, in effect, is an essential difference in outlook and political philosophy.'[78]

It is hard to deny that such thinking accurately represented a significant strand in historic Liberal thought. But it is more questionable whether it was in step with the prevailing trend of public opinion, enthused as it was by the success of the wartime managed economy to believe that the postwar state could continue to play an active role to the benefit of the individual citizen. There was altogether less in Liberal National pronouncements about the need for social reform based on the sort of radical interventionism of which the Liberal party had once appeared to be the spearhead. Indeed, while Liberal Nationals had begun by supporting the Beveridge Plan of 1942, looking forward to 'the establishment by all parties of the principle of freedom from want on a lasting basis',[79] their position was now more equivocal. Rowland Hunt, the party's General Secretary, writing in its house journal the *New Horizon*, went so far as to suggest that Beveridge's proposals, 'which, it must be noted, are now the official policy of the Sinclair Liberals', were absolutely contrary and opposed to Liberalism and, 'if adopted in this country would be Hitler's last triumph, for Britain would then become a completely totalitarian state'.[80]

Instead, Liberal Nationals tried to convince the electorate that social progress could best be maintained through continuing partnership with Churchill's 'liberalised' Tory party. As Simon proclaimed, the Conservatives were now totally different from the reactionary Tories whom a united and powerful Liberal party had fought and beaten four decades earlier. He went further: 'The immense improvement brought about between the two wars in the standard of life and in the provision for those who needed help most was the result of the legislation of a National Government in which Conservatives predominated.'[81] This was a sentiment for which many modern revisionist historians would now have considerable sympathy, but it did not reflect the ideas of the majority of the population in 1945. For those voters the 1930s already stood, not as an example to be upheld and emulated, but as the Devil's Decade, an era of depression, dole queues and the Jarrow Hunger March. If this was the case, then Liberal Nationals were unlikely to benefit from their ever closer alliance with the Conservatives, for they were 'accessories to all the criminal negligence of the Tory Government before the war'.[82]

The twenty-point Liberal National manifesto closely followed that of the Conservatives. It began by pledging national unity under Churchill's leadership in the vigorous prosecution of the war against Japan. Cooperation was called for with the United States, Russia and all the other United Nations, both to secure the permanent destruction of Germany's power to wage war and to build a future system of world security. In the domestic arena the party would work for the earliest possible restoration of individual rights and liberties. Enterprise and industry should be freed from bureaucratic control and restrictive practices eliminated, while the small man would be given every opportunity to establish and extend his own business. Encouragement would be given to home ownership and there were promises of higher standards of health and nutrition, as well as the complete implementation of the 1944 Education Act and the introduction, as soon as possible, of schemes for National Insurance and Family Allowances.[83] As with the Conservative document, the unimaginatively titled *Mr Churchill's Declaration of Policy to the Electors*, there was much here to commend, but the priorities of the Liberal Nationals – international over domestic – were unlikely to inspire the electorate.

Not surprisingly, the party's campaign had three main and inter-related themes: the Liberal Nationals, working in close association with a modernised Conservative party, were now the only true voice of British Liberalism; the Labour party was the ultimate threat to Liberal values; and the Sinclair Liberals were at best the unwitting agents or at worst the clandestine future allies of the socialist menace. Speaking in Wrexham, Lord Rosebery proclaimed that he would remain a Liberal long after the Sinclair

Liberals had passed into the Labour party. They had already, he insisted, entered a pact with Labour, which was why they were opposing ten of the principal members of the Churchill government but not standing against no fewer than 26 former Labour ministers.[84] In nearby Denbigh Morris-Jones suggested that Sinclair's followers were 'nothing more than half-baked Socialists' who were getting ready to form a government with Clement Attlee.[85] In their predictable response the Liberals accused Liberal Nationals of being no more than closet Conservatives. The often heard cry that Liberals were divided amongst themselves was not in fact true, insisted Lord Samuel, because the Liberal Nationals were not Liberals at all. The Liberal National dissentients had become 'indistinguishable, in policy and action, from Conservatives' and had been 'written off as a total loss long ago'.[86] In Huddersfield Mabane was standing 'as an undisguised Tory', who had been backed by the local Conservative association even before he was nominated by what was still managing to call itself the Huddersfield Liberal Association. 'If it were not so pathetic, it would be amusing.'[87] Where no Liberal was standing, it fell to Labour to puncture the Liberal Nationals' Liberal credentials while presenting itself as the true heir of the radical tradition in British politics. A Liberal National was a man with a Liberal past and a Tory present, claimed Sir George Schuster's Labour opponent in Walsall. If they voted for Schuster, Walsall Liberals would not be voting for a Liberal at all. 'It is cashing in on a bit of tradition which is very strong in Walsall to call Sir George Schuster a Liberal.'[88]

In most constituencies, of course, the Liberal Nationals were irrelevant to the basic contest between Conservatives and Labour and thus to the ultimate outcome of the election. But they could not escape the anti-Conservative tide which swept across the country, bringing Labour to power with the first parliamentary majority in the party's history. For the Liberal Nationals the result was a disaster. Only 11 unequivocal adherents were returned to Westminster.[89] Sixteen seats were lost to Labour and the party was wiped out in English towns and cities. It did relatively better in Scotland, where the swing to the left was somewhat weaker, though Ernest Brown, defeated in Leith, was among the casualties. Other prominent names to lose their seats included Mabane, Schuster and Shakespeare. Even Simon's old constituency of Spen Valley fell to Labour. Perhaps the Liberal Nationals' one crumb of comfort was that there was little evidence to suggest that the Liberal party – itself reduced to a mere 12 MPs – had had any success in reclaiming the diminished 'Liberal vote' from them. No Liberal National seat fell to the Liberals.

It was clearly time for Liberal Nationals to consider their future, not least because there was now no pretence of the National Government which had given them their primary *raison d'être*. Here and there optimism persisted. Despite losing his seat in Huddersfield, William Mabane was much impressed by the party's new intake of MPs. They were 'very united and have their tails right up'. By contrast, the independent Liberals were, he believed, in a parlous position, facing grave financial difficulties after the loss of more than 70 deposits at the election.[90] Nationally, the party did its best to regroup and a number of new appointments were made. Henderson Stewart succeeded Brown as chairman of the parliamentary party, while Herbert Butcher, MP for Holland-with-Boston, took on the role of chief whip, with Niall Macpherson (Dumfriesshire) Scottish whip. In the Lords Rosebery was elected sessional chairman with Teviot chief whip. By the end of the year Mabane had become chairman of the party's executive committee, with Sir Leighton Seager as his deputy. The Liberal National Organisation itself moved in September from Old Queen Street to more modest premises on Lambeth Palace Road.

On the ground, however, the mood was far from buoyant. In Yorkshire, the party's area organiser, Ewart Sellars, quickly reached a gloomy conclusion. After visiting a number of Yorkshire constituencies he decided that a divided Liberal movement offered no hope and could only lead to further electoral defeats. He found a widespread feeling that Liberal National policies had no individuality to distinguish them from orthodox Liberals on the one hand and progressive Tories 'of the Quintin Hogg school' on the other. But at the same time he did sense a deep-rooted desire for a Liberal policy to counteract the excesses of socialism.[91] The party's agent in Huddersfield came across similar thinking:

> Liberals [are] very puzzled about the future of the Liberal National Party. People are asking what are its functions now that there is no National Government and the only answer I can give is 'To oppose Socialism and the trend towards Control and Nationalisation'. The answer to this I generally get is that this is also the policy of the other Liberal Party. One hears frequently that unless the two sections of the Liberal Party do now get together, both will cease to be effective forces.[92]

In Bradford South, where the Liberal Nationals had lost the seat at the General Election, the local party was clearly struggling to keep going despite offers of help from headquarters in London. According to Sir Herbert Holdsworth, the constituency's former MP, there could be no possibility of again going before the country as a separate party and he thought 'the time had come for all anti-socialists to consolidate'. Such a coalition, however, could not include the mainstream Liberals whose new leader (Clement Davies) and whip (Horabin) 'had strong leanings to Socialism'.[93]

The party's elder statesman, Lord Simon, no longer holding office in its organisation but, despite his 72 years, not without continuing political ambitions of his own, also favoured the Tory option. On 2 August he sent Churchill, scarcely yet accustomed to his new role as leader of the opposition, his thoughts on the future. Simon's first conclusion was that the result of the election seemed to indicate the voters' desire to return to a two-party system. Indeed, there was no reason to believe that either wing of the once great Liberal party would ever regain a position of effective power. The Labour government had revealed its socialist intentions, making clear the duty of the opposition to watch over personal liberties and preserve and protect individual enterprise and energy. 'No objects', suggested Simon, 'could more naturally appeal to the innate liberalism of the country, using that word in the sense in which it has long inspired both professed Liberals and the best thought of the modern democratic Conservative.' Indeed, the Conservative party was no longer the party it had been 40 years earlier, and Liberals and Conservatives had 'reached an identity of purpose which ought to be openly acknowledged'. Simon's implication was clear. The moment had come for the amalgamation of the Conservative and Liberal National parties and, though he wrote as an individual, he had 'reason to believe that many Liberal Nationals agree with me'.[94]

In practice, then, most Liberal Nationals concluded that they could no longer continue as an independent party. The only realistic alternatives were reunion with the orthodox Liberals or an even closer association than already existed with the Conservative party. Rather surprisingly in view of the impasse reached in the negotiations of 1943–4, the party opted first to investigate Liberal reunion. The main determinant of this choice was clear evidence of a deterioration of the relationship with the Conservatives, particularly at constituency level. Even at the General Election arrangements between the two parties had often been difficult. In Scotland talks had gone on for many months in order to reach an understanding as to which constituencies the Liberal Nationals wished to contest, and who were to be their candidates in these constituencies. The Conservatives'

Scottish whip had found himself continually referred from one Liberal National official to another without resolution. 'One was very apt to find that one was talking to the wrong person and to be referred to another' and 'in Dumfriess-shire [sic] and in the Western Islands they continued to contradict themselves repeatedly time after time regarding what they were going to do.'[95] Despite a clear disparity in size and resources several Liberal National associations had been reluctant to play second fiddle to the big battalions of the Conservative party. In Wrexham the local activists were determined not to fall in line behind a Tory candidate 'without putting up a jolly good fight for our own man first'.[96] So while the Conservatives had already selected a candidate to carry their standard, the Liberal Nationals not only went ahead and chose their own, but then persuaded the Tories to withdraw on the grounds that a Liberal National was more likely to capture a seat with a strong Liberal tradition.

The outcome of the General Election nationally had placed a searching question-mark over all such calculations. Disillusioned Conservatives, anxious for scapegoats for their worst electoral performance since 1906, began seriously to question the value of their partnership with the Liberal Nationals. In particular, did a Liberal National standing with full Conservative backing really have the ability to attract the support of a wider proportion of the electorate than a straightforward Tory? The Conservatives' Political Secretary for Scotland believed that on balance this was the case – but the evidence was scarcely compelling:

> As regards Liberal National candidates attracting votes which would not be given to Unionist candidates, I think that in some cases this would happen because practically every Unionist would vote for the Liberal National candidate if that course were recommended by the Unionist Association, while there are undoubtedly Liberals who would not vote for a Unionist candidate. In Montrose Burghs I think that the Liberal National Member would undoubtedly get more votes than would a Unionist candidate, both for the reason just given and also because there is practically no Unionist organisation there owing to the support given for very many years to a Liberal candidate in that constituency.[97]

In individual constituencies, however, local Conservatives, frustrated by the self-denying electoral ordinance which in many cases meant that they had not contested the seat since 1929, were beginning to take matters into their own hands. In Inverness-shire the Liberal Nationals had failed to respond to repeated Conservative attempts at co-operation with the result that the local Unionist committee was now considering the adoption of a Unionist candidate. In Luton, where the Conservatives had originally decided to delay selecting a candidate, 'rumours were current that the Liberal Nationals were preparing to select their own candidate right away, which was naturally causing a good deal of resentment'. In Newcastle East the Conservative association announced its intention to adopt a candidate regardless of any views expressed by party headquarters.[98] Even in Mabane's old seat of Huddersfield the semi-dormant Conservative party was beginning to stir. At the opening of the local party's new premises in July 1946, the presiding officer declared that it was 'time that we Conservatives asserted ourselves. I am sick and tired of bowing down to other parties. If I had my way I would ask you to put up a Conservative candidate in Huddersfield.'[99] The following January the Tories duly adopted a prospective candidate of their own. The worry in many constituencies was that any further deference to the Liberal Nationals might lead to the complete atrophy of the local Conservative organisation:

> Where a Liberal candidate has been supported by the Unionists for very many years the Unionist organisation is bound to have suffered and to be not so extensive or efficient as in a constituency where there have habitually been Unionist candidates.[100]

The problem was exacerbated by the fact that local Liberal National parties were, in general, in no position to take over the responsibilities of propaganda and political education which the Conservatives had voluntarily surrendered to them. This was 'seriously prejudicing the future prospects of the Unionist party, and of opposition to Socialism in the constituencies concerned'.[101]

In this situation of mounting Conservative dissatisfaction, several Liberal National associations had also begun to take independent action and explore the possibility of reunion with what were still commonly called, despite the fact that he was no longer their leader, the Sinclair Liberals. In Dumfriesshire negotiations were proceeding between the sitting Liberal National MP, Niall Macpherson, and representatives of the party which had opposed him at the General Election only a few months earlier. Speaking to the Scottish Liberal Club in Edinburgh in February 1946 on the theme of 'the future of Liberalism', Henderson Stewart argued that the defeat of Churchill the previous summer had created an entirely new situation. Claiming that he was speaking for the whole of the Liberal National parliamentary party, he suggested that the time was ripe for an 'all-round, sincere reconciliation among true Liberals'. Henderson Stewart's message was clearly addressed primarily to the right wing of the Liberal party and he expressed concern at the left-leaning tone of some of that party's leaders. His aspirations were certainly wide-ranging:

> It is said by some of our critics that the Liberal Nationals have no thoughts save to ally themselves with the Conservatives. How foolish! We look much further afield. I see gradually emerging, before this Parliament has completed its term, a realisation that Labour rule is a menace which at all costs must be ended; and out of that realisation a coming together of enlightened Conservatives (of whom there are a great many in this new House), of vigorous Independents, of disillusioned Right Wing Labour men and Liberals of all groups. There, could it be fashioned, is the democratic force of tomorrow; there, if we but act wisely, is the future vehicle of true constructive Liberalism![102]

Nationally, more formal negotiations were initiated following an open letter from Ernest Brown to the *Glasgow Herald* in May. On behalf of the Liberal party, the Duke of Montrose responded with the offer of talks in London on 23 May.[103]

The Liberal Nationals had to tread carefully. 'The attempts at fusion ... are bound to cause offence to Unionists and make it more difficult for the Liberal Nationals to secure Unionist support in the constituencies where in the past they have relied upon it.'[104] The danger was obvious that, should the talks end in failure, the Liberal Nationals would find it difficult, if not impossible, to then negotiate a renewed agreement with the Tories. The Liberal National leadership was therefore careful to present the talks on Liberal reunion – at least to the Conservatives – as the first step in the creation of a broad anti-Socialist coalition, a first step which only they, and not the Tories, could secure. 'We finally had to agree', noted the Conservatives' vice-chairman, J.P.L. Thomas, 'but did not approve this plan as we did not think that they are right in assuming that the Sinclair Liberals would sooner work with them than with the leaders of the Conservative Party.'[105] An important meeting of leaders from the Conservative and Liberal National parties had taken place on 21 March at Conservative

Central Office. Here the Liberal Nationals had done their best to present their case. Lord Teviot argued that a number of Sinclair Liberal MPs were getting very dissatisfied with their party and might come over to the Liberal Nationals in the not distant future. But 'any indication of liaison with the Conservative Party, *under that name*, might stop this movement'. The name was, in fact, the problem. Teviot believed that the sooner the two parties – Conservatives and Liberal Nationals – could get together 'under the same umbrella' the better, but John Maclay, MP for Montrose Burghs, stressed that an attempt to link up at the present time might set back the movement towards Liberal unity 'which was demonstrating itself all over the country'.[106] On this somewhat duplicitous basis, therefore, the negotiations between Liberals and Liberal Nationals proceeded.

The leaders of the Liberal party were equally cautious. Sinclair could see the obvious advantages of fusion. The inclusion of Liberal Nationals would shift the Liberal party's internal balance to the right and more to his personal liking. Furthermore, with its own parliamentary party reduced to just 12 MPs (11 following Horabin's defection in October 1946), Liberalism was losing credibility as a national political force. The addition of recruits from the Liberal Nationals would mean that 'people would begin to take the Liberal Party seriously again'.[107] Reunion in Scotland, where the Liberal Nationals held three seats (five, if Murdoch Macdonald and Jacko MacLeod are included) and the Liberals none, 'would have a most heartening effect'.[108] But there was an obvious downside to such calculations. Any additional numerical strength from the Liberal Nationals would be largely cancelled out if their sitting MPs were subsequently challenged in their constituencies by Conservatives, an almost inevitable outcome unless Liberal-Liberal National fusion was achieved on the sort of basis which the Liberal Nationals sought. That basis would involve on-going partnership with the Conservatives, thereby undermining the independence which all Liberal leaders, Sinclair included, still regarded as beyond negotiation. Furthermore, the party's elder statesman, Lord Samuel, warned that the inclusion of the Liberal National group might have a damaging impact upon Liberal activists and left-leaning radicals. He preferred to think in terms of individual Liberal Nationals voluntarily declaring themselves in agreement with Liberal policies and rejoining the mainstream party.[109]

For all the reservations on both sides, there were early signs that the negotiations might bear fruit, at least within individual constituencies and that these outcomes might develop a bandwagon effect across the country. A resolution had already been passed in March at a conference in Plymouth recommending the union of the Devon and Cornwall Liberal Federation and the South-West Area Association of the Liberal Nationals.[110] In Huddersfield it was clear that local activists were more concerned with propagating the gospel of Liberalism than with the precise party label under which they campaigned. After co-operation in the municipal elections of 1946 the two local associations took the decision to amalgamate in March 1947 and to affiliate to the Liberal Party Organisation.[111] In July 1946 it was reported to the Manchester Liberal Federation that negotiations in Burnley had led to a fusion of the two parties and affiliation to the LPO. The Burnley party was now pressing for reunion at a national level.[112] Around the same time reunion was announced in the London area, again on Liberal rather than Liberal National terms, although the Liberal Nationals subsequently tried to recreate a separate Liberal National association for the capital to replace the officers who had thrown in their lot with the Sinclair party.[113] For the Liberals, Frank Byers, who had recently succeeded Horabin as chief whip, responded to the news from London by trying to draw a distinction between the Liberal National leadership and the party's rank-and-file. The vast majority of the latter were, he suggested with some justification, 'firm believers in Liberal principles, who found themselves in the Liberal National Party largely by the chance of local circumstances. They are determined to see a strong, independent Liberal Party having pacts with neither Tory nor Socialist.'[114]

In Scotland, too, there were early signs of progress. This time it was apparently the Liberal Nationals who were making the running, so much so in fact that there were Liberal fears that their chief negotiator, Lady Glen-Coats, chairman of the Scottish Liberals, was being out-manoeuvred by Henderson Stewart for the Liberal Nationals. The latter put forward a plan for a new Liberal party in Scotland to be called the Scottish United Liberal party to which both existing organisations should become affiliated. On 27 October the Scottish Liberal party and the Scottish Liberal National association issued a joint statement setting forth the basis of fusion to be submitted to their respective organisations. By this stage, however, negotiations at a national level had broken down and, without endorsement from headquarters for further action, the Scottish Liberal National association had to admit in early December that the quest for reunion had been abandoned.[115]

The negotiations that really mattered – those between the principal figures in the two parties – never came near to success. A declaration on reunion issued by the Liberal Nationals following their annual conference in Edinburgh in June 1946 was purposefully ambiguous. It stressed that the existing Labour government represented the antithesis of all that gave Liberalism meaning. In such circumstances the overriding duty of all Liberals was to secure its overthrow:

> This being the predominant issue, it followed, as a matter of practical politics, that, in order to achieve this end, Liberals, while maintaining their independence as a Party, should be prepared to co-operate with all other political forces whose primary object is the same.[116]

Just as in 1943–4, 'independence' was the key question as far as the Liberal leadership was concerned, but whether and in what sense it could be maintained in a process of cross-party co-operation to defeat the Labour government was far from clear. In particular, would a reunited Liberal party be free to put up candidates against Labour *and* Conservative MPs at the next general election?

Frank Byers sought to sweep away the Liberal Nationals' obfuscation. To the latter, he claimed, 'independence' apparently meant the closest possible alliance with the Conservatives, including electoral pacts, for the sake of defeating the socialists. But this type of 'independence' presupposed that there was no real difference between Conservatives and Liberals, which was far from the case.[117] The Liberal chairman, Philip Fothergill, was worried that the Liberal Nationals were only concerned to bring as much of the Liberal party as possible into an anti-socialist coalition in order to improve their own negotiating position with the Tories. The Edinburgh Declaration was duly considered by the executive of the Liberal Party Organisation and clarification sought. An increasingly acrimonious exchange of letters ensued between Fothergill and Mabane. Finally, it was Mabane who brought matters to a close:

> Your letters make it clear that before any discussions can take place we must agree to a tactical decision (relating to the candidates at the next general election). To insist on such a conclusion before negotiations are even started stultifies them in advance by making freedom of discussion impossible ... We are forced with regret to conclude that no further purpose would be served by pressing the matter further.[118]

The *Manchester Guardian*, whose sympathies remained decidedly Liberal, even if it had not endorsed the Liberals at the last election, rejoiced at this outcome and questioned why the attempt to involve the party in an 'ignoble subjection to Conservative aims' had ever been made. As for the Liberal Nationals,

> they have not been a success as recruiting sergeant for the party to which they owe their existence, and though a great future can never await them, they might find that things would go better for them individually if they changed their name to one more in keeping with their position.[119]

Throughout the summer of 1946 the Conservatives awaited the outcome of all these discussions. Their readiness to go along with the Liberal National strategy is best explained by their acceptance of the attractions of a broad anti-socialist coalition of which, according to the Liberal Nationals, a Liberal-Liberal National pact would be an essential first stage. Despite the 'landslide' Labour victory of 1945, it was only the British electoral system which gave Attlee his overwhelming parliamentary majority. Labour still polled less than 50 per cent of the popular vote and less than the aggregate total of the Conservatives and Liberals. In such a situation the temptation for Conservatives to see electoral salvation lying in some form of association with the Liberals – whatever the latter's own wishes – was intense. The alternative was that the Liberals would continue to take votes which might otherwise accrue to the Tories. Sir John Reynolds, a defeated Conservative candidate in Bolton, was 'not so sanguine about the future. Whilst the Liberals still hoped for a comeback they would always be a menace.'[120] Churchill himself wrote to his newly appointed Party Chairman, Lord Woolton, in August 1946 to stress the desirability of a broad alliance between the opposition parties. Within this, he regarded the Liberal Nationals as being of particular importance. 'We must treat them properly for they have been loyal allies.'[121] The Leader's thinking on an anti-Labour front was echoed in the more advanced sections of the Conservative party. After the 1945 debacle, many Tories believed that their party would in future always struggle to compete with Labour unless it secured a more progressive image – unless, in fact, its 'liberal' wing became more prominent.

In September 1945 a letter had appeared in the *Spectator* from Quintin Hogg, MP for Oxford and a leading light in the wartime Tory Reform

Committee. Claiming 30 or 40 supporters in the Commons, Hogg suggested that the policies in which he believed showed 'no striking differences from the Liberals' and suggested that 'if only the Liberals would come and help ... we could, together, capture the Conservative Party'.[122] By early 1946 informal discussions were taking place inside a small committee of Conservatives and Liberals, chaired by Peter Thorneycroft, Tory MP for Monmouth. It was decided to draw up a statement for joint signature entitled *Design for Freedom*. Such was the progress made that in November Liberal headquarters felt obliged to deny rumours of a Liberal-Conservative pact.[123] Meanwhile the progressive Conservative MP, Harold Macmillan, was pursuing similar ends through different means. Securing re-election to the Commons in November 1945 after defeat at the General Election, he began to argue for a change in the party's name as the word 'Conservative' failed to reflect the sort of policies he was keen to advocate and which alone would attract former Liberal voters. Macmillan aired his ideas at Conservative rallies during the summer of 1946 and, in a speech in September, suggested the possible creation of a 'new democratic party'. Writing in the *Daily Telegraph* the following month, he called upon Conservatives and Liberals to come together 'to promote a policy, not of passive anti-Socialism, but of an active and dynamic character'.[124]

The notion of a broad anti-socialist coalition would continue to permeate Conservative thinking for several years to come. But the failure of talks on Liberal reunion clearly meant that such an alignment was unlikely to begin with reconciliation between the severed wings of the old Liberal party. Indeed, having indulged the Liberal Nationals over the previous months as they engaged in negotiations about which most senior Tories had harboured serious doubts, many in the Conservative hierarchy were now ready to agree that 'the time has come when it must be made clear that the present position is NOT satisfactory and can NOT continue'.[125] The new approach was soon evident. Following a preliminary discussion between Woolton and Mabane (Mabane had served as Woolton's wartime parliamentary secretary at the Ministry of Food), a more formal meeting between Woolton, Mabane and Teviot took place on 25 October 1946. Here the Liberal Nationals confirmed that a complete break had occurred in their talks with the Liberals which would be announced in the press. With the Liberal Nationals' options thus further reduced, the Tory Chairman was well placed to drive whatever bargain he wished. Indeed, when Teviot suggested that it was unfortunate to find Conservative candidates being adopted in what he considered to be traditional Liberal

National seats, Woolton responded that he was not prepared to withhold support from Tory organisations which were seeking to re-establish themselves 'now that the Gentleman's Agreement between parties was ended'. He brushed aside Teviot's complaint that the nomination of a Conservative candidate for the forthcoming by-election in the Scottish Universities seat was making co-operation impossible:

> I told them that I thought the party was entirely justified in putting up Walter Elliot for the Scottish Universities: we had waited for a long time whilst there had been negotiations with the Liberal Party, and could reasonably assume that their minds were running along the lines of re-uniting with the Liberal Party: there was, therefore, no reason why we should defer the development of our own power until they had decided which way they were going to jump, and as far as I was concerned I should wait no longer.

Woolton went further. He personally would welcome a new agreement 'in a form appropriate to present circumstances'. But the Liberal Nationals would be well advised to 'make up their minds at once as to whether they were going to associate with the Liberals or with us'. If additional pressure were needed, Woolton suggested that jobs might be found for competent Liberal Nationals in the Conservative organisation but, 'if they delayed for two or three months, I should have completed my staff and would then undertake no obligation in the event of amalgamation'. Having precious little with which to bargain, Teviot and Mabane soon agreed to Woolton's proposals. Conversations would begin between the chief whips of the two parties with a view to the formation of a united 'Conservative and Liberal' opposition; in the event of agreement between the parliamentary parties Teviot and Mabane would have it confirmed in those constituencies represented by Liberal Nationals and in such others in which there was an operative Liberal National organisation; and these constituency amalgamations would be effected under the title of 'United Conservative and Liberal Associations'. The outcome of all this, Woolton predicted, might be a small break-away among Liberal Nationals but 'I do not know where they will go when they break'.[126]

Thereafter progress towards an agreement was rapid with Woolton confiding to Churchill that an important step could now be taken towards the 'Union Party we both desire'.[127] The Conservatives were fully aware of the weakness of the Liberal National position. 'The Lib Nats', noted the

Tory chief whip, James Stuart, 'are almost completely dependent upon us for their very existence (i.e. qua organisation, etc). I am not, therefore, *too*, worried by their complaints: without the Tories, where would they be?'[128] For their part, the Liberal Nationals understood that, the longer they delayed, the more their residual position in the country was likely to be eroded. The Conservatives 'could no longer hold up the adoption of candidates in constituencies with a Liberal National tradition but no Liberal National organisation'.[129] Ernest Brown, disappointed to have been passed over in favour of Mabane for the chairmanship of the party's executive committee and, at 66 years of age, reconciled to the end of his Commons career, did not believe that the Liberal Nationals could survive. The best that they could hope for would be to persuade the Conservatives to change their name.[130] By March 1947 the outline of an agreement was in place. Only on the issue of a joint organisation in parliament did the Liberal Nationals manage to hold their ground, arguing that it was not possible to change their title in the present parliament. But they agreed that, at the next general election, both their existing MPs and future candidates should stand as Liberal Unionists, a curious title granted its use in the late nineteenth century by a body that was later swallowed up by the Conservatives shortly before the outbreak of the First World War. The most significant provisions related to the position in the constituencies and formed the basis of the Woolton-Teviot Agreement, announced in May. In constituencies where each party already had an organisation, a combined association should be formed under a mutually agreed title designed to indicate a community of effort and purpose. In constituencies where only one of the parties had an organisation, that body should consider including in its membership all who supported joint action against socialism, and modifying its title accordingly. And, in constituencies where combined associations were seeking a candidate, a joint list would be prepared by the two parties' headquarters in consultation.[131] After an effective life of nearly 16 years, it seemed that the Liberal National party might be coming to an end.

5

The Long Road to Extinction, 1947–68

In so far as the history of the Liberal National party has yet been written, most accounts regard the Woolton-Teviot Agreement of 1947 as marking the end of its independent existence. John Ramsden, for instance, writes of the pact creating 'a single party'.[1] Such an approach is not without merit. Over much of the country the Liberal National tradition quickly evaporated, disappearing completely or surviving only in the antiquated nomenclature by which what were usually unequivocally Conservative candidates chose, or in some cases, were obliged, to present themselves to the electorate. The Liberal National label was sufficient to confuse or intrigue potential voters, particularly those of a younger generation for whom the disputes and divisions of the 1930s were an unknown episode in the Liberal party's history, but it had little continuing political significance. It was but an historical curiosity, 'the fossil remains of a conflict long ago with the Labour Government of 1929–31 and of a desperate closing of ranks on the Right after the Labour victory of 1945'.[2]

Against such an interpretation must be set the fact that, notwithstanding Woolton-Teviot, the Liberal National party still had more than two decades of theoretically independent existence before it, a longer life than it had had before the agreement of 1947 was reached. Throughout this period, the party retained the form and appearance of a national organisation with officers, finances and parliamentary and extra-parliamentary structures separate from those of the Conservatives. A diminishing band of candidates stood under one variant or other of the Liberal National device at each general election up to and including that of 1966. It was not in fact until May 1968 that the Liberal National Council was finally wound up and the party's residual members and assets were formally incorporated into Conservatism. While it would be perverse to suggest that Liberal

Nationalism remained a powerful force in British politics through the 1950s and 1960s, these last years of its history have their own interest and significance, and are well worth examining.

*   *   *

'There is no question of either side relinquishing its identity', insisted Woolton at the press conference called to announce the details of his agreement with Teviot. 'We are merely aiming at a closer co-operation of like-minded persons in the constituencies, thus broadening the basis of association activities.'[3] In practice, the Conservative approach was far more calculating than the Party Chairman's words implied. Stephen Pierssené, General Director at Tory Central Office, was quite clear that Woolton-Teviot was the first step towards 'the final amalgamation of the Liberal Nationals with our Party'. It would, however, be a mistake '*at this stage*' to give the impression that the Conservatives were swallowing up their allies. After all, the retention of the word 'Liberal' in the title of joint associations was designed to attract some degree of right-wing and moderate Liberal support. Such support would be less likely if the Liberal Nationals closed down their headquarters and took the Conservative whip in parliament. But 'after the next election I think it is probable that both these events will happen'.[4]

Woolton-Teviot was in fact part of a broader Conservative strategy which had its eye firmly on the bigger fish, the Liberal party itself. Announcing his agreement with the Liberal Nationals, Woolton had added that there was now no major issue separating Liberalism from Conservatism. 'They are both expressions of the same political philosophy.' The old quarrels between the two parties that used to enliven political life in earlier days were now 'just ancient and meaningless feuds'.[5] Speaking in Ayr just days later, Churchill dwelt upon the same theme. It was a mistake for Liberals to waste their time in abusing the Conservatives. They should concentrate their fire on their common opponents in the Labour government.[6] Whether, however, the Liberal Nationals would prove an asset to the Tories in this broader campaign was open to doubt. Liberal activists tended to view Liberal Nationals with the venomous distaste which the doctrinal purist reserves for the heretic, but would not waste on the non-believer. Some indeed, with one eye on the internal party struggle between economic and social Liberals, were only too glad to see the Liberal Nationals draw ever closer to the Conservatives. According to Richard Rowe, prospective Liberal candidate for Nottingham South, the Liberal party had undergone a 'perplexing transformation' over the previous decade. 'It had shed the "Liberal-Nationals" finally and, I hope, irrevocably, and with them laissez faire capitalism.'[7] Thus, according to Lady Rhys Williams, the 'curious thing' was that the Liberal Nationals were 'right out' of the process of Conservative-Liberal relations, 'chiefly because most of their members are *persona non grata* to the Liberal Headquarters, who are much more friendly to the Tories proper than to the Liberal Nationals!'[8]

There were early signs of the Conservatives' strategy bearing fruit. Up and down the country joint associations came into existence. In constituencies such as Dunstable, Bideford and North Angus there emerged so-called 'Liberal and Conservative associations'. At this distance in time it is not easy to determine precisely how these came into being. According to Liberal commentators such joint associations derived from meetings at which actual Liberals were either greatly outnumbered or even excluded. Even the Liberal Nationals sometimes played only a token part in the proceedings. Bideford witnessed the 'usual manoeuvre':

a public meeting announced to form a Liberal-Conservative Association. The President and Chairman of the local Liberals turn up with a band of Liberals. The meeting's Tory Chairman announces that at a previous meeting (which no Liberal had ever heard about) the style of address for the new Liberal-Conservative organisation was decided. The local Liberal President, the indefatigable Miss Hutchinson, thereupon makes her protest, is called a liar by a gallant voice in the body of the hall and is asked to leave by the Chair. Whereupon, 26 Liberals sweep out and the phoney meeting proceeds – with no reporters present, for the local reporters had been refused admittance![9]

Similarly, in North Angus 'less than a dozen Unionists' met in Montrose to form a Unionist and Liberal association. When one Liberal told the meeting that these men were acting in an unconstitutional manner, he was requested to leave. 'No doubt the formation of this Association will be hailed by the Tory machine as another victory for freedom and democracy.'[10]

By contrast, Conservatives and Liberal Nationals sought to defend the legitimacy of the new arrangements. The newly appointed secretary of the joint organisation in Cannock insisted that a United Association of Conservatives and Liberals had only been set up after proper discussion between Liberals, Liberal Nationals and Conservatives. Its officers included a Conservative chairman, a Liberal vice-chairman and a Liberal National vice-president. A prospective parliamentary candidate was adopted by a completely free and open meeting of around 500 members of all three parties. Only then, while arrangements were proceeding for the adoption of a united candidate, did the West Midlands Liberal Federation announce that the local Liberal association was against the proposals. This, however, was 'the first time the Press or the public had heard of the existence of an independent Liberal association' and it was reported that the meeting at which a hostile statement was issued by this unknown Liberal association was attended by just six men and one woman.[11] In the face of such conflicting testimony, what seems beyond dispute is that the Conservatives were able to take advantage of the long-term collapse of the Liberal party's organisational infrastructure in many constituencies. Liberal party headquarters protested strongly against the inclusion of the word 'Liberal' in the titles of these new associations, but on the ground the party was often in no position to resist this usurpation of its identity.

That said, the Conservative approach certainly had a strong appeal for many right-leaning Liberals, concerned by the performance of the Labour government. During a by-election campaign in Edinburgh East in November 1947 a lengthy discussion took place at a meeting of the division's Liberal association. Many members expressed the view that, with the country passing through a serious crisis, the fight should be between socialism and anti-socialism. 'It was noticed that both the Liberal National [and Conservative] and the Scottish Liberal Party's candidates were standing as Anti-Socialists.'[12] In November 1949 the somewhat unlikely figure of Cyril Osborne, the right-wing Conservative MP for Louth, wrote to the *Manchester Guardian*, calling for a united Conservative-Liberal front to oppose the Labour government. The *Guardian* was predictably dismissive of Osborne's initiative, calling upon the Tories to offer Liberals a free fight in 50 or 70 seats to prove their sincerity.[13] What was striking, however, was that a quarter of the large postbag prompted by Osborne's letter came out in his support – this in the context of the newspaper's strongly 'Liberal' readership.[14]

The concept of joint Liberal-Conservative associations certainly helped confuse the political situation for many voters. Nowhere was this more evident than in Pembrokeshire where Gwilym Lloyd-George enjoyed the support of the local organisations of the two parties. 'I have never been a Liberal-National', he insisted, 'and I am not one now.'[15] This was technically true, but Lloyd-George certainly behaved like a Liberal National, even speaking on Conservative platforms to cries of 'Judas' from traditional Liberals. But amid rumours of a Liberal split and suggestions that a breakaway group would support an independent Liberal candidate at the next general election, the Pembrokeshire Liberal Association gave the sitting member a renewed vote of confidence. Only, in fact, when Lloyd-George spoke in support of a Conservative and National Liberal candidate in the Bradford South by-election of December 1949 was the Liberal whip in the House of Commons finally withdrawn from him.[16] Even so, Lloyd-George was formally re-adopted for the General Election of 1950 by a joint meeting of the Pembrokeshire Liberal and Conservative Associations with no dissenting votes recorded.[17] Such anomalous situations reflected both the weakness of independent Liberalism in this period and its lack of success in clearly defining its own identity.

In constituencies where there was a genuine Liberal National presence, the process of amalgamation envisaged by Woolton-Teviot often proceeded less smoothly than had been assumed. Conservatives looked to the example of Huntingdon, where a movement towards amicable union was already well advanced by the time Woolton-Teviot was announced, as a model to be followed elsewhere, but this was far from being the case. In a minority of constituencies no agreement proved possible. In Newcastle East, last contested by the Conservatives in 1924, 'we tried hard to come to an arrangement with the Liberals but found them quite impossible, and they have adopted a Sinclair Liberal candidate'.[18] In Denbigh it was known that the sitting Liberal National MP, Sir Henry Morris-Jones, would not be standing at the next general election. This, combined with the recommendations of the national agreement, clearly afforded local Conservatives, who had last contested the seat back in 1929, the opportunity to re-assert themselves. After considering the text of the Woolton-Teviot document, the Denbigh Conservative Association suggested the creation of a small sub-committee consisting of an equal number of Conservatives and Liberal Nationals to consider a process of merger on the basis suggested by the two Central Offices and proposed that the resulting joint body should be entitled the 'Conservative and Liberal National Association'.[19] There seemed every reason for such an outcome. Indeed, at a meeting of the joint negotiating committee the Liberal Nationals confessed their own weakness. Alderman Oswald Jones admitted that they had no effective organisation to match that of the Tories. While Morris-Jones had many personal followers, these did not constitute an organised body. For the Conservatives, Alderman J.D.H.

Osborn magnanimously responded that fusion should be on the basis of numerical equality, a 'generous gesture' gratefully accepted by the Liberal Nationals.[20] Thereafter, however, the Liberal Nationals prevaricated, fusion was delayed and it was the minor party which eventually seized the initiative and nominated a candidate to succeed the sitting MP. The Conservatives surprisingly acquiesced. The new candidate, Emlyn Garner Evans, who had stood as a Liberal in the constituency in the General Election of 1945, committed himself to the defeat of the Labour government and, on that basis, secured the unanimous approval of Denbigh Tories at their 1948 AGM.[21] Thus, when the election was held in February 1950, Garner Evans stood – contrary to the spirit of Woolton-Teviot – as a National Liberal candidate without any formal reference to the local Conservative association in his affiliation, though he did enjoy that body's full support.

Elsewhere, the Conservatives were less reticent in imposing themselves. In the adjoining constituency of Wrexham Conservative resentment at playing second fiddle to the Liberal Nationals had been building up for some time. The mood at a meeting of the Conservative Executive Committee, shortly before the Woolton-Teviot Agreement was announced, was very clear. A succession of speakers argued against amalgamation and in favour of the adoption of a Conservative candidate. According to one local alderman, 'we should adopt our own candidate and let other organisations support us if they so wished'.[22] But Woolton-Teviot forced Wrexham Tories to agree to further discussions with the Liberal Nationals. Even so, it was argued that the Conservative delegation to such talks should emphasise to the Liberal Nationals that '*we* were in the strong position in that we have the organisation and the members'.[23] For some months the two parties in the division maintained a 'united front' against socialism, whilst holding on to their separate organisational identities. But the Conservatives were not to be thwarted. In July 1948 a joint selection committee put forward the name of Richard Lamb as a suitable prospective candidate. The Conservative Divisional Council agreed that, in the event of Lamb being adopted, he should be asked to stand as a 'United Conservative and Liberal National'. Almost as an after-thought it was pointed out that 'the Liberal National Association would have to be consulted in the matter'. The following year it was again the Tories who took the lead in deciding that Lamb was not, after all, a suitable choice.[24] Finally, in the summer of 1949 the inevitable logic of the situation was accepted and it was agreed that the two organisations should amalgamate as the Wrexham Conservative and National Liberal Association. 'We are absorbed by the

Conservative Association', admitted Edna Hughes, whose father had been the driving force in establishing the Wrexham Liberal National Association more than a decade earlier. Had the two existing associations been disbanded and then reformed as a new joint association with mutually agreed rules and procedures, she might have believed otherwise.[25] As it was, the Conservatives emphasised that members of the Liberal National Association would be eligible to serve as officers of the new association, and upon its Executive Council and various committees, 'only under the existing rules of the Conservative Association'.[26]

Even in constituencies where the Liberal Nationals were struggling to survive there was often a reluctance to surrender institutional independence. In Bradford South a meeting of the party's officers decided to issue a defiant statement to the press of their determination to carry on, notwithstanding the observation of one of those present that the association had 'no candidate in view and neither effective set of officers nor effective women's organisation and he failed to see that the association could keep going long under such conditions'.[27] Efforts to secure co-operation between Bradford Conservatives and Liberal Nationals over municipal elections in 1948 quickly broke down.[28] Not in fact until February 1949 did the Liberal Nationals agree in principle to the formation of a joint association 'while maintaining our own identity'. Sir Herbert Holdsworth, the division's former MP, suggested that he would want an assurance from the Conservatives that they were prepared to support the best candidate 'whether Conservative or Liberal'. But the Liberal National Chairman was more realistic:

> as we had no definite names of Candidates to offer at the May Municipal Election nor for the next General Election and that the Conservatives had adopted candidates for all but four of the twenty wards and in all four parliamentary divisions [in Bradford], we had agreed to support their nominees who would be styled 'Conservative and National Liberal' candidates in the event of the formation of the Joint Association.[29]

In the West Riding seat of Brighouse and Spenborough it needed the personal intervention of Lord Woolton to moderate the over-enthusiasm of local Tories. The constituency was a new creation, the product of boundary changes, and took in parts of the old seats of Elland and Spen Valley. With slightly more of the new division coming out of Conservative-held Elland, local Tories felt entirely justified in nominating a candidate of their own. But Spen Valley held particular significance for the Liberal Nationals as the former seat of John Simon, though it had been lost in the General Election of 1945. In a move designed to pre-empt a Conservative candidature, a body calling itself the Brighouse and Spenborough Liberal Association was quickly formed early in 1949 and adopted William Woolley, the former Liberal National MP for Spen Valley. 'They ignored and treated with sarcasm' the Conservatives' offer of a joint selection process, complained J.W. Sutcliffe, the local Conservative chairman.[30] Woolton, however, was clear that, if his agreement with Teviot were to have any meaning, it must not be a one-way process. The Liberal vote might be small, but it could be an important factor in winning the next election. 'A Conservative with Liberal support or a Liberal with Conservative support will have a better chance than either would have in a three-cornered fight'. But 'you cannot have co-operation on the basis of "take all and give nothing"' and the Liberal Nationals had a 'very strong moral' claim on the new seat. They must not be 'squeezed out of their last remaining seat in Yorkshire'.[31] Sutcliffe recognised where his duty lay. 'You are Chairman of the Party', he wrote to Woolton, 'and if you say our persistence will yield damage to the national interest we are capable of sinking our "partisan" feelings and not opposing Mr Woolley.'[32] Even so, he expected trouble from the Spenborough end of the division, where many Conservative members were threatening resignation and the withdrawal of their subscriptions, and 'certainly will not work for Woolley'.[33]

Notwithstanding such difficulties, by the time of the General Election of 1950 around 60 local mergers had taken place and at the election over 50 candidates stood under such varied labels as National Liberal and Conservative, Conservative and National Liberal, Liberal and Conservative, and Conservative and Liberal – the 'liquorice allsorts' as they were contemptuously dubbed by Clement Davies.[34] Inevitably, however, the actual Liberal National component concealed by these titles was considerably diluted. In many cases Conservative candidates were chosen by the newly constituted joint associations; in others, a new type of candidate came forward who could claim little connection with the internal Liberal quarrels of the 1930s which had given the Liberal National party its original identity and coherence. The Conservatives noted that a 'nominally amalgamated Association' had been formed in Dundee. But out of a total membership of around 7000 just 20 were Liberal Nationals. The agreed candidate for Dundee West, H.J. Scrymgeour-Wedderburn, had 'always been a Unionist' and had even been a Unionist MP in the past. 'Everyone interested in these matters knows this, and even if he agreed to call himself a Liberal-Unionist, which is extremely unlikely, he would be laying himself open to criticism for political dishonesty.'[35] Even more bizarre was the adoption of Churchill's son Randolph by the joint association in Leslie Hore-Belisha's old seat of Plymouth, Devonport. According to the sitting Labour MP, Michael Foot, a true blue Tory had boarded the train at Paddington, only to alight in Plymouth 'half a Liberal'.[36] Advising his father, who proposed to come to speak for him, Randolph suggested emphasising his 'Liberal past ... Show how most of the principles for which Gladstone, John Morley and, to some extent, Lloyd George stood, have today been incorporated in Conservative thought.'[37] In Luton, where the fusion of the two parties was more amicable and the resulting joint association more genuinely reflective of two independent and distinct political traditions than in many other constituencies, the candidate selected was the wartime Radio Doctor, Charles Hill, who in 1945 had contested the Cambridge University seat as an Independent. Hill later recalled that, in his opinion, the old Liberal party – and in Luton the Liberal National party was in effect the Liberal party – had lost all relevance to the modern world and, in any case, had no independent chance of victory. But, for a man of working-class origins, the 'traditional Liberal emphasis on the freedom of the individual, on free trade and on the dangers of monopoly and privilege appealed to me', while the Conservative party had 'widened its appeal, lowered its barriers and widened its outlook'.[38] On this basis Hill accepted nomination as a 'Liberal-Conservative'. At the election he insisted emphatically, 'I am not a National Liberal'.[39] His intention was to stand 'on an enlightened progressive platform which affords an opportunity for Liberals and Conservatives to combine to bring an end to Socialism, without a return to reaction'.[40]

At a national level the Liberal Nationals continued much as before. An interesting report on co-partnership and profit-sharing in industry was prepared in time for consideration by the party's annual conference in Harrogate in June 1948. 'A New Climate in Industry' contained recommendations on employee share-holding, profit sharing and joint discussions between management and labour on all matters affecting the status and interests of the worker and the fortunes of his firm.[41] Woolton urged Macmillan to attend this conference as an expression of the newly formalised partnership between the two parties.[42] The conference looked forward to the election of a new Conservative-Liberal National government pledged to establish laws and conditions under which competitive free enterprise could function vigorously, effectively and with social justice. A programme of denationalising the industries taken into public ownership by Labour would be needed but could not be implemented until the overwhelming mass of the electorate had been convinced by practical experience that such a course was necessary for the country's economic survival. There should also be a commitment to reduce taxation by £1000 million. 'This cannot be done all at once, but it should be the determined aim.'[43] By resolution the party also agreed to change its name from 'Liberal National' to 'National Liberal', the logical title that had been eschewed in 1931–2 because of its resonance with the Coalition Liberal supporters of Lloyd George a decade earlier.

Over the following two years the National Liberals' most common refrains remained the need for a united front to defeat socialism and criticism of the mainstream Liberal party for endangering this unity by insisting on its independence and 'attempting to produce an independent policy where, fundamentally, no difference existed'.[44] In a message to Lord Rosebery, Churchill spelt out the common position of the two parties:

> All of us who are opposed to Socialism wish to preserve liberty and free enterprise. You and I believe that only in this way can our country become prosperous enough to maintain and improve the social services which our two historic parties, each in its own way, helped to bring to maturity. We know that Socialism will cripple the very enterprise which has made us a great people and provides the funds for social progress ... Division or dissipation of energy would be fatal.[45]

In response Liberal spokesmen continued to pour scorn on the National Liberals' on-going pretensions to institutional independence. Speaking in the House of Lords, Samuel likened them to Jonah inside the belly of a Conservative whale. Teviot was

> not aware that the process of deglutition has been completed and the process of digestion is very far advanced. We observe these facts as we remember a similar case of the Liberal Unionists in previous generations, who were swallowed up and disappeared for ever, and we beware accordingly.[46]

THE LONG ROAD TO EXTINCTION, 1947–68 167

*   *   *

With the approach of another general election National Liberals were keen to regularise their relationship with the Conservatives. While Woolton-Teviot had covered the position in the constituencies, the parliamentary situation remained more vague. In particular, it was not clear what the whipping arrangements would be for MPs elected under joint labels nor had the future status of such a parliamentary group been defined. Clarification would afford National Liberals more security for themselves and more credibility with the electorate, while perhaps strengthening their claims to ministerial posts in any future Conservative government. For some, clarification meant abandoning their remaining claims to an independent existence. Lord Simon no longer held office within the party, but had not abandoned his own hopes of a further government appointment. He and Churchill were near-contemporaries and, if the Tory leader could still aspire to head a peacetime cabinet, so too could Simon hope to serve as Lord Chancellor within it. Simon calculated that the position of the National Liberals after the next election would only be significant if the Conservatives failed to gain an independent Commons majority. Should that majority be secured, Churchill would be in a position, if he so chose, to ignore them completely. 'When it comes to making a Ministry', Simon warned Lord Teviot, 'there are always more horses than oats.' Simon felt particularly isolated as a National Liberal peer in the upper chamber. As he complained in July 1949, 'the fact is that there is no Liberal National Party in the House of Lords and in saying so I am not blaming anybody. I am merely registering the fact.' Thirteen peers nominally accepted the National Liberal whip, but the majority were elderly or inactive and they never met as a group to confer on policy or tactics. There were many days when only Simon and Teviot (both now in their mid-70s) were present in the upper chamber to represent the party's interests. Simon's logic was as impeccable as it always had been throughout his long political career. While it had been 'quite right to form the Liberal Nationals into a Party in 1931 … there is no independent future for those who carry this name'.[47]

Such reasoning persuaded Simon that the time was ripe for a renewed approach to Churchill. Accordingly, in late 1948 he declared that it was now his wish 'publicly to enrol myself under your banner as a Conservative'.[48] Churchill responded cautiously and asked Simon to consider whether or not a change of party label might deprive him of his ability to attract Liberal votes, particularly at by-elections.[49] Simon agreed to abide by Churchill's advice, but reiterated his frustration at being 'somewhat isolated, when I so much agree with the general line which you and your followers are taking'. Stressing his past links with the Tory leader – 'for after all we were Liberals together' – Simon hinted that he would appreciate being taken more fully into the counsels of the Conservative party.[50] This Churchill was ready to concede and, during 1949, Simon began to attend some meetings of the Tories' Consultative Committee, the shadow cabinet of the day, advising on such legal and constitutional issues as the Republic of Ireland Act and India's wish to become a republic while retaining membership of the Commonwealth. Almost certainly, Churchill's cautious attitude was determined by his on-going hope of winning over the mainstream Liberal party, with several of whose leading figures, including Sinclair and Lady Violet Bonham Carter, his personal relations had always been warmer than with Simon. Allowing the latter into the Conservative ranks at this stage might well have jeopardised such plans.

Simon was not the only prominent National Liberal to be thinking in terms of joining the Conservatives. James Henderson, the party's candidate in East Dundee, called at the Conservative party's Edinburgh headquarters and announced his wish to 'call himself an out-and-out Unionist and have nothing further to do with the National Liberals'. According to Henderson there were several other National Liberal members and candidates, including Henderson Stewart the MP for East Fife, who felt the same way, but who were restrained from following their instincts by Teviot, who liked being chairman of a party, and by Jack Maclay, MP for Montrose, who liked being chairman of a parliamentary group. Henderson was particularly concerned about the position of a defeated National Liberal candidate. 'He indicated that a failed Unionist candidate would have some claim upon the Unionist Party, while a failed National Liberal candidate would have no ground to stand upon anywhere.'[51]

For the majority of National Liberals, however, regularising their relationship with the Conservatives should not involve a complete loss of their separate identity. Maclay tried to appeal to Woolton on the basis of the Conservative party's self-interest. A more formal arrangement, he suggested, would be more effective in attracting Liberal voters at the coming election. 'The charge against the National Liberals', he conceded, 'is that they are merely the tools of the Conservative Party, and that any Liberal ideas they may have will be swamped by the major party.' If, however, it was made clear to wavering Liberal voters that the National Liberals' partnership with the Tories was in fact the *only* chance of making their Liberal ideas effective and that a formal structure of co-operation would ensure 'the fullest consideration and respect for their attitude and approach', then there might be a very considerable impact. National Liberal representation in the Conservative whips' office would, he urged, be a useful beginning.[52] But there was no good reason for the Tories to respond positively to these suggestions. The National Liberals now had little intrinsic power or even bargaining strength. Having abandoned the option of Liberal reunion, they had no obvious alternative to continuing co-operation with the Tories upon whom they were, electorally, completely dependent.

Conservative calculations were sharply focused on what would be most likely to bring them victory at the general election, where they would face an enormous task if they were to surmount Labour's 1945 majority. It was in the Conservatives' best interests to await the outcome of the election and then to assess the usefulness of the National Liberal connection in terms of broadening their own electoral appeal and review the relationship thereafter. Stephen Pierssené, the Tories' General Director, summed up his party's attitude:

Although the extent of Liberal support which we can attract to ourselves is problematical, I think that it would be a mistake from a short term point of view to encourage the National Liberals to abandon their separate existence and to join the Unionist Party. The short term point of view, I feel, is 'what is most likely to win the next election?' I am convinced that our present policy ... of attracting all the right wing Liberal support we can, is effectively splitting the Liberal Party and that those who follow an independent Liberal line will generally tend to split the anti Tory vote rather than the anti Socialist vote.[53]

Not surprisingly, Pierssené urged Woolton to stick for the time being with a loose rather than a formal arrangement, even if the complete absorption of the National Liberals was their inevitable destiny in the somewhat longer term.[54]

The nature of the Conservative-National Liberal relationship was well illustrated in the process by which the former's manifesto for the General Election of February 1950 was prepared. The National Liberals played no part in the drafting of the original policy statement, *The Right Road for Britain*, upon which the later manifesto, *This is the Road*, was based. But consultations were arranged with Teviot and Maclay to enable them to look over the draft document and the National Liberals subsequently sent in 'one or two useful ideas'.[55] According to Maclay, there was nothing in *The Right Road for Britain* with which he could possibly disagree and 'we believe that the general policies set out must commend themselves to our colleagues in the House and our supporters in the country'. But Maclay was keen to insert a recognisably 'liberal' tone into the Tory document. The difficulty was that the whole focus of political debate had shifted towards the idea of an interventionist state and a feeling existed that 'the Conservative Party is quite prepared to accept a high degree of state planning provided that it is in good hands!' Maclay understood that loose talk about a return to a free economy, and even about multilateral trade, would be 'dangerous', but he hoped that the Conservatives could still make it clear that their ultimate objective remained a free economy adapted to modern conditions and that regional and even bilateral trading arrangements were only temporary expedients. Just as important as the contents of the document was the need to make it clear to the public that consultations about it had gone beyond the Conservative party itself. This would enable the National Liberals to play an important role:

> We ourselves believe that there is still a large floating vote which is undecided as to how it will finally move. We think that it can be encouraged to move our way, if it can be brought to realise that the Conservative Party is willing and anxious to receive the constructive co-operation of elements outside recognised Conservative circles.[56]

The National Liberals' own manifesto, *Making Britain Great Again*, did little to offer a distinctive position in terms of policy and was more an attempt to justify their own existence. The 19 points of National Liberal doctrine were not easy to distinguish from the policies set out in the Conservative manifesto. 'At present', it argued, 'no contemporary difference of principle or aim between Liberals and Conservatives stands in the way of the full co-operation which the national situation demands.'[57] In stressing also that they remained true to the traditional Liberal faith, the National Liberals implied that the distinction between Conservatism and Liberalism had largely lost its meaning, an impression which Churchill also strove to convey. The Conservative leader's personal forward to the Tory manifesto, which linked the policies of the future government he hoped to lead with the 'spirit of Liberalism', had one eye on the partnership with the

National Liberals, but was also concerned to attract voters from the mainstream Liberal party. Churchill 'always seems to have at the back of his mind the idea that he will be able to gather the other Liberals to the fold', observed Lord Teviot. 'I feel he is unduly optimistic, as every single avenue of approach to them has met with a complete negative.'[58]

Teviot's scepticism was well justified. The Liberal party's decision to fight on as broad a front as possible and field as many as 475 candidates was a bitter disappointment. 'My fear', confessed one veteran Conservative MP, 'is that the infernal Liberals are going to queer our pitch all over the country.'[59] The Liberal strategy showed that the campaign to form joint Liberal-Conservative constituency associations had enjoyed very limited success outside the National Liberal wing of Liberalism. The aspiration of a united front against the Labour government remained unfulfilled.[60] One interesting exception, however, occurred in Huddersfield where the local Tories agreed not to contest the West division, while the Liberals agreed not to oppose the Conservatives in the East division. Liberals and Liberal Nationals had reunited in Huddersfield in 1947, very much on Liberal terms, but the arrangement of 1950, which remained in place until the General Election of 1964, in part reflected the continuing influence of National Liberal thinking in the town.[61]

Inevitably, the election of 1950 was primarily a contest between the Labour and Conservative parties. Indeed, the two parties dominated British politics between them in these years to a greater extent than was the case at any other time in the twentieth century. In 1950 they shared 89.6 per cent of the popular vote; in 1951 the figure was 96.8 per cent.[62] Nonetheless, the Conservative-National Liberal-Liberal relationship offered an interesting sub-plot to the main drama, and one which was not without significance for the final outcome of the poll. If the Liberals were to succeed in re-establishing their claim to be a significant political force, they needed to ensure that their identity was not contaminated by association with the National Liberals, still less with the Tories. Not surprisingly, Woolton became concerned that the Liberal campaign was less concerned with opposing the government and more focused on undermining the Conservative-National Liberal partnership.[63] By contrast, the Conservatives, and especially the National Liberals, saw advantage in blurring distinctions, even if this confused the voter. '*Nothing* suits these Independent Liberals so well as to be treated as the only spokesmen of Liberal opinion', argued Simon. 'It seems a pity to encourage this view when the contrary can be forcibly presented.'[64]

As the election approached, the Chairman of the Liberal Party Organisation, Lord Moynihan, suggested to Woolton that Conservative candidates and those who supported the Conservative party should be prepared to present themselves to the voters as Conservatives and that 'the name "Liberal" should not be used by them in order to confuse the issue'. Woolton responded, with some justification, that the National Liberals had as much right to employ the word 'Liberal' in their name as did anyone else.[65] At his adoption meeting in Woodford Churchill criticised the 'very small and select group of Liberal leaders who conceived themselves the sole heirs of the principles and traditions of Liberalism and believed themselves to have the exclusive copyright to the word "Liberal"'.[66] Two days later he and Rosebery issued a joint statement which suggested, somewhat half-heartedly, that 'Liberal-Conservative' candidates should use the prefix 'National' where a candidate from the mainstream Liberal party was also in the field. This was not enough to pacify Liberal headquarters and the option of legal action was briefly considered. But Clement Davies's protests were easily brushed aside when Churchill reminded him that he too had carried the Liberal National device for most of the 1930s. The Conservative leader would not therefore 'presume to correct your knowledge of the moral, intellectual and legal aspects of adding a prefix or a suffix to the honoured name of Liberal. It has certainly often been done before by honourable and distinguished men.'[67]

Perhaps the most significant National Liberal (or, strictly speaking, 'Liberal-Conservative') contribution to the campaign was made by Charles Hill, the candidate for Luton, who was assigned one of the Conservatives' radio broadcasts, Simon's offer in this direction having been politely declined. In his compelling voice and with skills honed during the years of war, the former Radio Doctor explained his hybrid candidature:

> I could find little real difference between the Liberal, not Socialistically inclined – there are some who are – and the progressive Conservative. I came to the conclusion that the real issue was between Socialism and Freedom; that Liberal ideas were more important than party labels ... That's why I am glad to be standing as a candidate with both Liberal and Conservative support, like many others who think as I do.[68]

In the event, while the political pendulum swung strongly in the Conservatives' direction, it did not move sufficiently to deprive Attlee of the reins of power. A battered, and in some cases exhausted, Labour cabinet was given a renewed mandate by the electorate, although the overall Labour majority in the new House of Commons was now reduced to just five seats. From more than 50 candidatures joint Conservatives and National Liberals were successful in just 16 seats, a less impressive performance than that enjoyed by the Conservative party as a whole, but a reflection of the nature of the seats contested rather than of any differential swing. Gwilym Lloyd-George, narrowly beaten in Pembrokeshire, was the one notable casualty. These 16 MPs now constituted themselves into the Liberal-Unionist group in the House of Commons and were soon joined by John Macleod, again elected as an unofficial Liberal with Conservative support in Ross and Cromarty and G.R.H. Nugent, the victorious Conservative in Guildford. Of the original 16, ten were of Liberal origin and six Conservative.[69] They were not, felt John Simon, 'individually a very distinguished lot'.[70]

*   *   *

The closeness of the electoral contest inevitably invited analysis of why Churchill had failed to recover power and of what might bring the Tories success the next time the country went to the polls. The intervention of so many independent Liberal candidates appeared to have been a crucial factor. Though the party had won only nine seats and lost 319 deposits – a 'defeat on a scale which it would be hard to parallel'[71] – 2.6 million Liberal votes had still been cast nationally. As figures such as Teviot had suspected, leading Conservatives had been over-optimistic about their ability to attract the Liberal vote. Anthony Eden was one who had believed that the Liberals were 'finished' as a party and that Liberals, particularly in the industrial north, would vote Tory.[72] While the statistics suggested that the party was indeed finished, at least as a serious contender for power, its capacity to damage the Conservatives' electoral prospects remained. Between them the Conservatives and Liberals had polled about 1.85 million more votes than the victorious Labour government.

To many the conclusion seemed obvious. *The Times* spoke of the 'national disservice' caused by Liberal intervention and suggested that the party could best serve the interests of Liberalism in the future by allowing its supporters to judge for themselves which of the two larger parties could do more to put the Liberal spirit into practice.[73] Simon was more explicit. If, as was widely assumed, the Conservatives had succeeded in maximising their own core vote, the problem now was 'how best to get those who voted Liberal to vote

Conservative next time'. Simon gently implied that the role of the National Liberals could be crucial, for the argument that Liberals should now support a liberalised Conservative party 'comes most effectively from those who have always been Liberals'. Furthermore, the real difficulty to be overcome was the traditional state of mind of 'so many Liberals that, whatever happens, they will not vote for a Tory'. In the recent election Simon had detected a tendency in Conservative circles to think that the National Liberals did not matter very much as 'they would support the Conservatives anyhow'. As a result, not enough had been made of the argument that voting for the independent Liberal party was not the only way for a voter to register his Liberal credentials.[74] Invited to discuss the question with the Conservative Chairman, Simon offered his services in approaching the official Liberal party to secure an electoral arrangement. He added that he thought it would now be an advantage if Churchill formally included him in the shadow cabinet, a suggestion which the Conservative leader resisted.[75] Simon was clearly concerned that, unless he was involved to protect the interests of the National Liberals, any Conservative pact with the official Liberals might be too favourable to the latter at the expense of his own group.

In practice, the Conservatives determined to approach the Liberals themselves. In March Churchill proposed the setting up of a shadow cabinet committee to 'go into all the questions open between Conservatives and Liberals to see what can be done to secure greater unity among the forces opposed to Socialism'.[76] The Labour Prime Minister poked fun at the Tory courtship of the Liberal party. Were the intentions of the Leader of the Opposition honourable or not, asked Attlee:

> He has been a very ardent lover of this elderly spinster, the Liberal Party. The elder sister – the National Liberals – was married long ago; she is now deceased. This now is the younger sister, but she is getting on. I can never make out whether the rt hon. Member for Woodford is going to play Petruchio or Romeo. He gives her a slap in the face, then offers her a bunch of flowers.[77]

It was a well-phrased jibe, capturing the almost schizophrenic nature of the Conservatives' attitude towards the Liberal party at this time.

But for the National Liberals this was no laughing matter. If the Tory strategy ended in success, this might fatally undermine the credibility of their claim to be a necessary bridge between the two political movements. When, in the spring, it was reported in the press that leading Tories, Harold

Macmillan, R.A. Butler and Duncan Sandys, were to open negotiations with Clement Davies, Simon voiced his alarm. Macmillan should not forget that, ever since 1931, the National Liberals had had a larger representation in the Commons 'than the other lot':

> If now the other Liberals are given a guarantee of 40 seats, or whatever it may be, I think the National Liberals may feel somewhat aggrieved, for, after all, it is these latter that have stood out for the sensible view to be taken by Liberals in the country and have done a great deal among their own people to get steady support for the Opposition.[78]

Undeterred, Churchill continued along his chosen path, telling the 1922 Committee of Conservative backbenchers that they had to obtain Liberal support, both as individuals and, if possible, as a party, not through a political deal but by proclaiming the fundamental principles upon which those who opposed socialism were agreed.[79] Yet such a deal, based upon the introduction of a scheme of electoral reform, seems to have been briefly considered. Macmillan, more than ever convinced of the need for a definite alliance with the Liberals, believed that there was a strong case for an experiment with Proportional Representation, restricted to the large cities. 'It could do no harm and might do good.'[80] Even Churchill was interested and, according to Nigel Fisher, made a moving but unsuccessful appeal to the 1922 Committee to be allowed to pursue an arrangement along these lines.[81] Churchill seems to have reasoned that PR would create the basis for permanent co-operation between Conservatives and Liberals and probably for the gradual absorption of the latter. Writing in *Liberal News*, 'Radical' suggested that Churchill's intentions were genuine and that he would not mind disbanding the National Liberals in order to secure an electoral deal, just as – the parallel was no doubt intentionally bizarre – Stalin had disbanded the Comintern during the war.[82]

During the summer of 1950 R.A. Butler was entrusted with the delicate task of taking the negotiations forward. Lady Violet Bonham Carter, increasingly doubtful whether her party still had an independent future, though continuing to set her face against joining the hated National Liberals, represented the Liberal party. The aim was evidently a pact for the next election and in June Butler drew up a discussion paper which he entitled an 'Overlap Prospectus of Principles'. At Central Office Woolton remained sceptical and the talks came to an end by the late summer.

Churchill, however, kept in touch with Clement Davies and it was rumoured that, without the agreement of the shadow cabinet, he was ready to withdraw Conservative candidates from around 40 constituencies. Senior Tories, including Woolton, were alarmed. 'I am having a very difficult time with Churchill', wrote the Conservative Chairman who claimed that the leader had even threatened to resign if he could not have his own way. 'He is determined to bring about some arrangement with the Liberals.'[83] Meanwhile the National Liberal leadership could only look on in confusion and dismay. Teviot's anxiety was only too evident:

> Rumours are spreading all over the place and I am in a very awkward position as no one so far has communicated with us. All I can say to those who are continually ringing up is that I know nothing. The answer to that is 'well you ought to' to which I reply I have nothing to say but will let them know if there is anything I can pass on.[84]

The negotiations between Conservatives and Liberals appear to have petered out because Clement Davies would not contemplate a national agreement – or perhaps, more precisely, because he knew that important sections of his party would not let him contemplate it. But the fact that talks got as far as they did suggests that the idea of an electoral pact was not as chimerical as has sometimes been suggested. Woolton even reported that Davies was happy for further negotiations to be 'conducted on the constituency level' and that it would be 'best if they arose spontaneously'.[85] Some further progress was indeed made. The 'Huddersfield formula' was extended to Bolton where the Conservatives agreed not to oppose the Liberal candidate in Bolton West, while the Liberals stood down in Bolton East. In three seats in rural Wales and in Dundee the Tories agreed to leave the field to the Liberals and, most publicly, Violet Bonham Carter, at this stage the leading Liberal advocate of an arrangement with the Conservatives, was not opposed in Colne Valley, with Churchill even speaking on her behalf in the election campaign.

But co-operation went no further, much to the relief of the National Liberals whose last remaining *raison d'être* would have been endangered by a more comprehensive Liberal-Conservative arrangement. Indeed, the National Liberals were now able to profit from the internal disputes and divisions within the mainstream Liberal party. The 1950 General Election had been a disillusioning experience for the latter. Many long-term Liberals now questioned their party's continued viability and the period before the country next went to the polls in October 1951 witnessed a number of significant defections, many of them to the National Liberals. Conscious of her party's relative impotence, Elizabeth Rashleigh, prospective Liberal candidate for Torrington, now joined the National Liberals, arguing that Liberals like herself had to decide whether they were 'for or against this [Labour] Government and I am against it'.[86] The National Liberal Organisation was able to publish a pamphlet in which Lord Milverton and eight former Liberal parliamentary candidates explained their conversion to National Liberalism. Apart from the internal disunity displayed by the parliamentary Liberal party, argued Milverton, the public was understandably confused about the real difference between Liberals and Conservatives – confused because on the big issues of the day there was no difference. Both shared 'a belief in individual liberty [and] a hatred of the principle of the omnipotent State and its interlocked monopoly of economic and political power'.[87] Milverton had become convinced that anti-socialist inter-party co-operation was essential if the liberal way of life was to be preserved.[88] Defections among Liberal peers in this period were particularly damaging. When Lords Reading and Rennell went over to the Tories, *Liberal News* was reduced to seeking comfort in the fact that at least they had not joined the National Liberals.[89]

By 1951 the National Liberals' position had clearly strengthened, not least because, in the absence of a wide-ranging Liberal-Conservative electoral pact, they once more appeared to be the Tories' best means of eating into the Liberal vote. With increasing indications that Attlee's government would not be able to survive a full term, Conservative agents were instructed to ensure that the pamphlet 'Who are the National Liberals' (subtitled 'What National Liberals Believe: a restatement of National Liberal Principles and Aims') got into the hands of Liberals in those constituencies where there was an influential Liberal element which was not yet co-operating with the Tories, but whose support could have a marked impact on the outcome of the next election.[90] But if the National Liberals' position was somewhat strengthened, their leaders were in no doubt that the party had to maintain its intimate ties with the Tories. Following a private meeting of the National Liberal Council in February 1951, Herbert Butcher, chief whip of the Liberal-Unionist parliamentary group, pledged further co-operation with the Conservatives to secure the defeat of the Labour government at the earliest possible opportunity. Geoffrey Shakespeare stressed that any future co-operation with 'the other sections of the Liberal party' must be on the basis of working under the 'inspired leadership of the greatest living Englishman' to resist the challenge of socialism which had already reduced Britain's fortunes to their lowest ebb.[91] By the summer the National Liberal-Conservative partnership seemed to be functioning more smoothly than at any time since the signing of the Woolton-Teviot Agreement four years earlier. Maclay now wrote to thank the Tory Chairman for his 'sustained understanding of the difficulties of our position and the unfailing help you have given in all our problems'.[92]

But the National Liberals' greatest advantage lay in the inability of the Liberal party to repeat its effort of 1950 in terms of the number of seats contested when Attlee called another general election for 25 October. At the outset it was reported that the Liberals already had 174 candidates provisionally adopted. Before long, however, many of these withdrew, while some impoverished constituency associations quickly came to the conclusion that they did not have the funds to support a contest. Eventually the party tried to present its predicament in terms of a considered strategy. But the fielding of just 109 candidates was less a case of a rational decision to fight on a narrow front than a matter of sheer financial necessity. It left the Liberals wide open to the cry that a vote for them was 'a wasted vote'. As a Conservative election leaflet put it, 'the Independent Liberal Party has no hope of power and to support a party without hope is itself a hopeless action'. The dearth of Liberal candidates meant that in many constituencies National Liberals and others standing under variegated joint labels were able to present themselves as the only available 'Liberal' option. In others plain Conservatives were able to play upon their 'Liberal' credentials, not least by reminding the voters of their on-going partnership with the National Liberals.

In Luton, Huntingdonshire, Central Norfolk, South Angus and East Fife, all of which had been contested by independent Liberals in 1950, the sitting Conservative and National Liberal MP had a straight fight against Labour. In Huntingdonshire it was claimed that the Conservative-National Liberal coalition now represented 'an almost impregnable barrier against Socialism'.[93] Joint candidates were put forward in all seven Sheffield seats. In none was there an independent Liberal opponent to lay an alternative claim to his party's traditions. *The Times* predicted that in Southampton's two seats many independent Liberals might withhold their votes or even support Labour. But 'even making allowance for that contingency the chances are that at least one of the two – both held by Labour in 1950 – will go to the combined Conservative-Liberal nominee'. [94] In Gateshead a joint Liberal-Conservative association, putting up candidates in the town's two seats, prompted the Liberals to recreate an independent Liberal association in July 1951.[95] But this did not translate into a Liberal challenge when polling day arrived. In Swansea West local Liberals tried to take advantage of evident dissension between Conservatives and National Liberals following the replacement of a joint nominee of National Liberal origins by one with a Conservative pedigree, but they again failed to field a candidate of their own since 'this was not the time'.[96]

Where a Liberal was still in the field it was the task of National Liberals and Conservatives to marginalise him and emphasise his irrelevance to the outcome of the election as a whole. In Denbigh, where E.H. Garner Evans still presented himself simply as the National Liberal candidate without any formal reference to the Conservatives in his affiliation, it was stressed that the choice facing the electorate was 'plain and direct':

> It is between a continuance of Socialist rule or the return to power of a broadly based government led by Mr Churchill – mainly Conservative in composition but one in which Liberal influence can be made effective by the co-operation of an ever increasing number of National Liberals. The Independent Liberal Party offers no alternative. In the present crisis of our affairs, true Liberals will refuse merely to sit on the fence.[97]

If not all Liberal voters were entirely seduced by the logic of this argument, it remained difficult to determine what the mainstream Liberal party now hoped to achieve.

The National Liberals' manifesto, *Britain and the Next Five Years*, followed predictable lines. Stressing that the purposes of modern Conservative policy were now the same as those in which all Liberals believed, it invited Liberals to join in close alliance with the Tories under Churchill's leadership. It highlighted the dangers on the international front and called for the more effective management of British industry with rewards for enterprise and initiative. The present level of public expenditure should be drastically lowered and steps taken to reduce tariffs and other restrictions on commercial expansion. An emphasis upon the basic freedoms of conscience, speech, enterprise and association was spelt out in traditionl Liberal terms, but this sat quite easily alongside Tory calls to set the people free from the supposed constraints imposed by the Labour government.[98]

Sensing the weakness of the Liberals, Teviot urged Liberal headquarters to advise Liberal voters in the more than 500 seats where no Liberal was standing to support a Conservative or National Liberal candidate. Otherwise, he claimed, the Liberals would be divided into three groups, one voting for socialism, one against socialism and one not voting at all, with the result that the 'effectiveness of Liberal influence will be dissipated'.[99] This proposal was rejected by Clement Davies, following advice from Samuel and Fothergill, who suggested that Davies should respond that Liberals did not wish to be reduced to the same political futility as the National Liberals – a response that risked being thrown back in the Liberal party's own face.[100]

As in 1950, Liberals were obliged to expend a considerable amount of their time trying to counter National Liberal arguments and what they interpreted as a deliberate attempt to confuse the electorate. With his characteristically dry humour, Herbert Samuel claimed that there was not enough Liberalism in the 50 or more joint candidates to 'equip a single Liberal member of a parish council'. These 'pretence Liberals' were merely usurping the Liberal name in order to pick up a few votes from unwary Liberals.[101] Liberal headquarters was even obliged to issue a statement denying the inherently unlikely story that Lord Simon would be speaking on behalf of Violet Bonham Carter in Colne Valley.[102] Even Labour, perhaps sensing that the distribution of the former Liberal vote might be crucial to the electoral outcome, joined in the debate with Attlee telling an audience in the same constituency that, every time Liberals had succumbed to Tory blandishments in the past, it had meant reaction and hard times for the people and the weakening of genuine Liberalism.[103]

Nationally, there was not much movement in the voters' preferences since 1950, but the political pendulum swung just sufficiently to the right to give Churchill a parliamentary majority of 17 seats, even though, by a quirk of the British electoral system, the Conservatives and their allies secured fewer votes than Labour. Nineteen candidates were successful under a variety of joint labels, an increase of three from the previous election. In Ross and Cromarty Macleod now won as an unequivocal National Liberal and Conservative candidate, while Gwilym Lloyd-George took over from a retiring Conservative MP in Newcastle North. The one outright gain by a joint candidate was in Bedfordshire South where, in the absence of a Liberal opponent, Norman Cole took the seat from Labour. In addition, jointly nominated candidates narrowly failed to take advantage of the absence of a Liberal opponent in Southampton Test and Leith. There was a moment of uncertainty in the formation of the new government when Churchill offered Clement Davies the ministry of education. The latter was tempted but, on the advice of senior colleagues, the offer was eventually declined. Had Davies's decision gone the other way, the remaining Liberal party might well have disintegrated with imponderable consequences for the National Liberals. As it was, Davies's tiny band survived to uphold their claim to be the only true descendants of the once great party of Gladstone and Asquith.

National Liberals, of course, had no comparable qualms about the offer of office. John Maclay became Minister of Transport and Civil Aviation, while Gwilym Lloyd-George was appointed Minister of Food, both outside the cabinet. There were also junior posts for Charles Hill and, after a short delay, James Henderson Stewart. Perhaps of equal importance was the appointment of the National Liberals' chief whip, Herbert Butcher, as the government's deputy chief whip with especial responsibility for relations with the six Liberal MPs who had survived another electoral drubbing. But, although Churchill restored many of his wartime colleagues to ministerial rank, no place was found for John Simon despite the vigorous part he had played in the election campaign.[104] Simon's disappointment was intensified when Churchill appointed to the Lord Chancellorship Gavin Simonds, an elderly Law Lord with no previous political experience.

The early 1950s were, arguably, the high point of the National Liberals' fortunes, certainly in the postwar era. The aggregate vote of the jointly nominated candidates came to over one million; for the first time this total vote exceeded that of the orthodox Liberal party; and, with a government majority of just 17 in the new House of Commons, there were even those prepared to suggest, at least in private, that the 19-strong Liberal-Unionist group now held the parliamentary balance of power. It was the National Liberals' contention that they were in a position to steer the new government in a distinctively 'Liberal' direction. Maclay had already described the ways in which this could be done:

> The group holds weekly meetings at which it considers, with particular reference to the Liberal point of view, the business before Parliament. The views of the group can be expressed by its members on the floor of the House; through attending Conservative committees [National Liberal MPs had first been invited to join the 1922 Committee at the beginning of the 1947-8 session[105]]; through the collaboration of the group's Whip in the preparation of the

combined Whip which members of the group receive; and by the chairman of the group to the Leader of the Conservative party.[106]

There were, of course, elements of illusion in this picture. Many – probably most – of the million votes secured by joint candidates had been given by Conservatives, sometimes indeed to Conservative candidates standing under a hybrid label. The notion of holding the balance of power implied the sort of coalition partnership in which the National Liberals had the option of withdrawing their support and bringing the government down. This did not exist in any but the most theoretical sense. National Liberals were as likely to support the government as were Tory MPs and the Liberal-Unionist group never collectively withheld its support during the 13 years of Conservative administration which now unfolded, although there would be individual cases of rebellion just as there were among Tories.

Furthermore, to suggest that the Conservative party of this era was 'liberalised' by its association with the National Liberals is problematical, not least because of the difficulty of defining precisely what 'liberalism' involved in the decade after World War Two. This was something upon which even the tiny band of Clement Davies's parliamentary followers failed to reach a consensus. What is true is that under figures such as Harold Macmillan, Anthony Eden and R.A. Butler the Conservative party moved further to the left than at any time in its history. Even Churchill, during the last active decade of his political career, made great play of his Liberal past His celebrated election broadcast of 1945, in which he claimed that Attlee's Labour party would need to employ the methods of the Gestapo to carry out its programme, is not remembered for its 'liberal' tone. Even here, however, Churchill stressed that there was 'scarcely a Liberal sentiment which animated the great Liberal leaders of the past which we do not inherit and defend'.[107] In the wake of the Suez Crisis of 1956 Liberals would hasten to distance themselves from Anthony Eden. Before that moment, however, many had been attracted by his 'brand of humane, liberal and progressive Conservatism, born in the trenches on the Western Front'.[108] But did any of this have anything to do with the National Liberals? It would be difficult to produce evidence suggesting that the Liberal-Unionist group was successful in shifting the government's thinking along 'Liberal' paths which it would not otherwise have followed. The Conservative party of the 1950s, especially its leadership, was already predisposed towards policies of the moderate centre ground and needed little prompting in this direction from its parliamentary allies.

Yet it is easy to be too dismissive of the National Liberals' importance. In the politics of the early 1950s the success of the Conservative party in appealing beyond its core vote does seem to have been a key factor in its electoral success. If it is misleading to speak of a million National Liberal votes in 1951, there was a body of electors prepared to support the Tories because of their 'liberalised' image, an image in which the partnership with the National Liberals was an important element. The evidence suggests that few Liberals, in the absence of a Liberal candidate in 1951, had felt obliged to abstain and that a clear majority of them transferred their support to the Conservatives. Something between 60 and 70 per cent of those who had supported Liberal candidates in 1950 seem to have moved over to the Tories when the possibility of a Liberal vote was no longer an option and it was noticeable that, in those constituencies where Liberals had stood in 1950 but did not do so a year later, the swing to the Conservatives was greater than elsewhere. Overall, this may have been enough to account for more than half the seats which the Tories now gained from Labour.[109] It seems reasonable to conclude that, as had been the case in the Conservative party of Stanley Baldwin in the 1930s, the Tories' partnership with the National Liberals was still, two decades on, helping to broaden their electoral appeal. In the climate of the early 1950s, moreover, this was not something which Conservative strategists would lightly discard. With the government's narrow parliamentary majority and with contemporary wisdom, based on the idea of the 'natural swing of the pendulum', suggesting that the next election would probably see a movement back to the left, Tories knew that every single vote might be important if they were to have any chance of holding on to power. On this basis the National Liberals remained an asset, however tenuous their independent institutional existence had become.

*　　*　　*

Notwithstanding their symbiotic partnership with the Tories, the National Liberals continued to maintain the outward form and organisational apparatus of an independent body through the National Liberal Organisation and the National Liberal Council in London, the continued publication of the house journal, *New Horizon*, and the holding of annual party conferences. The Liberal-Unionist parliamentary group occupied its own bench in the Commons and met regularly on Wednesday evenings when the House was in session. Maclay remained chairman of the group until 1956 when he was succeeded by James Duncan, MP for South Angus. The relationship between Conservatives and National Liberals on the ground, in individual constituencies, varied considerably, with the importance of the National Liberal component depending upon the party's inherent residual strength, the calculation of local Conservative managers and the identity of the sitting MP or parliamentary candidate. Where the Conservatives allowed a significant National Liberal element to persist, this was usually on the basis of electoral considerations – the old idea that a National Liberal candidate could appeal to sections of the electorate which a mere Conservative could never reach. Any change in the arrangements, suggested the Tories' Chief Organisation Officer at the beginning of 1954, would 'almost inevitably lead to independent Conservative candidates and the possible loss of constituencies'.[110]

The situation in Luton fell into this category. Through the 1950s Charles Hill steadily increased his majority, partly by making a special appeal to the Liberal vote in a constituency with a lingering Liberal tradition, but little sign of an independent Liberal party. At one time, indeed, Hill employed two agents, one Conservative and one National Liberal. In Denbigh, a marginal seat where the Liberals were seen as the main threat to continuing Conservative control, the National Liberals enjoyed a particularly favoured position. So certain were the Tories of the electoral importance of their allies that they acquiesced in playing second fiddle to a palpably unsatisfactory National Liberal MP, lest the assertion of their own claim to the constituency should alienate a body of voter support and hand the seat to their opponents. After the General Election of 1951 the local Conservative party chairman, Lt-Col. J.C. Wynne-Edwards, drew up a detailed appreciation of the situation from which he concluded that the key tasks for the future were to win over more Liberal votes and to strengthen the position of the National Liberals. Without hesitation, he ruled out any idea of the National Liberals' complete absorption into the Conservative party:

> The real value of the National Liberals to the anti-Socialist cause lies in their name which acts as a stepping stone for wavering Radicals. Absorption would mean the destruction of that inducement to cross the stream. It is in the real interests of the Conservative Party to reinforce the stepping-stone rather than to destroy it.[111]

Despite repeated evidence that the National Liberals' organisational position in the constituency was crumbling, this situation continued until 1958. Only then did the sitting member's descent into alcoholism force the Tories' hand. Even then, although a Conservative was adopted to stand as the 'Conservative and National Liberal' candidate at the next election, Wynne-Edwards remained keen that the National Liberals should not be thrown overboard. In the wake of the 1959 General Election he believed that they might now dissolve of their own accord. Yet, 'it would be to our advantage to keep in touch with them and through them with the considerable body of opinion which they represent'.[112] Denbigh Conservatives agreed that National Liberals should be offered the status of a group on the local Conservative association and numerically generous representation within it.[113]

More typically, the National Liberal tradition gradually faded away over the course of the 1950s. In several constituencies the 'and National Liberal' suffix was quietly dropped from the title of the local Conservative association. Dewsbury, Gateshead, Gloucester, Southampton and Normanton were last contested by jointly named candidates in 1951; Burnley and Walsall North in 1955. A hybrid candidate contested Motherwell for the last time in a by-election in 1954. Gwilym Lloyd-George was replaced by a straightforward Tory in Newcastle North when he accepted a peerage early in 1957. Very rarely did a new joint association come into being, although Merionethshire was contested by a joint candidate for the first and last time in 1955, following the formation earlier that year of a new National Liberal association.[114] If this was an attempt to broaden the Conservatives' appeal in the constituency, it failed. The candidate finished fourth behind Labour, the Liberals and Plaid Cymru.

Elsewhere hybrid labels were maintained, even if they no longer had much meaning. They did little harm and still had an irritant value at least as far as the mainstream Liberal party was concerned. In all his experience of constituencies, declared the Liberal agent in Sheffield in 1952, 'there was none so dead as Sheffield'. But 'Mr D.E. Moore and others reminded him of the Con-Lib millstone round Sheffield Liberals' necks and their long experience of such difficulties'.[115] By the time that the youthful Michael Heseltine contested the Gower division of Glamorganshire as the Conservative and National Liberal candidate at the General Election of 1959, the National Liberal suffix was just 'an historic relic; it played no part in the campaign'.[116] In Bradford the joint label was maintained into the 1960s, but the *Bradford Onlooker*, the magazine of the Bradford Conservative and National Liberal Association, contained little if any evidence of an ongoing National Liberal tradition. Arthur Tiley's election leaflet for Bradford West in 1966 still contained the 'Conservative and National Liberal' banner, but only the word 'Conservative' appeared in bold capital letters. Quite simply, the National Liberal party now lacked the institutional infrastructure to renew itself as it failed to recruit a new generation of local activists or sustain its grassroots organisation. After all, if the modern Conservative party was as liberalised and as like themselves as National Liberals claimed, it surely made sense for new recruits to join the overwhelmingly larger component of the electoral alliance.

Most National Liberals did little to resist the overpowering Conservative embrace. 'I never for one moment imagined that I would ever be a Conservative', confessed Sir Herbert Janes, a leading figure in the creation of a joint organisation in Luton. But when he retired to Worthing, where there was no National Liberal organisation, and received a request for help from Conservative Central Office, he had 'no alternative'. Janes really was convinced that the Conservative party had changed sufficiently to encompass the Liberal beliefs which he had espoused throughout his life, 'although if any of the old toryism should emerge I should be right against it'.[117] Only occasionally was there evidence of National Liberals struggling to maintain their independent identity. In Wrexham a small group led by Edna Hughes and Councillor Trevor Hanmer continued, in the face of a somewhat insensitive local Conservative party, to insist that National Liberalism should be recognised as a separate and valuable tradition within the activities of a genuinely joint enterprise. Meetings of the joint association revealed increasing dissatisfaction and irritation with the suffocating dominance of the Wrexham Conservatives. In July 1952 members of the National Liberal group raised the issue of Miss Hughes's salary and status. She had been appointed 'Organiser' with the specific brief of maximising the 'Liberal' component of the joint vote, but her position had become 'most unsatisfactory and reflected a tendency to neglect the interests of the National Liberals'.[118] Not only were 13 of the 15 officers of the joint association in 1953 Conservatives, but the junior partners also believed that they were being subjected to unnecessary and heavy-handed slights. Among their complaints were that details of the National Liberals' annual conference were not brought to the association's attention; National Liberal literature was not circulated in the constituency; and no National Liberal speakers were ever invited to Wrexham. Edna Hughes had 'no illusion as to [the Conservatives'] ultimate goal – the extinction of all

Liberals and any avowed intention of co-operation should be closely scrutinised and tested by counter-proposals'.[119] Finally, in August 1953, following a carefully prepared meeting of sympathisers, a group of Wrexham National Liberals decided to end their partnership with the local Tories. Their declared purpose was 'to preserve their independence and safeguard Liberalism as an operative factor in the political life of this country'.[120]

Momentarily, it seemed that the Hughes-Hanmer initiative might merge into a broader National Liberal movement to reassert the party's independence and inherent Liberalism. From the annual assembly in Hastings in March 1954 there emerged an eponymous group which looked to produce a 'distinctive Liberal policy which would bring about the union of all Liberals'.[121] 'The Hastings Group are getting on with policy and plans but it is all very hush-hush', confided Edna Hughes. 'There is some hope that Joint Associations may disappear.'[122] While insisting that the modern Conservative party was the ally of Liberalism, the group showed signs of divergence from some aspects of the government's programme. A series of articles and pamphlets followed whose free-market ideas seemed in some ways to anticipate the Conservatism of a later generation – this at a time when figures such as Butler and Macmillan were positioning the Tories firmly within a consensual (critics might suggest corporatist) centre ground. A pamphlet produced by the Hastings Group in September 1954 urged the establishment of a royal commission to investigate trade union practices with an emphasis on the rights of individual trade unionists. It was further suggested that the National Coal Board should lease out its pits to private enterprise and there were calls for a system of 'contracting in' to union membership and a secret ballot every five years on political affiliation. It was also proposed that all government departments should be ordered to cut their costs by 5 per cent annually over a four-year period and that the annual cost of the welfare state should be reduced by not less than £100 million over the same period. As a sop to mainstream Liberals it was argued that the single transferable vote should be tried out, at least for one general election, failing which the electoral system should be investigated by a royal commission.[123]

But the National Liberal leadership viewed such developments as the Hastings Group and the rebellion in Wrexham with understandable caution. Any genuine reassertion of independence risked alienating the party's Conservative allies with the inevitable prospect of subsequent electoral extinction. No sitting National Liberal MP could expect to hold on to his seat in the face of Tory opposition. Apart from some cautious support from Henry Morris-Jones, the former MP for neighbouring Denbigh, the Hughes-Hanmer revolt received no endorsement from the National Liberal Organisation in London, much to Edna Hughes's disgust, and was doomed to failure. The rebellion in Wrexham petered out, while the Hastings Group soon lost momentum.

Only one National Liberal MP experienced serious difficulties as a result of being expected to act as lobby fodder for a Tory government. Frank Medlicott, the member for Norfolk Central, was in many ways an archetypal Liberal. His nonconformist religious faith was at the heart of all his political beliefs and he was also a committed temperance campaigner. He had in fact stood, unsuccessfully, as a Liberal candidate in Acton as long ago as the General Election of 1929. But his views gave rise to an uneasy relationship with his local constituency association. Medlicott opposed hanging, warned of the dangers of drink and protested against the cruelty of the Grand National with its annual tally of equine casualties. Most problematically, in a rural constituency dominated by prosperous Conservative farmers, he spoke out against blood sports. But the issue which brought matters to a head was the Suez Crisis of 1956. For many Liberals of this era Suez was a watershed, all the more poignant because of Prime Minister Anthony Eden's well merited reputation, dating back to the 1930s, for championing the principles of liberal internationalism. The government's conduct in the autumn of 1956 put an end to any lingering suggestion that the Conservative and Liberal parties might one day coalesce. The image that the Conservatives had been fostering for more than two decades that they had become the most appropriate repository for the remnants of British Liberalism was finally shattered. Violet Bonham Carter later admitted that she had 'almost persuaded' herself 'during the 51–56 Government that Toryism was shading into Liberalism'. After Suez, however, she concluded that there had been a 'reversion to type'.[124]

If the National Liberals really had represented the Liberal conscience of the Conservative party, then Suez was surely the moment for that conscience to be stirred. In practice, however, the group of Liberal-Unionist MPs all seem to have accepted Eden's conduct with the single exception of Frank Medlicott, who abstained on a motion of confidence on 8 November and then sent an open and critical letter to the Prime Minister. The MP soon came under severe pressure in his constituency and the following May it was announced that he would not be standing for re-election. Medlicott was not willing to play the role of 'party hack, prepared to throw overboard everything in which he believes if only he can cling to his seat in parliament'.¹²⁵ He subsequently rejoined the Liberal party and served as its Treasurer under Jeremy Thorpe.

As the rebellion in Wrexham and the emergence of the Hastings Group revealed, the possibility of Liberal reunion remained in the minds of some National Liberals in the early 1950s. In one sense this had now become a more likely proposition than ever before, as the General Election of 1951 had witnessed the defeat of the remaining left-wing Liberal MPs including Megan Lloyd George. Over the course of the next parliament the small band of Liberal MPs smiled benignly on much of the legislative programme of the Churchill government. Indeed, the 1951 election was scarcely over before Maclay reported to Woolton that the National Liberals were being approached by Liberals all over the country and that he was thinking hard about 'how best to consolidate what is still a very fluid position'. Maclay suggested that an approach might be made via the Liberals' 'very sensible and well balanced' chief whip, Jo Grimond.¹²⁶ But at the same time long-standing animosities remained. When Churchill suggested that Violet Bonham Carter might consider standing for parliament again, but this time as a National Liberal, her response could hardly have been more emphatic. 'I said "Never. They have never stood or fought for anything and had earned the contempt of all Parties. I shld. find it easier to stand as a Conservative if I did make a change."'¹²⁷

Some of the calls for reunion coming from National Liberals were on the old basis that all Liberals should now unite with a modern Conservative party that was 'dedicated to conserving and restoring those liberties which were ... the bedrock of Liberal faith'. Lord Rosebery was still reiterating this theme as late as 1955. The consequence of separation, he claimed, was

> A long and humiliating sequence of defeats and a total of nearly 400 lost deposits by Liberal Parliamentary candidates and the reduction of Independent Liberal representation to an insignificant fragment, comprising six members, five of whom were unopposed by Conservative candidates and three of whom at least owe their presence in Westminster to active Conservative support.¹²⁸

But the possibility of a genuine coming together of the Liberal diaspora, outside the embrace of Conservatism, was also discussed. An article in *New Horizon* claimed to discern stirrings within the ranks that suggest a growing desire for independence from Conservative domination and – strangely as it will seem to a straight Liberal – their own traditional Liberal instincts and faith are seeking new expression.[129]

The Liberal whip in the House of Lords, Lord Rea, showed interest and urged that reunion should at least be discussed,[130] while as late as September 1956 Clement Davies was being kept informed of a 'private plan ... to unite the milling Liberal factions at all costs'.[131]

None of this came to anything. Suez served to drive a renewed wedge between the two groups while, under its new leader Jo Grimond, the Liberal party, at least after the General Election of 1959, set about repositioning itself on the centre-left of British politics in such a way as to render the idea of Liberal reunion impractical. In any case, absorbing the Liberal party was not the priority for Conservatives that it had been in the late 1940s. They probably assumed that the Liberal party would now fade away of its own accord without the need to expend undue energy in laying claim to the corpse. In the context of the early 1950s this was not an unreasonable proposition. When, against the calculations of contemporary psephologists, the Tories defied the electoral pendulum and not merely won the General Election of 1955 but did so with an increased parliamentary majority, their confidence in their ability to prevail on their own was no doubt enhanced.

In the run-up to that election a minor stir was occasioned by the publication of the memoirs of Henry Morris-Jones, the former National Liberal MP for Denbigh who, only the previous year, had served as chairman of the party's executive committee. Perceptive readers noted a revealing passage:

> The Liberal National Party was never intended to be permanent. It is today, as the National Liberal Party, a shadow of its former self, overwhelmed by the Tory machine ... A decision, on the part of both [Liberal and National Liberal] Parties as to their future is now imperative.[132]

Liberals were delighted by this confession. One who claimed to deplore the spectacle of a 'now practically spineless group of old friends blind to the facts of life', declared that National Liberalism was dead. 'That fact has been obvious for some time, but the official recognition of its present status was notable coming from [such an] authoritative source.'[133]

Dead or not, four candidates at the election stood as 'National Liberals', eight as 'National Liberals and Conservatives', and a further 33 others used such varied labels as 'Conservative and Liberal' and 'Conservative and National Liberal'. In what was the dullest election of the post-war era, the National Liberals played an unexceptionable role. Reviewing the contest the Nuffield historian later concluded that, although the party issued a separate manifesto – 'Freedom for the Future' – nothing in it or in the election addresses of National Liberal candidates called for separate treatment outside his account of the Conservatives' activities.[134] The manifesto declared the National Liberals' aims to strengthen Britain's position in a free and peaceful world, to strengthen the national economy and to increase the rights and liberties of the individual. All of this was dependent on a strong Conservative government, while only the continued co-operation of Conservatives and National Liberals could ensure that constructive Liberal and Conservative thinking was translated into effective policies and action. Overall, with the country experiencing mounting prosperity, the National Liberals benefited from a moderate swing in the government's favour which gave the new Prime Minister, Anthony Eden, an overall majority of 58 seats in the new House of Commons. With ten fewer nominations than in 1951, joint candidates secured 21 victories, two more than at the previous election. Arthur Tiley won the new seat of Bradford West, while Joan Vickers regained Hore-Belisha's old seat of Plymouth, Devonport from Labour.

Many, however, now wondered whether there was any longer a need for the Conservatives' so-called 'associates' to maintain their separate identity, or whether the moment had not come to 'tidy up the question of nomenclature'. Could they not now all be called Conservatives, asked one correspondent to *The Times*. 'If not, can anyone tell me in what respect they differ from any Conservative member?'[135] In response Teviot and Maclay did their best to explain. The National Liberal Council outside parliament and the Liberal-Unionist group within it, they suggested, provided what the independent Liberal party could not – a means of making Liberalism a continuing and effective force in the life of the nation.[136] The problems with this argument have already been rehearsed. But before long another telling doubt would be added. For the first time since 1931 the Liberal party's parliamentary representation had not been reduced at a general election. In itself it was a questionable basis from which to draw much comfort, but over the next few years the green shoots of Liberal recovery were less easy to deny. Between Torquay in December 1955 and Galloway in April 1959 Liberals contested 19 by-elections. Only one deposit was lost and in seven contests the party came first or second. Perhaps independent Liberalism was not dead after all.

On a positive note, the elevation of Harold Macmillan to the premiership in January 1957 resulted in the appointment of two members of the Liberal-Unionist parliamentary group to the cabinet. As Chancellor of the Duchy of Lancaster, Dr Charles Hill found himself in charge of the government's information and propaganda strategy, no easy task in the wake of the Suez fiasco of the previous year. For a time, he became an indispensable adviser to the Prime Minister whose own experience of broadcasting and communications was limited. Promoted to the Ministry of Housing, Local Government and Welsh Affairs in October 1961, Hill proved altogether less successful. John Maclay, who had resigned from Churchill's government in May 1952 when his health broke down under the pressure of work, had returned to office during the Suez Crisis as Minister of State for Colonial Affairs. Now Macmillan appointed him Secretary of State for Scotland. His promotion was in part party-political. The Liberals posed a more serious threat to Conservative domination in Scotland, especially in agricultural areas, than was the case in most English constituencies. Having a National Liberal in charge was something of an insurance policy for a government which still felt more comfortable employing the title 'Unionist party' north of the border. At all events, Maclay embarked upon more than five years of diligent, if unspectacular, administration, turning the Scottish Office into an agent of regional policy designed to reinvigorate the country's industrial economy.[137]

Mark Bonham Carter's celebrated by-election victory at Torrington in March 1958 rightly occupies an almost iconic position in the history, and more particularly the revival, of the Liberal party. It was the Liberals' first by-election gain since 1929 and, with hindsight, stands as one of the first tangible signs that the process of long-term decline could be arrested and indeed reversed. But the by-election was also a seminal moment in the history of the National Liberals. The seat, originally under the guise of South Molton, had been held, except for five years in the 1920s, by the George Lamberts, father and son, since 1891. Lambert senior had been among the original defectors to the Liberal National cause of 1931. He was succeeded by his son in 1945 and it was the father's death at the beginning of 1958 which, by elevating the younger Lambert to the peerage, occasioned the by-election.

The choice of a successor exposed the fragility of the National Liberals' claim still to exist as a viable political force. The young Anthony Royle was selected as the National Liberal and Conservative candidate, but was widely regarded as an unreconstructed Tory. Bonham Carter, grandson of Asquith and the first Liberal to contest the seat since 1950, spared no effort in disparaging Royle's double-barrelled label. Dubbed 'Mr Facing-Both-Ways', Royle found his party affiliation, designed to appeal to two separate traditions in a constituency where 'the word Liberal still has a palpable magic', something of an embarrassment. He was scarcely helped by an intervention from his predecessor. Speaking on Royle's behalf, Lord Lambert praised political 'cross-breeds', adding that he himself put 'National Liberal' before 'Conservative' because he believed quality should always be on top.[138]

Victory over a National Liberal candidate was particularly sweet for the Liberals, one of their first clear successes in the internecine Liberal struggle that had been going on for the best part of three decades. Lady Violet Bonham Carter purred at her son's win and later recalled 'the strange sense of being a member of an army of liberation entering occupied territory which for years had been ruled by quislings and collaborators and that their day was over once and for all'.[139] In fact, the Liberal victory is best explained in terms of the mid-term unpopularity of the Conservative government. But the 'National Liberal factor' inevitably came under scrutiny as observers sought to explain the transformation of a 9000 government majority into a narrow win for Bonham Carter. *The Times* suggested that many Liberal voters, who had been prepared to maintain their loyalty to a Lambert, no matter which variant of Liberalism he espoused, were less instinctively disposed to accept the Liberalism of anyone else standing under National Liberal and Conservative colours.[140] But, granted that the original Liberal Nationals were now a dying breed, where did this leave the National Liberal party?

> It is conceivable that Conservative Central Office may well have been wondering, in their studies of the problems that face them in a general election, whether the National Liberals might prove a useful counter to the Liberal revival. But does Torrington suggest that the electorate refuse to be deceived when a fundamentally Conservative candidate makes a marriage of convenience with Liberalism? Would

the Conservative Party be any worse off if it frankly flew its own colours?[141]

Torrington, indeed, gave ammunition to those Tories who believed that it was time for the National Liberals to be wound up. 'As regards the "bridge to us" aspect', noted one Conservative official, 'I have always been of the opinion that any Liberal convert would much rather come direct than mess about with the Lib Nats whom he regards with as much abhorrence as I do.'[142]

Not surprisingly, the National Liberals' manifesto for the General Election of 1959 singled out the Liberal party for special criticism. The first question for Liberals to ask themselves, it suggested, was whether a party could win sufficient seats in the new parliament to form and maintain a government capable of fulfilling its promises. The best that the Liberal party could hope for was to hold the balance between the two major parties. But how might the Liberals use this position?

> This would recreate the situation which existed after the general elections of 1923 and 1929 ... Power without responsibility is an ugly thing described by an ugly name, and as precedent proves those who exercised it would, at the first opportunity, be given short shrift by the nation.

In practice, claimed 'Britain's Future: Socialism or Liberty?', there were only two truly distinctive features in independent Liberal policy, and both were potentially disastrous. One was to give up nuclear weapons and entrust the ultimate defence of the country to the United States. 'Never before has any party advocated that the ultimate defence of these islands should be left to the discretion of a foreign Power, however friendly.' The second was the Liberal commitment to proportional representation. 'Such a system would paralyse the effectiveness of government and have a debilitating effect upon our democratic institutions.'

Supporting the Liberal party in the postwar era had been a futile exercise. Now it might well prove dangerous by letting in a Labour government. Real Liberal progress, suggested the National Liberal manifesto, had been secured by the past eight years of Conservative government:

Scarcity has been replaced by plenty; austerity has given place to abundance; we are a better fed and better housed nation; building society deposits, national and other forms of savings are bigger than ever before, and millions of workers are enjoying for the first time middle-class standards of material comfort.

At the end of a decade of unprecedented affluence, it was difficult to dispute this description. Whether it amounted to 'Liberalism' was more open to question. But the National Liberals had no doubts:

The nation is becoming what Lord Rosebery, the last Liberal Prime Minister of the nineteenth century, described as the Liberal aim: 'A great property-owning democracy' whose citizens enjoy more liberties than they have known for more than twenty years.[143]

Benefitting again from a swing in the government's favour which saw Harold Macmillan's parliamentary majority increase to 100, jointly nominated candidates were successful in 20 of the 40 seats which they contested. Making allowance for the by-election loss in Torrington, no Liberal-Unionist seat changed hands compared with the General Election of 1955 and no new seats were gained. It was, however, striking that Torrington itself was now recaptured by a straightforward Conservative. It was hard to derive much evidence from these results to support the contention that the Conservatives were continuing to draw significant electoral advantage from their partnership with the National Liberals. Yet when in a 1961 by-election the Conservative candidate saw his majority slashed in the former National Liberal seat of East Fife, it was suggested that the Liberals had eaten into the genuinely Liberal vote which had previously supported the National Liberal MP.[144] Similarly, the Liberals made a point of targeting the seat of North Mearns and Angus when it was announced that the sitting 'Liberal and Unionist' member would not be standing again and that he would be replaced by a Tory candidate.[145]

An article in *The Times* in May 1962 prompted the last round of what had become a fairly regular debate in its correspondence columns as to whether the National Liberals were serving any useful purpose by clinging to their theoretically independent, but increasingly tenuous, existence. While recognising that there were still a handful of constituencies in which 'hybrid candidatures' retained some validity, *The Times* concluded that 'National Liberalism as a self-consciously maintained political entity has served its turn for the anti-Socialist forces and for the immediate future ... has done all the good it is likely to do for the Conservative Party'.[146] In response Julian Ridsdale, MP for Harwich, did his best to restate the National Liberals' traditional case. The threat of socialism, he claimed, was still real enough, as had been shown in a speech by James Callaghan in the recent Commons debate on the Budget, with which the leader of the Liberal party had expressed sympathy. For those who did not wish to aid this 'debacle for the country of turning back to Socialism with Mr Grimond's support', there remained ample justification for keeping the National Liberal Organisation in being as an expression of the traditional Liberal values of those whose last desire was to see another socialist government.[147] For the mainstream Liberal party, Donald Wade sought to deflate the National Liberals' exaggerated pretensions. They were now, he insisted, indistinguishable from Conservatives and it was about time that they honestly admitted this fact to the British electorate by dropping their distinctive title.[148]

But it was the changing political scene which finally destroyed National Liberalism's remaining *raison d'être*. By the early 1960s the notion – of which the National Liberals had been the tangible expression – of a broad front of Conservatives and Liberals in opposition to a perceived 'socialist threat' had largely lost its meaning. This reflected changes in both the Labour and Liberal parties. Hugh Gaitskell, chosen to succeed Attlee in 1955, proved to be the most right-wing leader in the Labour party's history up to that date. Though he died suddenly in January 1963, the Labour government headed by Harold Wilson, narrowly elected to power in October 1964, did not inaugurate a second phase of socialist advance, building on the earlier achievements of Attlee's postwar administration. At the same time the Liberal party was looking less and less like a potential electoral partner for the Tories. As early as the autumn of 1961 the Conservative party publication *The Councillor* complained that, while it had been customary to regard Liberals as anti-socialists, particularly on local councils, recent experiences 'point to second thoughts'.[149] The Conservative Campaign Guide for the 1964 General Election argued that Liberal policies had moved increasingly leftwards with Liberal MPs voting more and more with the Labour party. Indeed, 'whenever they have voted so far in the present Parliament they have supported the Socialists with five out of every six votes'.[150]

For a time, in fact, in the early 1960s, the Liberals, enjoying their best by-election performances for more than 30 years, seemed to pose a greater threat to the Conservative party than did Labour. *The Times* well captured the Tories' dilemma:

When the Conservative Party was fighting with Labour in the dismemberment of the carcase of the old Liberalism, there was obvious advantage in establishing its Liberal appeal and emphasising its old Liberal associations and Liberal converts. But today might not the claim to Liberalism, with its often bogus ring in the ears of floating voters, merely suggest that Liberalism has important qualities that Conservatism lacks? Can a party convincingly attack principles or policies or attitudes it advocates itself?[151]

Under Jo Grimond's leadership the Liberals had finally abandoned the ambiguous political stance that had characterised the party in the Clement Davies years. Grimond's aim was to reposition Liberalism as a radical, non-socialist party of the left. One feature of this repositioning was an assault on the comfortable Liberal-Conservative electoral alliances, which had long existed in local politics, often under the label 'Progressives' and in many cases predating the split of 1931. For younger Liberals in particular such arrangements had no place in the modern party. In 1962 Michael Meadowcroft was appointed Local Government Officer by the Liberal Party Organisation with the specific task of ending these pacts. Meanwhile the majority of Liberals acquiesced in the leader's partly overt, partly clandestine, quest for a partnership with the non-ideological wing of the Labour party.[152] But that quest never got far enough to prompt right-leaning Liberals to consider the option of affiliation with the National Liberals as some predicted. In this transformed political climate the question now was whether National Liberalism served 'any useful purpose, or whether it may not be positively damaging'.[153]

The party was one of the more inconspicuous victims of Macmillan's famous 'Night of the Long Knives' in July 1962 when the Prime Minister, apparently reacting in a state of near panic to a series of political and electoral reverses, sacked a third of his cabinet. Not only did the National Liberals lose their two remaining cabinet ministers, Charles Hill and Jack Maclay, but also the Minister of State at the Home Office, David Renton who, at just under 54 years of age, might reasonably have expected promotion rather than the sack. The elevation of Niall Macpherson to be Minister for Pensions and National Insurance provided only partial compensation. In fact Maclay left office readily enough, though his friends were shocked by the suddenness of his dismissal. About a year earlier he had told Macmillan that he would like to retire from the Scottish Office, at some time in the reasonably near future convenient to the Prime Minister, in order to spend more time with his seriously disabled wife.[154] Hill, by contrast, was very upset. 'It was painful', recorded Macmillan, 'but he is really *not* up to it.'[155] Renton, assured that he would return to office when circumstances allowed, knew in his heart that his ministerial career was over and that he was perhaps paying the price for having earlier turned down an offer to become Solicitor General.[156]

The *New Horizon* expressed its dismay at what had happened. Only two members of the Liberal-Unionist parliamentary group now held office in the Conservative government. It was suggested in the press that the dismissals had been the cause of a serious row between the National Liberal party and its Tory allies. For this, suggested the *Daily Telegraph*, there was no justification. 'No party – even if it sails under five aliases – has a prescriptive right to be represented in the Administration, as a bonus for supporting the Government.' Even so, the *Telegraph* hoped that the Conservatives would not over-react to 'the National Liberal outburst'. The Woolton-Teviot Agreement might be becoming more and more of a dead letter, but no advantage would come from hastening its demise. Indeed, 'it would be suicidal on the eve of a ticklish General Election to alienate the always large section of Liberal thought which prefers Tory democracy to Socialism, even disguised as radicalism'.[157]

For the National Liberals Herbert Butcher sought to quash any suggestion of a quarrel with the Conservatives. Macmillan had simply conducted a cabinet reshuffle, as he was entitled to do, and the *New Horizon* had, with equal right, expressed regret at the departure of Maclay, Hill and Renton. But this should not be taken as indicating any rift. The role of the National Liberals, Butcher suggested, remained clear. It was to ensure that the policies which had been followed by successive Conservative governments headed by Churchill, Eden and Macmillan were not replaced by the policies of socialism. In future, the danger might come not from 'direct Socialist attack' but as a result of 'confusion arising from independent Liberal infiltration'. Butcher had no doubt that, as in the past, the two parties would again co-operate at the next general election to ensure that 'the ideals which Conservatives and National Liberals share are again triumphant'.[158]

But such arguments increasingly failed to convince. If the National Liberals were any sort of asset to the government, the fact could not be escaped that they were a diminishing one. At the time of the attack in the *New Horizon*, the Liberal-Unionist group claimed a membership of 22. Of these, one, Group Captain Richard Collard, MP for Norfolk Central, soon died. Among the remainder, Sir Richard Nugent in Guildford and Sir John Gilmour in East Fife had been elected as Conservatives and their membership of the group was regarded as no more than a 'vestige of the past'.[159] With no realistic prospect that any other constituencies would ever convert to National Liberalism and every likelihood that the group's remaining MPs would, when they either died or stepped down from the Commons, be replaced by Conservatives, only one long-term outcome seemed possible. By contrast, one feature of the Liberal revival was the re-emergence of local party organisations in areas in which National Liberals had for long held a monopolistic claim on the party label. In the former Liberal stronghold of Swansea West, for example, where the local Liberal party had disappeared after the split of 1931–2, leaving the field free to Liberal Nationalism, a new association was formed in 1961 and a Liberal candidate was in place for the general election three years later.

The process of extinction was greatly hastened by the General Election of 1964. The Liberal-Unionist parliamentary group had already been significantly depleted in the course of the 1959 parliament. By-elections in Dumfries (December 1963), following Macpherson's elevation to the peerage as Lord Drumalbyn, and in East Fife (November 1961), necessitated by the death of Henderson Stewart, saw Conservative candidates succeed the former members. Charles Hill, who had himself decided that the National Liberal 'organisation and designation' were now 'anachronisms' and that the right moment to 'change our local name' would be when he retired from his constituency, left the House of Commons to become chairman of the Independent Television Authority in June 1963.[160] But the change to a Conservative candidate could not save his Luton seat from falling to Labour in November 1963. Following the death of R.C.M. Collard, Ian Gilmour was horrified to read in the local press that he had been selected as the 'Conservative and Liberal' candidate for the Central Norfolk by-election in November 1962. After consulting the local party chairman, he at least succeeded in changing his designation to 'Conservative and National Liberal'. Then, after securing victory, Gilmour determined to face realities. The local party organisation was 'entirely or virtually entirely Conservative in all senses except name'. Gilmour got rid of the National Liberal suffix as quickly as he could and prepared to stand as a plain Conservative in the General Election.[161] Similarly, Joan Vickers in

Plymouth Devonport and N.J. Cole in South Bedfordshire, where the 'hybrid label' was now proving an 'embarrassment', dropped the joint designations under which they had campaigned in 1959.[162] In Denbigh the change of Geraint Morgan's affiliation from 'Conservative and National Liberal' to 'Conservative' passed largely unnoticed with only the *Western Mail* remarking that the constituency's 53,000 electors 'must be thankful that the confusion of the Liberals and National Liberals has now been removed'.[163] Elsewhere long-serving National Liberal and Unionist MPs, Captain James Duncan in South Angus and Sir Colin Thornton-Kemsley in North Angus, who had served as chairman of the parliamentary group since 1961, stepped down and were replaced by Conservatives. Many other constituencies, previously contested under joint labels, including six seats in Sheffield, were now offered Conservative candidates.

As a result, just 19 candidates stood under one variation or other of the joint party label, considerably fewer than at any of the elections of the 1950s and only half the total in 1959. Of sitting MPs Sir William Taylor was beaten in Bradford North as was M.N. Shaw in Brighouse and Spenborough, the seat which had been reserved for the National Liberals as compensation for the disappearance of Simon's Spen Valley constituency back in the late 1940s, and which was narrowly captured in a 1960 by-election. This left just six successful candidates – Herbert Butcher in Holland-with-Boston, David Renton in Huntingdon, Julian Ridsdale in Harwich, Greville Howard in St Ives, Arthur Tiley in Bradford West and Alan Hopkins in Bristol North-East. In addition, John Osborn (Sheffield, Hallam) and Sir Peter Roberts (Sheffield, Healey), though elected as Tories, chose to align themselves with the Liberal-Unionist parliamentary group.

* * *

Rather as had been predicted in Roger Fulford's fictional account, the last years of the National Liberal party were tainted by corruption. The key figure was the Pontefract architect, John Poulson. Many years before his more celebrated association with the Tory Home Secretary of the early 1970s, Reginald Maudling, Poulson seems to have befriended and bankrolled Herbert Butcher, National Liberal MP for Holland-with-Boston and the party's long-serving chief whip. It was the architect's cash which subsidised the National Liberal Forum, the party's monthly discussion group at the Caxton Hall which Butcher had revived in 1946. The National Liberal party had obvious attractions for Poulson. Its declining strength and consequent shortage of funds made it easy for him to advance within its ranks, while its ever closer association with the Conservatives afforded him the opportunity to meet some of the leading politicians of the day. Most meetings of the Forum were of an unexceptionable nature. Just occasionally, however, it was used for significant policy statements. It was from this platform in January 1964, for example, that Enoch Powell denounced the 'hocus pocus' prices and incomes policy of his own government and called for a reassertion of the priority of the market. It was at the same venue in November 1960 that Poulson had his first fateful meeting with Maudling, then a rising young minister in the Macmillan government. Poulson himself used the Forum to espouse his views of economic liberalism that were markedly out of kilter with the mainstream Conservative thinking of the day. It is not clear what the new Tory leader Edward Heath would have made of the words of introduction delivered by Poulson in November 1966:

> We remain steadfast to the Asquith tradition, believing in free enterprise, open competition, the widest practical application of free trade, prudence in public expenditure and taxation, personal liberty, and the realistic expression of the social conscience by adequate provision for those in need of help, without the bogus benevolence of a so-called Welfare State and its distribution of universal benefits regardless of need.[164]

Poulson's self-interested generosity – what has been called his 'open cheque book technique' – soon brought its rewards. In 1961 he was appointed joint vice-chairman of the executive of the National Liberal Council and three years later he became chairman. Only Poulson's unquenchable ambition can explain his continuing readiness to pour money into a patently declining concern. In March 1967 he contributed his first article to *New Horizon*, ridiculing the election of Jeremy Thorpe to replace Jo Grimond as leader of the Liberal party – 'the viking-by-adoption gave way to the ventriloquist-by-profession'.[165] The following year he took control of the journal, transferred its operation to his London office and promptly presided over its demise.

Poulson's cash may have kept the National Liberals going somewhat longer than would otherwise have been the case. Nonetheless, by the mid-1960s it was only too apparent that the party was fading away. The parliament elected in October 1964, however, was not the time for a significant reappraisal of the relationship between the Conservatives and their now much diminished allies. With a parliamentary majority which fell for a time to a bare three seats, Harold Wilson's Labour government was always likely to seize any suitable moment for a further appeal to the electorate. So the National Liberals fought one more election when the country again went to the polls in March 1966. Only nine constituencies were contested by hybrid candidates, although three further jointly selected nominees chose to stand as Conservatives. In some of these nine, moreover, the National Liberal component had, for all practical purposes, lost its meaning. In Wrexham, for example, it amounted to little more than securing the signature of Edna Hughes, the elderly daughter of the founder of the local National Liberal party, on the nomination papers of the Conservative and National Liberal (but in practice Conservative) candidate, Griffith Pierce.[166] Of the six seats held in 1964 Holland-with-Boston, vacated by Herbert Butcher, was now fought and won by a Tory while, in the face of a substantial national swing to Labour, both Bradford West and Bristol North-East were lost.

This left just three 'Liberal Unionist' MPs in the new parliament – David Renton in Huntingdonshire, Julian Ridsdale in Harwich and John Nott, newly elected for St Ives. Of these Nott could scarcely claim any Liberal pedigree. As an aspiring Conservative politician he had arrived in St Ives to be interviewed as a potential candidate by what he supposed would be the local Conservative association, only to discover that his designation would in fact be 'National Liberal and Conservative' and that the former's influence was still strong, even in the mid-1960s.[167] With such a tiny parliamentary force, however, it was time to face realities. When David Renton had first raised the possibility of submerging the National Liberals' identity within the Conservative ranks, he was met with R.A. Butler's insistence that it was wrong to throw away an asset, however small.[168] Now, finding himself the leader of his group, Renton seized the initiative. With a minimum of fuss the National Liberal Council was disbanded in May 1968 and the party's accumulated funds of around £50,000 were handed over to the Conservatives.[169] After an existence of almost 37 years the National Liberal party passed into history.

6

Conclusion

The National Liberal Forum held its final meeting in March 1968. The office of the National Liberal Organisation closed that Easter, leaving its Treasurer (Lord Drumalbyn) and Chairman (John Poulson) to deal with any outstanding matters. Then, meeting in London on 14 May 1968, the National Liberal Council resolved to dissolve itself. Born into the age of Baldwin and MacDonald, the party had managed to survive into the era of Edward Heath and Harold Wilson. The following month saw the publication of the final issue of the party's journal, *New Horizon*. Under the heading 'Mission Accomplished' the editor, Dominic Le Foe, reviewed the history of the National Liberal movement. The decision to break away from the Liberal party in 1931 had been 'crucial and highly significant'. The actions of Sir John Simon and his followers 'removed the Liberal Party as it had been from the political chess board, but opened up the whole question of the distribution of the Liberal vote'. That issue remained important after 1945 but now 'the old Liberal ideals ... became twice as precious under a Socialist government as ever they had been under the nineteenth-century Tories'. At this point the National Liberals began to exercise a 'telling influence'. Two decades later the Conservatives had come through a 'majestic rethinking of philosophy and strategy'. Their platform was now immensely more progressive than anything the independent Liberal party had proposed in the early 1950s, when they too could have thrown in their lot with the Tories. But, with 'the transformation of the Conservative Party being completed', it was 'probably inevitable' that the National Liberal role would disappear.[1]

David Renton, as the last leader of the parliamentary party, took up the same theme. For 30 years, he claimed, the National Liberals had fulfilled an important role in National and Conservative governments and, as one whose association with the party had spanned its entire history, he was 'proud of the part which our movement has played in the history of our times'. Now, however, its two principal justifications had passed. By 1946 the General Agreement on Tariffs and Trade had been accepted by all parties and the free trade versus protection controversy, which had split the Liberal movement in 1932, had ceased to be an issue in British politics. 'Everyone now believes in protection to some extent and in the lowering of world trade barriers, so long as it does not lead to dumping.' The threat of socialism remained, but the National Liberals' alliance with the Conservatives was now firmly consolidated. Moreover, now that the Liberal party 'has proclaimed itself as the alternative party of the Left and has indeed become largely a gathering of Radical extremists, there are few Liberals of the old and true tradition remaining to be disillusioned or to need a bridge to cross over from it to a party which more truly represents their aims and ideas'. Thus the National Liberals 'achieved much in their time, but that time has passed'.[2]

Can such claims be sustained? This book has argued that the National Liberals did indeed exercise a marked influence over the course of British politics for a period of about a quarter of a century, but the emphasis is somewhat different from that presented by Le Foe and Renton. Though there are clear links between the two, the pre- and post-Second World War periods need to be considered separately. Notwithstanding the denigration of their opponents, the Liberal Nationals were a significant political force in the 1930s. Indeed, without them, the National Government would not have been possible. Their impact was both negative and positive — negative from the point of view of the mainstream Liberal party and positive from that of the Conservatives.

Orthodox Liberals never quite knew how to respond to the Liberal Nationals. Some could not easily bring themselves to accept that the Liberal National defection was anything other than temporary. Some thought it best to ignore their existence on the grounds that publicity would only give credence to their otherwise spurious claims to legitimacy. Still others sought refuge in ridicule with Isaac Foot comparing their relationship with the Tories to that of the 'janissaries and eunuchs of the royal palace'.[3] But Liberals as a whole found it far more difficult to take the Liberal Nationals seriously and to recognise the damage that they were doing to their cause. The Liberal Nationals 'were considered more of a minor nuisance than anything else', recalled one veteran of a succession of unsuccessful Liberal election campaigns. 'Somehow one never thought that they would last.'[4]

Of course, the decline of the Liberal party was already well advanced by the early 1930s and many crucial developments had taken place long before the Liberal Nationals came on to the scene. But the party remained a significant factor in British politics at least in terms of its voting strength in the country. At the General Election of 1929 the Liberals had managed to secure almost a quarter of the popular vote. Liberalism was still a significant force over much of the country. Thereafter, however, the party continued to decline in a way that seemed to point to inevitable extinction. At the General Election of 1951 the party returned only six MPs on the basis of fewer than three-quarters of a million votes, less than 2.6 per cent of the total. In this process the role of the Liberal Nationals seems beyond question.

The most obvious impact was the immediate loss of around half of the Liberal party's parliamentary strength. 'The presence in Parliament of a little more than 30 Liberal Members who advocate tariffs', declared the *Liberal Magazine* with scarcely disguised incredulity, 'is an amazing fact. Even a year ago nobody would have believed it.'[5] But the reluctance of the orthodox party to challenge Liberal Nationals in their constituencies in the General Election of 1935, together with the cancellation of that scheduled for 1939–40, means that the true impact of the schism of 1931–2 did not become fully apparent until after the Second World War. Of all the constituencies which had been represented by Liberal National MPs during the 1930s, the mainstream Liberal party managed to mount a challenge in just 14 in the General Election of 1945. In two of these constituencies, Montgomeryshire and Eye, the sitting Liberal National member had gone back into the Liberal fold and was safely returned to Westminster. In Denbigh and the Western Isles the Liberal candidate managed to secure second place. But in the remaining ten contests Liberals came bottom of the poll. In other words, in the majority of Liberal National seats independent Liberalism had been wiped out as a significant political force.

Ever since it slipped into third party status the Liberal party has objected to attempts to define it in relation to its rivals in the Conservative and Labour parties. As Frank Byers explained in 1946, 'Liberalism does not offer a middle way between Toryism and Socialism, but a distinctive, positive way of its own which is opposed to both, and which offers the nation an escape from the obnoxious choice between monopoly capitalism and collectivism'.[6] Suitably modified, a similar statement might be offered by a Liberal Democrat in our own day. Yet for many voters, including Liberal ones, locating Liberalism on a linear progression between the left and right extremes of the political spectrum has always been part of their electoral understanding, especially once the Liberal party's aspiration became limited, at least for the foreseeable future, to holding the balance of parliamentary power. The Liberal Nationals' unequivocal declaration that they felt closer to the Conservative party of Stanley Baldwin than they did to the post-1931 Labour party thus had a definite appeal to many Liberal voters, however loudly the mainstream party tried to deny it. Furthermore, the idea that modern Conservatism *had* changed and that it was not the same as the party which Liberals had steadfastly opposed before 1914 was not without merit, as even orthodox Liberals would concede in their more unguarded moments. Speaking to the AGM of the Midland Liberal Federation in January 1937, Lord Trent admitted that 'one of the realities that we as a Party have to face in this country is that the very considerable left wing of the Conservative Party rank and file have borrowed our clothes while we were bathing'.[7]

As a result, at least before 1939, the Liberal Nationals were putting forward a credible claim to represent the only viable future for British Liberalism. Speaking in 1936, Hore-Belisha drew a parallel from the recent past:

> I remember when the Lloyd Georgian section was looked upon by the other section as unorthodox, and then it became orthodox and considered the others heretics. The day may not be far distant when the Liberal Nationals will be regarded as the true preservers of our tradition.[8]

The Liberal National challenge was all the more real granted the increasingly parlous state of the mainstream party. A stiff upper lip in the face of all adversity and an unswerving, if illogical, confidence that better times would one day return became part of the stock-in-trade of official Liberal party pronouncements in the dark middle decades of the twentieth century. In private, however, Liberal strategists were often more ready to face reality. 'We must anticipate that scores of constituency organisations will disband', warned Ramsay Muir in the wake of the General Election of 1935. Muir even believed that it might be necessary for his party to abandon its claim to the name 'Liberal', which had been 'defiled by the Simonites'.[9] For many the arguments in favour of a National Government increased rather than diminished as the decade progressed, granted the ever-worsening international situation, and not all Liberals approved of

Sinclair's attempts to emphasise his party's opposition. 'I don't think it is at all realised', warned J.A. Spender only weeks before the outbreak of European war, 'how deeply the dissent from his lead has cut into the party and sent its members into the Tory or Simonite camp.'[10]

Nor is it necessary to interpret the Liberal National defection in purely cynical terms. There had been much talk of Liberal-Conservative cooperation in 1924 following Asquith's decision to allow a minority Labour government to take office. Even Lloyd George had then spoken to Churchill of the possibility of supporting a future Conservative government in the way that Liberal Unionists had backed the Salisbury administrations of the 1880s and 1890s.[11] Experience since 1924, together with the perceived gravity of the political and economic crisis of 1931, made it almost inevitable that Liberals would once again sincerely disagree about the right course to take. Indeed, some sort of party realignment was clearly on the cards. As Harold Macmillan later recalled, 'Great indeed were the changes which the shock of the crisis brought about in the minds of men with regard to economic and political theories'.[12] As early as December 1929 Churchill predicted that all three parties would 'go into the melting pot within the next two years and come out in an entirely different grouping'. One of the reasons for this was that, whatever was happening to the Liberal party, 'the Liberal doctrine is spreading'. Churchill believed that 'quite half the members of the Labour Cabinet are Liberals'.[13]

If not cynical careerism, there was certainly a strong dose of political realism in the thinking of the Liberal Nationals. By the time of the crisis of 1931, more than a decade and a half had passed since the Liberal party had last presided over the country's government and Liberal Nationals were convinced that there was no foreseeable likelihood of the party regaining power. Participation inside the National Government, however, at least offered a practical opportunity to exert Liberal influence over government policy. Meanwhile, purist Liberals could dream idly of the day when their party on its own would recover the strength it had enjoyed in the era of Gladstone and Asquith. The words of a Liberal National pamphlet, published shortly before the outbreak of the Second World War, are instructive:

> As Liberals we stand (as Liberals have always stood) first and fundamentally for the improvement of the condition of the people. We naturally believe that this can best be achieved by the fullest exercise of Liberal influence in the conduct of public affairs. But we

are practical-minded Liberals. We face the situation as it is. One of the hard facts to which it would be folly to shut our eyes is that a Liberal Party Administration, such as we had before 1914, is not a practical possibility at the present time. What, then, should Liberals do? Should we take up an attitude of absolute and permanent opposition to all other Parties and to any partnership in a National Government? Ought we to run the risk of losing everything because we cannot get everything?[14]

In this way Liberal Nationals were anticipating (and, more importantly, giving an answer to) a debate that would dominate later decades of the Liberal party's history – whether the party should cling to its ideological purity or seize any appropriate opportunity to work in combination with other parties. If the occasion arose, insisted David Steel in 1975, it was important that Liberals should be ready to join with others for the more effective promotion of liberalism and not behave 'like a more rigid sect of the exclusive brethren'.[15] Though Steel's thoughts were fixed on a possible realignment of the political left, the parallel, in strategic terms, with the Liberal Nationals should be obvious.

The corollary of all this is the impact which the Liberal Nationals had on the fortunes of the Conservative party and, more particularly, on the sort of Conservatism that was in the ascendant in the 1930s. It was easy for Liberal Nationals to exaggerate the influence which the participation of less than three dozen MPs could have in the face of the massed ranks of the Tory party and to take credit for policies which would have been implemented with or without their presence. The Liberal National group 'meet together every week and we go through the Bills', explained Clement Davies for the benefit of his electors. 'If there is something in them that offends our Liberal conscience, we go round to see the Minister. We do the best we can to get the best measures for the people.'[16] But, as has been argued above, the impact of the Liberal Nationals was not just a function of their numbers in the House of Commons. The Conservative party of Baldwin and Chamberlain was willing to 'liberalise' its policies for altogether broader reasons than simple parliamentary arithmetic.

With hindsight it is reasonable to describe the inter-war years as a period of Conservative domination. The party was in power either alone or in combination for all but two brief periods of minority Labour government. But contemporary Tories lacked any long-term confidence about their party's prospects. It seemed to them that the logical outcome of a universal franchise in the context of a mass working-class population was socialist rule. If this outcome was to be avoided, the declining Liberal party – or at least the still considerable Liberal vote – held the key. 'Few Conservatives doubted the desirability of opposing Labour candidates with a combined "anti-Socialist" Conservative and Liberal vote.'[17] But precisely how this was to be achieved was the subject of considerable debate within the Tory ranks. The outcome of the General Election of 1929 seemed to confirm the Conservatives' worst fears. As Thomas Jones, who listened to the results as they came through with Baldwin in 10 Downing Street, noted: 'It became plain as the night wore on that LG's 500 stage army had put dozens of Labour men in by taking enough votes away this time from Conservatives'.[18] Participation in a National Government and partnership with the Liberal National group offered the solution for which Baldwin and others were looking. Standing on a 'National' rather than a Conservative platform, and using the Liberal Nationals to tap into the Liberal vote, offered the prospect of significantly broadening their party's appeal while keeping the socialist threat at bay. The electoral history of the 1930s seemed to confirm the success of this strategy. The percentage of the popular vote secured by the government in both the General Elections of 1931 and 1935 was not equalled at any other contest of the twentieth century.

But the Conservative-Liberal National alliance offered Baldwin a further, and equally important, opportunity. It enabled him to move the centre of gravity of the administration towards the political middle ground, in line with his own instincts as a progressive, consensual Tory. This made possible the effective sidelining of the Conservative right wing. A *Times* leader, in the wake of the General Election of 1935 and the subsequent reconstruction of the government, offered a perceptive assessment of what was going on. Noting that the Liberal National and National Labour groups between them were contributing seven ministers to a cabinet of 22, but only 41 MPs out of a government total of 434, it also drew attention to the fact that, in reshaping his administration, Baldwin had 'not called to his assistance any fresh representative of Right-wing views' from a pool of around 50 or 60 Conservative MPs. This, it believed, was the correct course as it conformed to the broad-based appeal of the National Government.[19] Baldwin, suggested one MP, is 'just not interested in anything except ensuring in a vague way that the Conservative party is always in control and that it operates as far to the left as possible'.[20] Simply expressed though it was, this sentiment contained more than a grain of truth.

*   *   *

Many of these ideas were still present after 1945, but the political context in which they persisted was significantly different. Most obviously, the Liberal Nationals, or National Liberals as they soon became, were a much weaker force than they had been before the war. Diminished as a parliamentary group, deprived of its most obvious *raison d'être* with the passing of the National Government and unable to recover from the wartime erosion of its organisational infrastructure, the party had lost the credibility of an independently viable political force to which it had previously laid claim. Early in 1946 the Conservative Central Office carried out an enquiry into the Liberal National organisation in those constituencies contested by the party at the recent General Election. It found that in only six cases was it possible to describe the Liberal National position as 'fairly strong', indicating a local party membership of over 100. In the majority of cases the description was 'none', 'poor' or 'ineffective'. In sum, 'Liberal National organisations appear mainly to exist only on paper ... There appears to be a tendency for them to deteriorate, but to be clinging as long as possible to what they know to be a "sinking ship".'[21]

But the Conservative position had also changed; their electoral hegemony of the inter-war years was now a thing of the past. Indeed, the General Election result of 1945 seemed to confirm the party's worst fears about its natural place in the electoral hierarchy. If the Conservatives were to have any chance of returning to power, they would need to explore every avenue to extend their appeal to the electorate. In this scenario the Liberal Nationals, however weak their intrinsic position, could still play an important role. Internal party research suggested to the Conservatives that there was a considerable correlation between the profile and outlook of floating voters – that is, those who alone could return the party to government – and those who were basically Liberal supporters.[22] Just as in the 1930s, therefore, 'the Conservatives were keen to construct a similar social and political coalition of anti-Socialist forces'.[23] And, notwithstanding the often strained relationship between Liberals and Liberal Nationals, the latter occupied a potentially vital part in the Tory plan. As Lord Woolton explained to a Conservative MP, 'I am certain that if we can secure the full support of the Liberal Nationals throughout the country, we shall provide a bridge over which many "Sinclair" Liberals may pass without any detrimental effect on their political consciences'.[24] In addition to asking about the state of Liberal National organisation, the 1946 enquiry referred to above had also posed the question, 'To what extent do you consider that a Liberal National would attract Liberal votes which would in no circumstances be given to a Conservative candidate?' To this replies varied, but the most common answer was 'to a small extent'.[25] Such, however, was the Tory plight after 1945 that no assistance, however small, could be ignored. By 1950–51, moreover, the overall electoral position had become so tight as to render the National Liberal factor potentially decisive. The loss or gain of a relatively small number of votes could now make all the difference between a Labour and a Conservative government.

As in the 1930s, therefore, the post-war Conservative-National Liberal partnership, cemented in the Woolton-Teviot Agreement of 1947, was one of mutual advantage. Now, for Conservatives it was part of a desperate quest to recover power. Allowing the National Liberals to retain at least a semi-independent identity and organisation was a way of emphasising that the fight against socialism transcended party political boundaries.[26] For the National Liberals, on the other hand, the pact offered an escape route from probable extinction. With the decline of the mainsteam Liberal party continuing apace, moreover, National Liberals were even better placed than before the war to insist that theirs was the only viable means of promoting Liberal ideas in government. As one local official put it:

[Liberals] cannot wait for any more promised revivals of the Liberal party round the corner. The crisis is upon us and calls for the best team-work to help the nation and not merely to shout from the touchline for another five years. We Liberals turn to the one leader who can rescue us – the greatest Liberal of our time. He leads the Conservative party – the one party that can displace the Socialists and give the country more Liberalism than any Liberal Government gave in the last century.[27]

Not surprisingly, many Conservatives remained unhappy about the new arrangements. As far as they were concerned, the National Liberals were little more than a nuisance, complicating the activities of local Tory associations but offering very little in return. Having given way to their junior partners in the General Election of 1945, the feeling among Conservatives in the Clayton division of Manchester was one of 'Never again'.[28] But the majority view – that the National Liberals could still contribute to increasing the Tory vote – prevailed throughout the 1950s as Conservatives strained to make themselves more appealing to one-time

Liberal supporters, with Churchill in particular missing no opportunity to emphasise his own Liberal past.[29]

The suggestion that there was now little to differentiate Liberalism from modern Conservatism was, of course, hotly disputed. For the Conservatives it involved a measure of intellectual contortion, talking the Liberal language of 'freedom' and 'liberty' – 'setting the people free' as their 1951 manifesto proclaimed – while in practice progressively accommodating much of the post-war settlement of the Attlee government within their own policies and programme.[30] To the same proposition Liberal and National Liberal spokesmen took up predictably differing stances. According to the latter's elder statesman, Lord Simon, 'the proudest claim that Liberals can make today is that their creed has so largely permeated national policy as to be accepted and acted upon by the opponents of Socialism, even though they do not call themselves Liberals'.[31] By contrast, Roger Fulford, writing on this occasion as a Liberal partisan rather than as an author of fiction, insisted that 'Liberals cannot be Tories':

> With increasing persistence this dangerous nonsense is being dinned into our ears by the parrots of the Conservative Party. It is nonsense because it is not true; it is dangerous because, if it was generally believed and put into practice, it would lead to a division of British politics on a class basis.[32]

At the end of the day, of course, it all depended upon what constituted true Liberalism and to this fundamental question the leading spokesmen of the orthodox party failed to give a single and unequivocal answer in the decade after the end of the war. Certainly, the parliamentary Liberal party tended to look favourably upon most of the doings of Churchill's government in the years 1951–5. When a group of more radical Liberals decided to quit the party in 1956, they complained that since 1951 their leaders had 'presented what seems to us the extraordinary spectacle of a Liberal Parliamentary Party giving general support to a Tory government'. This was 'an indication of the general drift to the Right which has led each of us to sever his connection with official Liberalism'.[33]

In any case scope remained for continuing confusion among ordinary voters as to what was Liberalism and what was not. At the General Election of 1950 in Pembrokeshire Gwilym Lloyd-George stood as a Liberal with Conservative support. He denied that he was a National Liberal, but was widely regarded as such and he joined the Liberal Unionist parliamentary

CONCLUSION 213

group when elected for Newcastle-upon-Tyne North in 1951. Yet in neighbouring Carmarthenshire Rhys Hopkin Morris also enjoyed tacit Conservative support, but took the Liberal whip in the House of Commons. Indeed, it was striking that of the six Liberal MPs returned to Westminster in 1951 only Jo Grimond in Orkney and Shetland had prevailed in the face of Tory opposition. In other words most members of the parliamentary Liberal party probably owed their survival to the indulgence of the Conservatives – precisely the state of affairs for which they always ridiculed the National Liberals. Arguably, the Tories had made a tactical mistake in seeking, unsuccessfully as it turned out, an anti-socialist alliance with the Liberal party. An aggressive campaign in the late 1940s and early 1950s to eliminate the Liberals' parliamentary representation might have destroyed the orthodox party's viability as a national political force, leaving the National Liberals as the leading claimant to the historic Liberal tradition.

As the 1950s progressed and as the Liberal party increasingly donned the image of a non-socialist party of the left, so too the Conservatives' attitude towards it also necessarily changed. The argument now became that all that was best in Liberalism had long since been absorbed into Conservative philosophy while the Liberal party itself had gone astray. Leading Tories now sought to deter moderate Liberal voters from supporting Grimond's party by presenting it as dangerously left-wing and the very denial of true Liberal values, 'advocating policies similar to those put forward at one time or another by the Socialists'.[34] In such a situation the National Liberals inevitably became an asset of diminishing value. Yet even as late as 1967 Conservative Central Office was still receiving enquiries about the possibility of establishing new joint Conservative and National Liberal associations to 'encourage disenchanted influential members of the Liberal party' to jump ship.[35] Significantly, however, the advice now given was that such potential Liberal defectors should be encouraged to join the Conservative party directly.[36]

National Liberalism in fact was now fading away. Unable to renew itself, it came over time to suffer the fate that probably awaits the junior component in any political alliance – a loss of identity in the mind of the voter in favour of the senior partner.[37] The partnership, of course, had never been one of equals. In one of the sketches in which he delighted, Winston Churchill once drew the Conservative party as a kangaroo with its National Liberal 'baby' looking out from its pouch.[38] Incapable of surviving on its own, this infant was bound one day to die.

Yet for the National Liberals there may have been life after death. The party had provided one means by which an individualist, market-orientated tradition had survived through an era in which all the main parties sought to adapt to the Keynesian-Beveridgite consensus of ever greater state intervention. Particularly after 1945, the strand of 'economic liberalism', looking back to Gladstonian financial orthodoxy, was always stronger among the National Liberals than it was within the mainstream party, where 'social Liberalism' tended to have the upper hand. The National Liberals' statement of policy for the General Election of 1951 would not have been out of place in the Conservative party of the 1980s. As *The Times* summarised:

> The need for more efficient management in industry, an acute sense of personal responsibility, and active incentives for capital, management and labour is urged. The means must be found by voluntary negotiation between management and labour to allow increased effort to reap increased reward. Pointing out that today central and local government take nearly half of all the people earn, the document states that the present level of public expenditure, which discourages effort, hinders enterprise, and makes personal saving almost impossible, can and should be drastically reduced.[39]

At this time Conservatives too were speaking a similar language, but in government after 1951 they increasingly strove to occupy the consensual, interventionist middle ground. Against such a trend the National Liberals' Hastings Group of 1954 made a brave but ultimately futile protest.

By the time that the National Liberal party disappeared, the Conservatives were once more in opposition. The Labour government had secured a parliamentary majority of 96 at the General Election of 1966, leaving Prime Minister Harold Wilson to proclaim, with some credibility, that he had transformed his party into the natural party of government. However faintly, isolated voices began to seek explanations of where the Tories had gone wrong. Writing in the last ever issue of *New Horizon,* the Conservative and National Liberal candidate for Wrexham, Griffith Pierce, had no doubts. Condemning bodies such as the Bow Group as 'young Fabians of the Right', he described the pernicious influence of the Tory left:

> The retirement of Churchill saw these men drive the Conservative Party into a sordid rat race with Socialism; the battle cry of 1950 was

exchanged for a squalid contest as to which Party could offer the most for nothing which, being translated, means who best could relieve the individual of responsibility and, inevitably, of liberty. So, eventually, the people, who could no longer see the difference, voted for a change which merely altered the name of the current administrators of bureaucratic paternalism.[40]

Frequently derided by her critics as a nineteenth-century Liberal, Mrs Thatcher, in trying to arrest and reverse this pattern of events, should perhaps be seen as a reincarnation of the National Liberal tradition.

Notes

Introduction
1. R. Fulford, *The Right Honourable Gentleman: A Satire* (London, 1945), pp. 70–1.
2. Ibid., pp. 88–9.
3. Ibid., pp. 91, 129.
4. The party was called 'Liberal National', rather than the more obvious 'National Liberal', to avoid association with Lloyd George's group of Coalition Liberals who took the latter title between 1918 and 1923. But the 'Liberal Nationals' were formally renamed 'National Liberals' in 1948 and, even before then, the style 'National Liberal' had frequently been used. To add to the confusion, the main nationwide membership organisation of the orthodox Liberal party between 1877 and 1936 was known as the National Liberal Federation, while the National Liberal Club, founded in 1882, was designed to offer a London club for supporters of the Federation. When in 1936 it was suggested that the name 'National Liberal Federation' should be dropped, the *Liberal Magazine* protested that the proposal was 'too childish as well as having the unpleasant associations of "running away"' [*Liberal Magazine*, vol. XLIV, no. 512, May 1936]. Within a matter of weeks, however, it had been agreed that the NLF should be replaced by the Liberal Party Organisation.
5. M. Gillard and M. Tomkinson, *Nothing to Declare: The Political Corruptions of John Poulson* (London, 1988), p. 89.
6. Ibid., p. 90.
7. Among exceptions, note should be made of G. Goodlad, 'The Liberal Nationals, 1931–1940: the problems of a party in partnership government', *Historical Journal* 38, 1 (1995), pp. 133–43; and of N. Cott, 'Tory cuckoos in the Liberal nest?', *Journal of Liberal Democrat History* 25 (1999–2000), pp. 24–30. Cott's article is of particular relevance since it seeks to place the Liberal Nationals within a well-established centrist strand of Liberal thought which was pragmatic, consensual and coalitionist in orientation. There are also some important, but brief, observations in J. Ramsden, *The Age of Balfour and Baldwin 1902–1940* (London, 1978) and J. Ramsden, *The Age of Churchill and Eden 1940–1957* (London, 1995).
8. D. Brack et al. (eds), *Dictionary of Liberal Biography* (London, 1998), pp. 121–3.
9. *Liberal News* 24 Feb. 1950.

10. R. Douglas, *The History of the Liberal Party 1895–1970* (London, 1971), p. 233.
11. R. Skidelsky, *Politicians and the Slump: The Labour Government of 1929–1931* (London, 1967), p. 385.
12. See, for example, D. Butler and A. Sloman, *British Political Facts 1900–1975* (London, 1975), pp. 183–5.
13. A. Marwick, 'Middle opinion in the thirties: planning, progress and political "agreement"', *English Historical Review*, vol.LXXIX, no. CCCXI (1964), p. 297.
14. R. Muir, *The Record of the National Government* (London, 1936), p. 7.
15. Lord Boothby, *Recollections of a Rebel* (London, 1978), p. 84.
16. A. Marwick, *Britain in the Century of Total War: War, Peace and Social Change 1900–1967* (London, 1968), p. 208.
17. N. Branson and M. Heinemann, *Britain in the Nineteen Thirties* (London, 1971), p. 2.
18. Cato, *Guilty Men* (London, 1940).
19. *Liberal Magazine* June 1947.
20. Marwick, 'Middle Opinion', pp. 289–90.
21. M. Foot, *Aneurin Bevan*, vol. 2 (London, 1973), p. 213.
22. Cooper to Clarissa Eden 21 Aug. 1952, cited J. Charmley, *Duff Cooper* (London, 1986), p. 236; N. Nicolson (ed.), *Harold Nicolson: Diaries and Letters 1939–45* (London, 1967), pp. 333, 407.
23. Bracken to Lord Beaverbrook 16 March 1939, cited C.E. Lysaght, *Brendan Bracken* (London, 1979), p. 160.
24. J. Vincent (ed.), *The Crawford Papers* (Manchester, 1984), p. 585; R.R. James, *Anthony Eden* (London, 1986), p. 295.
25. B. Webb diary 9 June 1940, Chadwyck-Healey microfiche edition (Cambridge, 1978).
26. A.L. Rowse, *All Souls and Appeasement* (London, 1961), p. 16.
27. British Library, Irwin MSS, Eur C 152/18, Chamberlain to Irwin 12 Aug. 1928.
28. *The Times* 12 Jan. 1954.
29. *Liberal News* 9 March 1951.

1 Origins, 1916–31

1. National Liberal Organisation, 'About the National Liberals' (3rd edition, April 1962).
2. Variations on these figures appear in other works. More than was the case in any other election of the twentieth century, the precise party allegiance of a number of successful candidates is impossible to determine.
3. G. Dangerfield, *The Strange Death of Liberal England* (London, 1936), p. 10.
4. T. Wilson (ed.), *The Political Diaries of C.P. Scott 1911–1928* (London, 1970), p. 419.
5. E. Hopkins, *Charles Masterman: Politician and Journalist – The Splendid Failure* (Lampeter, 1999), p. 185.
6. K. Middlemas (ed.), *Thomas Jones: Whitehall Diary*, vol. 1 (London, 1969), p. 278.
7. D. Close, 'The realignment of the British electorate in 1931', *History* 67 (1982), p. 402.
8. Wilson (ed.), *Scott Diaries*, p. 440.

9. D. MacCarthy (ed.), *H.H.A.: Letters of the Earl of Oxford and Asquith to a Friend*, vol. 2 (London, 1933), p. 85.
10. Memorandum by Lloyd George 18 Nov. 1924, cited P. Rowland, *Lloyd George* (London, 1975), p. 615.
11. House of Lords Record Office, Lloyd George MSS, G/17/11/19, Lloyd George to C.P. Scott 10 Feb. 1926.
12. Manchester Central Library, E.D. Simon MSS, M/11/11/5 addnl, diary 4 June 1925.
13. D. Cregier, *Chiefs Without Indians* (Washington, 1982), p. 207.
14. M. Hart, 'The decline of the Liberal party in parliament and in the constituencies', Oxford D. Phil. (1982), p. 230; C. Cook, 'Liberals, Labour and local elections', in G. Peele and C. Cook (eds), *The Politics of Reappraisal 1918– 1939* (London, 1975), pp. 169–70.
15. Lloyd George MSS, G/17/11/8, Lloyd George to Scott 27 Dec. 1923.
16. E.D. Simon MSS, M/11/11, diary 21 Jan. 1924.
17. P. Harris, *Forty Years in and out of Parliament* (London, n.d.), p. 97.
18. MacDonald diary 9 May 1924, cited D. Marquand, *Ramsay MacDonald* (London, 1977), p. 320. Users of MacDonald's diaries are asked to state that 'the contents of these diaries were, in Ramsay MacDonald's words, "meant as notes to guide and revive memory as regards happenings and must on no account be published as they are"'.
19. Rowland, *Lloyd George*, p. 612.
20. D. Howell, *MacDonald's Party: Labour Identities and Crisis 1922–1931* (Oxford, 2002), p. 20.
21. R. McKibbin, *The Evolution of the Labour Party 1910–1924* (Oxford, 1983), pp. 120–1.
22. B. Pimlott (ed.), *The Political Diary of Hugh Dalton 1918–40, 1945–60* (London, 1986), p. 37.
23. J. Barnes and D. Nicholson (eds), *The Leo Amery Diaries 1896–1929* (London, 1980), p. 361.
24. Wilson (ed.), *Scott Diaries*, p. 468.
25. J.A. Spender, *Sir Robert Hudson: A Memoir* (London, 1930), p. 174.
26. K. Robbins, *Sir Edward Grey* (London, 1971), p. 360.
27. J. Campbell, *Lloyd George: the Goat in the Wilderness* (London, 1977), p. 230.
28. D. Dutton (ed.), *Odyssey of an Edwardian Liberal: the Political Diary of Richard Durning Holt* (Gloucester, 1989), p. 102.
29. G. Tregidga, *The Liberal Party in South-West Britain since 1918* (Exeter, 2000), p. 45.
30. R. Douglas, *The History of the Liberal Party 1895–1970* (London, 1971), p. 206.
31. Dutton (ed.), *Odyssey*, p. 103.
32. A.J.P. Taylor (ed.), *My Darling Pussy: The Letters of Lloyd George and Frances Stevenson 1913–41* (London, 1975), p. 121.
33. J. Wallace, 'The political career of Walter Runciman, first Viscount Runciman of Doxford', University of Newcastle Ph.D. (1995), p. 320.
34. Wilson (ed.), *Scott Diaries*, p. 494.
35. Note by Samuel 13 Feb. 1929, cited B. Wasserstein, *Herbert Samuel: A Political Life* (Oxford, 1992), p. 303.

36. A.J.P. Taylor (ed.), *Lloyd George: A Diary by Frances Stevenson* (London, 1971), pp. 245–6.
37. MacDonald diary 6 Nov. 1928, cited Marquand, *MacDonald*, p. 483.
38. Wilson (ed.), *Scott Diaries*, p. 493.
39. E.D. Simon MSS, M/11/11/5, diary 18 June 1929.
40. Ibid., M/11/11/5, diary 27 July 1929.
41. Ibid., M/11/11/5 (496), Simon to R. Hutchison July 1930 (not sent).
42. Flintshire Record Office, Morris-Jones MSS 10, diary 6 Feb. 1930.
43. University of Newcastle Library, Runciman MSS 221, Runciman to Fitzherbert Wright 25 Nov. 1929.
44. Ibid., 224, A. Beechman to Runciman 18 Dec. 1929.
45. British Library, Irwin MSS, Eur C 152/8, Lane Fox to Irwin 22 Dec. 1929.
46. Lloyd George MSS, G/3/5/24, Beauchamp to Lloyd George 26 Dec. 1929.
47. Ibid., G/3/5/25, Lloyd George to Beauchamp 3 Jan. 1930.
48. Wasserstein, *Samuel*, p. 307.
49. MacDonald diary 3 Feb. 1930, cited Marquand, *MacDonald*, p. 529.
50. C. Davies to J.H. Lewis 3 June 1930, cited J.G. Jones, 'Advice from a friend: David Lloyd George, Sir John Herbert Lewis and the aftermath of the political crisis of 1931', *National Library of Wales Journal* xxx, 3 (1998), pp. 323–4.
51. Morris-Jones MSS 10, diary 6 Feb. 1930 and 11 March 1930.
52. E.D. Simon MSS, M/11/11/5 (496), diary 16 July 1930.
53. H. Samuel, *Memoirs* (London, 1945), p. 200.
54. E.D. Simon MSS, M/11/11/5 (496), Simon to Hutchison July 1930 (not sent).
55. Morris-Jones MSS 10, diary 9 July 1930.
56. Ibid., diary 21 July 1930.
57. Ibid., diary 23 July 1930.
58. Bodleian Library, Oxford, John Simon MSS, SP 249, fo.93, Simon to Lloyd George 25 Oct. 1930; Viscount Simon, *Retrospect* (London, 1952), p. 163.
59. *Manchester Guardian* 16 Jan. 1931.
60. John Rylands University Library of Manchester, MacDonald MSS, RMD/1/14/132, MacDonald to Lloyd George 29 Sept. 1930.
61. John Simon MSS, SP 249, fos 5–8, diary 20 Nov. 1930.
62. Ibid., SP 249, fos 12–13, D. Rowland Evans to Simon 20 Nov. 1930.
63. Ibid., SP 249, fos 14–17, diary 27 Nov. 1930.
64. *Observer* 2 Nov. 1930, cited G. Searle, *Country Before Party: Coalition and the Idea of 'National Government' in Modern Britain 1885–1987* (London, 1995), p. 156.
65. Simon MSS, SP 249, fos 45–6, memorandum of meeting with Neville Chamberlain 1 Dec. 1930; University of Birmingham Library, Chamberlain MSS, NC 2/22, diary 5 Dec. 1930.
66. Liverpool Record Office, Holt-Durning MSS, 920 DUR 14/27/189, L. Jones to R. Holt 9 Jan. 1931.
67. Chamberlain MSS, NC 2/22, diary 21 Nov. 1930.
68. Simon MSS, SP 249, fo. 106, Simon to Sinclair 11 Dec. 1930.
69. Morris-Jones MSS 10, diary 11 Dec. 1930.
70. Ibid.
71. N. Chamberlain to H. Chamberlain 14 Dec. 1930, cited R. Self (ed.), *The Neville Chamberlain Diary Letters*, vol. 3 (Aldershot, 2002), p. 228.

NOTES 221

72. Lloyd George to Lansbury 16 Feb. 1931, cited Campbell, *Goat*, p. 283.
73. Churchill Archives Centre, Cambridge, Thurso MSS 1/17/4, Sinclair to V. Finney 19 March 1931.
74. Morris-Jones MSS 10, diary 21 Jan. 1931.
75. Ibid., 10, diary 27 Jan. 1931.
76. MacDonald diary 28 Jan. 1931, cited Howell, *MacDonald's Party*, p. 199.
77. Irwin MSS, Eur C 152/19, Lane Fox to Irwin 28 Jan. 1931.
78. Chamberlain MSS, AC 5/1/527, A Chamberlain to Ida Chamberlain 17 Jan. 1931.
79. Ibid., NC 18/1/728, N. Chamberlain to H. Chamberlain 1 March 1931; P. Williamson, *National Crisis and National Government: British Politics, the Economy and Empire 1926–1932* (Cambridge, 1992), p. 207; J. Barnes and D. Nicholson (eds), *The Empire at Bay: the Leo Amery Diaries 1929–1945* (London, 1988), p. 112.
80. *Punch* 4 Feb. 1931.
81. Morris-Jones MSS 10, diary 10 Feb. 1931.
82. Chamberlain MSS, NC 18/1/725, N. Chamberlain to Ida Chamberlain 8 Feb. 1931.
83. *Sunday News* 1 March 1931.
84. *The Times* 4 March 1931.
85. British Library, Reading MSS, Eur F 118/101, Simon to Reading 2 March 1931.
86. Chamberlain MSS, NC 18/1/729, N. Chamberlain to Ida Chamberlain 7 March 1931.
87. Morris-Jones MSS 12, diary 16 March 1931.
88. Morris-Jones MSS 10, diary 17 March 1931.
89. *The Times* 19 March 1931.
90. Morris-Jones MSS 10, diary 25 March 1931; Churchill Archives Centre, Cambridge, Hore-Belisha MSS, HOBE 1/1, diary 24 March 1931. Morris-Jones gives a figure of 34 voting for Lloyd George.
91. *The Times* 26 March 1931.
92. Barnes and Nicholson (eds), *Empire at Bay*, p. 158.
93. Chamberlain MSS, NC 18/1/733, Chamberlain to Ida Chamberlain 5 April 1931.
94. Chamberlain to Ida Chamberlain 18 April 1931, cited Self (ed.), *Neville Chamberlain Diary Letters*, vol. 3, p. 255.
95. Morris-Jones MSS 10, diary 7 May 1931.
96. Bodleian Library, Oxford, Grigg MSS, microfilm 1003, N. Chamberlain to Grigg 8 May 1931.
97. Reading MSS, Eur F 118/101, Simon to Reading 2 June 1931.
98. Simon MSS, SP 178, fo. 2, Sinclair to Simon 27 June 1931.
99. Ibid., SP 68, fos 92–3, Simon to Sinclair 26 June 1931.
100. *The Times* 29 June 1931.
101. Hore-Belisha MSS, HOBE 1/1, Simon to Hore-Belisha 26 June 1931.
102. Ibid., HOBE 1/1, diary 26 June 1931.
103. Ibid., HOBE 1/1, diary 29 June 1931.
104. Taylor (ed.), *Darling Pussy*, p. 144; F. Owen, *Tempestuous Journey: Lloyd George, His Life and Times* (London, 1954), p. 717.

105. Harold Nicolson, unpublished diary 22 July 1931, cited R. Skidelsky, *Oswald Mosley* (London, 1975), p. 248. Percy Harris later wrote of Hore-Belisha: 'His handicap as a politician is that he has no fixed political creed ... He started as an ardent Radical, then became a leading figure in the Liberal National group, practically its founder, left them and became an independent, and now is a Conservative.' *Forty Years*, pp. 110–11.
106. *Sunday Observer* 28 June 1931.
107. *The Times* 30 June 1931.
108. House of Commons Debates, 5th Series, vol. 254, cols 1657–68.
109. For the formation of the National Government see Williamson, *National Crisis* and S. Ball, *Baldwin and the Conservative Party* (New Haven, 1988).
110. Samuel, *Memoirs*, p. 205.
111. Morris-Jones MSS 10, diary 7–11 Sept. 1931.
112. R. Bassett, *1931: Political Crisis* (London, 1958), p. 187.
113. Williamson, *National Crisis*, p. 354.
114. R. Muir, *The Record of the National Government* (London, 1936), p. 29.
115. Simon MSS, SP 68, fo. 118, Simon to MacDonald 1 Sept. 1931.
116. J. Wrench, *Geoffrey Dawson and Our Times* (London, 1955), pp. 292–3.
117. Williamson, *National Crisis*, p. 393; *The Times* 12 Sept. 1931.
118. Chamberlain to Grigg 16 Sept. 1931, cited Self (ed.), *Neville Chamberlain Diary Letters*, vol. 3, p. 30.
119. House of Commons Debates, 5th Series, vol. 256, col. 729.
120. Morris-Jones MSS 12, diary 14 Sept. 1931.
121. G. Schuster to Irwin 9 Oct. 1930, cited P. Williamson and E. Baldwin (eds), *Baldwin Papers: A Conservative Statesman 1908–1947* (Cambridge, 2004), p. 238.
122. *The Times* 17 Sept. 1931.
123. Morris-Jones MSS 10, diary 7–11 Sept. 1931.
124. Barnes and Nicholson (eds), *Empire at Bay*, p. 204.
125. Ibid.
126. Hore-Belisha MSS, HOBE 1/1, diary 18 Sept. 1931.
127. Runciman MSS 303, Runciman to H. Runciman 28 Sept. 1931.
128. Simon MSS, SP 68, fos 127–8, Simon to Lord Inchcape 24 Sept. 1931.
129. Morris-Jones MSS 12, diary 23 and 30 Sept. 1931.
130. *The Times* 3 Oct. 1931.
131. Ibid., 5 Oct. 1931.
132. Ibid.
133. Sankey diary 5 Oct. 1931, cited D. Wrench, '"Cashing in": the parties and the National Government, August 1931-September 1932', *Journal of British Studies* xxiii, 2 (1984), p. 146.
134. *The Times* 6 Oct. 1931; Morris-Jones MSS 12, diary 5 Oct. 1931. Morris-Jones suggests an attendance of 22.
135. Simon MSS, SP 68, fo. 163, Simon to MacDonald 5 Oct. 1931.

2   Crossing the Rubicon, 1931–35
1. Sir I. Jennings, *Party Politics*, vol. 2 (London, 1961), p. 61.
2. Speeches in Cleckheaton, reported in *Cleckheaton Guardian* 10 Nov. 1922 and *Yorkshire Observer* 14 Nov. 1922.

3. J. Simon, *Three Speeches on the General Strike* (London, 1926), p. 5.
4. G. Tregidga, *The Liberal Party in South-West Britain since 1918* (Exeter, 2000), pp. 64, 62.
5. C. Cross (ed.), *Life with Lloyd George: The Diary of A.J. Sylvester 1931–45* (London, 1975), p. 43. Yet it is also likely that Lloyd George's split from the Samuelites made it less necessary for some Liberals to join the Simonite camp.
6. J. Ramsden, *The Age of Balfour and Baldwin 1902–1940* (London, 1978), p. 325.
7. *Evening Standard* 28 May 1930. See also Gwilym Lloyd-George MSS (seen when in possession of Viscount Tenby, now in National Library of Wales), notes for memoirs: 'One sometimes got the impression that in politics, as in law, he was willing to speak to almost any brief and would ruthlessly devote all his mental energies to the task so long as it lasted.'
8. 'Ephesian', 'Simon: a study in silk', *The People* 25 Sept. 1927.
9. E. David (ed.), *Inside Asquith's Cabinet: From the Diaries of Charles Hobhouse* (London, 1977), pp. 229–30.
10. House of Lords Record Office, Samuel MSS, A/89/56, M. Asquith to Samuel 20 Sept. 1932; Beatrice Webb diary 18 Oct. 1931; M. Foot, *Aneurin Bevan*, vol. 2 (London, 1973), p. 246; University of Birmingham Library, Chamberlain MSS, NC 18/1/918, Chamberlain to H. Chamberlain 22 May 1935.
11. Lord Crawford and Balcarres, quoted in C. Bridge, *Holding India to the Empire: The British Conservative Party and the 1935 Constitution* (London, 1986), p. 21.
12. Bodleian Library, Oxford, Simon MSS, SP 67, fos 23–4, Simon to Lord Inchcape 21 Nov. 1930.
13. Viscount Simon, *Retrospect* (London, 1952), p. 170.
14. D. Marquand, *Ramsay MacDonald* (London, 1977), p. 556.
15. *Yorkshire Observer* 27 March 1931.
16. Manchester Central Library, papers of the Manchester Liberal Federation, M 283/4, 1/2, meeting of the executive committee of the Exchange division 15 Dec. 1930.
17. P. Clarke, *Hope and Glory: Britain 1900–1990* (London, 1997), p. 155.
18. R. Skidelsky, *Politicians and the Slump* (London, 1967), p. 229; M. Stocks, *Ernest Simon of Manchester* (London, 1963), pp. 93–4; *Liberal Magazine*, vol. XLI, no. 443, Aug. 1930.
19. Skidelsky, *Politicians and Slump*, p. 292.
20. National Library of Wales, Clement Davies MSS, C/1/16, Davies to S. Clement-Davies 3 Nov. 1943.
21. *The Times* 7 Oct. 1931.
22. Simon, *Retrospect*, p. 171.
23. Election address 7 Oct. 1931, *Liberal Magazine*, vol. XXXIX, no. 458, Nov. 1931.
24. R. Douglas, *History of the Liberal Party 1895–1970* (London, 1971), p. 222.
25. J. Wallace, 'The political career of Walter Runciman, first Viscount Runciman of Doxford', University of Newcastle Ph.D. (1995), p. 335.
26. Flintshire Record Office, papers of the Flintshire Liberal Association, D/DM/350, minutes of meeting of executive committee 8 Oct. 1931.
27. Walsall Local History Centre, papers of the Walsall Liberal Association, 31/1/3, minutes of meeting of executive committee 29 Sept. 1931.

28. Ibid., minutes of meeting of executive committee 8 Oct. 1931.
29. Samuel MSS, A/82/27, Leckie to Samuel 31 Oct. 1931.
30. J. Barnes and D. Nicholson (eds), *The Empire at Bay: The Leo Amery Diaries 1929–1945* (London, 1988), p. 187; T. Wilson, *The Downfall of the Liberal Party* (London, 1966), p. 370.
31. Simon MSS, SP 69, fos 36–7, Hutchison to Simon 11 Oct. 1931.
32. National Archives, MacDonald MSS, PRO 30/69/1753, diary 6 Oct. 1931.
33. *The Times* 2 Nov. 1931.
34. I. Hunter (ed.), *Winston and Archie* (London, 2005), pp. 196–7.
35. P. Williamson, *National Crisis and National Government: British Politics, the Economy and Empire, 1926–32* (Cambridge, 1992), p. 483. Cf. A.J.P. Taylor, *English History 1914–1945* (Oxford, 1965), p. 334: 'If Samuel had spoken for 72 Liberals after the general election of October 1931, he would have counted for something.'
36. *Liverpool Post and Mercury* 5 Nov. 1931.
37. Cambridge University Library, Baldwin MSS, vol. 45, fos 197–8, Simon to Baldwin 2 Nov. 1931.
38. Simon MSS, SP 69, fos 55–6, Hore-Belisha to Simon 5 Nov. 1931.
39. British Library, Reading MSS, Eur. F118/131, note of telephone conversation between Simon and Maclean 30 Oct. 1931; Samuel MSS, A/84/3, note by Samuel; H. Samuel, *Memoirs* (London, 1945), p. 214.
40. *The Times* 3 Nov. 1931.
41. Flintshire Record Office, Morris-Jones MSS 12, diary 3 Nov. 1931.
42. *Liverpool Post and Mercury* 12 Nov. 1931.
43. Morris-Jones MSS 12, diary 2 Nov. 1931.
44. *Liverpool Post and Mercury* 20 Nov. 1931.
45. *The Times* 30 Jan. 1932.
46. Ibid., 10 Feb. 1932.
47. Simon MSS, SP 71, Simon to I. Macpherson 5 Feb. 1932.
48. *The Times* 16 March 1932.
49. Ibid., 6 April 1932; T. Stannage, *Baldwin Thwarts the Opposition* (London, 1980), pp. 88–9.
50. *The Times* 27 May 1932.
51. *Yorkshire Post* 11 July 1932.
52. Morris-Jones MSS 13, diary 5 July 1932.
53. Simon MSS, SP 73, fo. 50, Hore-Belisha to Simon 7 Sept. 1932.
54. Stonehaven's New Year message, *Conservative Agents' Journal* Jan. 1932, cited Stannage, *Baldwin Thwarts Opposition*, p. 27.
55. Stannage, *Baldwin Thwarts Opposition*, p. 25.
56. R. Self, *Neville Chamberlain: A Biography* (London, 2006), p. 174.
57. Samuel MSS, A/89/26, MacDonald to Samuel 10 Sept. 1932.
58. Ibid., A/155/VIII/48, R. Muir to Samuel 22 April 1932.
59. Papers of the Manchester Liberal Federation, M 283/4, 1/2, meeting of the executive committee of the Exchange division 6 April 1932.
60. University of Newcastle, Runciman MSS 254, Simon to Runciman 16 Sept. 1932.
61. Self, *Chamberlain*, p. 174.
62. Chamberlain MSS, NC 7/11/25/35, Runciman to Chamberlain 21 Sept. 1932.

63. Morris-Jones MSS 13, diary 23 Sept. 1932.
64. Runciman MSS 254, Shakespeare to Simon 23 Sept. 1932.
65. Churchill Archives Centre, Cambridge, Hore-Belisha MSS, HOBE 1/1, Hore-Belisha to Chamberlain 23 Sept. 1932.
66. Morris-Jones MSS 13, diary 26 Sept. 1932.
67. Runciman MSS 254, Shakespeare to Runciman 27 Sept. 1932.
68. G. Shakespeare, *Let Candles Be Brought In* (London, 1949), p. 141.
69. Samuel MSS, A/89/81, note from Simon 28 Sept. 1932; Bodleian Library, Oxford, Sankey MSS, Eng. hist. c509, fo. 130, note by Sankey.
70. B. Wasserstein, *Herbert Samuel: A Political Life* (Oxford, 1992), pp. 360–1.
71. Viscount Snowden, *An Autobiography*, vol. 2 (London, 1934), p. 1029.
72. Baldwin MSS, vol. 46, fos 59–61, Simon to Baldwin 28 Sept. 1932.
73. Simon MSS, SP 73, Shakespeare to Simon 30 Sept. 1932.
74. Morris-Jones MSS 13, diary 5 Oct. and 14 Dec. 1932.
75. A.J.P. Taylor (ed.), *My Darling Pussy: The Letters of Lloyd George and Frances Stevenson 1913–41* (London, 1975), pp. 193–4.
76. Simon MSS, SP 73, Baldwin to Simon 26 Oct. 1932.
77. Morris-Jones MSS 13, diary 5 Oct. and 30 Nov. 1932.
78. Ibid., 14, diary 2 Jan. 1933; Stannage, *Baldwin Thwarts Opposition*, p. 39.
79. H. Nicolson, *King George The Fifth: His Life and Reign* (London, 1952), p. 498.
80. Ramsden, *Balfour and Baldwin*, p. 118.
81. P. Williamson, *Stanley Baldwin* (Cambridge, 1999), p. 347.
82. Ibid., p. 348.
83. E. Granville, 'The Liberal resignations', *Contemporary Review* Nov. 1932, p. 543.
84. J. Ramsden, *An Appetite for Power: A History of the Conservative Party since 1830* (London, 1998), p. 265.
85. D. Wrench, '"Very peculiar circumstances": Walter Runciman and the National Government, 1931–3', *Twentieth Century British History* 11, 1 (2000), pp. 61–82.
86. Viscount Templewood, *Ambassador on Special Mission* (London, 1946), p. 10.
87. British Library, Templewood MSS, Eur. E240, Hoare to Lord Willingdon 22 Jan. 1932.
88. Morris-Jones MSS 13, diary 10 Nov. 1932.
89. T. Jones, *A Diary with Letters 1931–1950* (London, 1954), pp. 25–6.
90. Chamberlain MSS, NC 18/1/759, Chamberlain to H. Chamberlain 24 Oct. 1931.
91. Ibid., NC 7/6/19, Chamberlain to Arthur Chamberlain 11 Feb. 1932.
92. A.J.P. Taylor (ed.), *W.P. Crozier: Off the Record, Political Interviews 1933–1943* (London, 1973), p. 7.
93. Morris-Jones MSS 13, diary 28 Nov. 1932.
94. Churchill Archives Centre, Cambridge, Thurso MSS II, 1934/37, Samuel to Sinclair 30 Oct. 1933.
95. House of Lords Record Office, Lloyd George MSS, G/19/7/6, notes on the political situation 26 Nov. 1933.
96. *The Times*, leading article 20 Dec. 1933.
97. Memorandum by Lord Lothian 16 Nov. 1932, cited M. Baines, 'The Samuelites and the National Government: a study in Liberal survival, August 1931 – November 1933', University of Lancaster M.A. thesis (1983), p. 73.

98. Stannage, *Baldwin Thwarts Opposition*, p. 104.
99. *Yorkshire Post* 18 July 1932; West Yorkshire Archive Service, Sheepscar Library Leeds, papers of the Yorkshire Liberal Federation, WYL 456/2, annual general meeting 27 Jan. 1934.
100. Papers of Manchester Liberal Federation, M 283/1/8, meeting of Municipal Representation Joint Committee 20 Jan. 1927.
101. Tregidga, *Liberal Party in South-West Britain*, p. 65; Runciman MSS 224, C. Mallet to Runciman 1 Oct. 1929.
102. West Yorkshire Archive Service, Kirklees District Archives, Huddersfield, Mabane MSS, DD/WM/1/2, Mabane to Samuel and Simon 9 Nov. 1931; papers of the Huddersfield Liberal Association, WYK 1146/1/1/5, special executive committee meeting 9 Nov. 1931.
103. Papers of Huddersfield Liberal Association, WYK 1146/1/1/5, annual general meeting 15 March 1934.
104. *Montgomeryshire Express and Radnor Times* 27 Oct. 1931.
105. National Library of Wales, papers of the Montgomeryshire Liberal Association, C 1988/27/3, annual general meeting 27 Feb. 1932.
106. Ibid., executive committee meeting 21 Sept. 1935.
107. A. Wyburn-Powell, *Clement Davies: Liberal Leader* (London, 2003), pp. 53–4.
108. Bedfordshire Record Office, papers of Sir Herbert Janes, JN 330, memorandum on Luton's political situation, May 1946.
109. B. Doyle, 'Urban Liberalism and the "lost generation": politics and middle class culture in Norwich, 1900–1935', *Historical Journal* 38, 3 (1995), pp. 620, 634.
110. Papers of the Manchester Liberal Federation, M 283/1/6/4, Liberal Councillors meeting 25 July 1933; C. Cook, 'Liberals, Labour and local elections' in G. Peele and C. Cook (eds), *The Politics of Reappraisal 1918–1939* (London, 1975), p. 179.
111. *The Times* 31 Jan. 1933.
112. Papers of Manchester Liberal Federation, M 283/1/3/5, executive committee meeting 26 April 1933.
113. N. Smart (ed.), *The Diaries and Letters of Robert Bernays, 1932–1939* (Lampeter, 1996), p. 29.
114. *The Times* 1 Feb. 1933.
115. Ibid., 31 Jan. 1933.
116. Manchester Central Library, papers of the Lancashire, Cheshire and North-Western Liberal Federation, M 390/1/8, Lord Stanley to members of the federation c. Feb. 1933.
117. *Liberal Magazine*, vol. XLI, no. 473, Feb. 1933.
118. Sinclair to Harcourt Johnstone 17 Jan. 1933, cited G. De Groot, *Liberal Crusader: The Life of Sir Archibald Sinclair* (London, 1993), p. 101.
119. Morris-Jones MSS 14, diary 28 Feb. 1933.
120. *Liberal Magazine*, vol. XLII, no. 486, March 1934.
121. C.L. Mowat, *Britain Between the Wars 1918–1940* (London, 1955), p. 413.
122. R. Muir, *The Record of the National Government* (London, 1936), p. 54.
123. Ramsden, *Balfour and Baldwin*, p. 325.
124. 'Celticus', *Why Not Trust the Tories* (London, 1944), p. 13.
125. Marquand, *MacDonald*, p. 731.

126. A. Seldon (ed.), *How Tory Governments Fall: the Tory Party in Power since 1783* (London, 1996), p. 293.
127. Williamson, *National Crisis*, pp. 44–5.
128. Ramsden, *Balfour and Baldwin*, p. 326.
129. Self, *Chamberlain*, p. 224.
130. Sankey MSS, Eng. hist. c511, fos 82–3, MacDonald to Sankey 15 July 1934.
131. Ibid., diary 24 May 1933.
132. Simon MSS, SP 79, fo. 116, Simon to Mackenzie King 23 Oct. 1934.
133. Ibid., SP 77, fos 43–4, Simon to Lord Willingdon 29 Sept. 1933.
134. Smart (ed.), *Bernays Diaries*, p. 120.
135. Ibid., pp. 68, 71.
136. Ibid., p. 91.
137. MacDonald MSS, PRO 30/69/5/8, Chamberlain to MacDonald 13 Oct. 1933.
138. Baldwin MSS, vol. 46, fo. 103, memorandum by Stonehaven 1 Aug. 1934; *Liberal Magazine*, vol. XLII, no. 490, July 1934.
139. Granville, 'Liberal resignations', p. 539.
140. Hore-Belisha MSS, HOBE 1/1, incomplete diary entry 12 Feb. 1932.
141. Wolmer to Mackie 28 Dec. 1934, cited Bridge, *Holding India*, p. 134.
142. *The Times* 12 April 1933.
143. Ibid., 10 Oct. 1933.
144. Ibid., 14 Dec. 1933.
145. *Liberal Magazine*, vol. XLII, no. 484, Jan. 1934.
146. Stannage, *Baldwin Thwarts Opposition*, pp. 39–40.
147. Flintshire Record Office, Glynne-Gladstone MSS 945, Johnstone to Herbert Gladstone n.d. (but 1932).
148. Morris-Jones MSS 15, diary 5 June 1934.
149. Chamberlain MSS, NC 2/23, diary 5 Dec. 1934.
150. Morris-Jones MSS 14, diary 20 and 24 Nov. 1933.
151. Birmingham University Library, Avon MSS, AP 14/1/241, Simon to Vansittart 24 March 1933.
152. R. Bassett, *Democracy and Foreign Policy* (London, 1968), p. 371.
153. Kordt to Dirksen 29 Aug. 1938, cited E.M. Andrews, *The Writing on the Wall* (London, 1987), p. 40.
154. Mrs Madariaga to T. Jones 15 April 1938, cited Jones, *Diary with Letters*, p. 403.
155. Baldwin MSS, vol. 121, fos 83–4, Ormsby-Gore to Baldwin 8 Oct. 1933.
156. Morris-Jones MSS 13, diary 7 April 1932.
157. Ibid., 12, diary 2 Nov. 1931.
158. P. Harris, *Forty Years In and Out of Parliament* (London, n.d.), p. 101.
159. Smart (ed.), *Bernays Diary*, p. 125.
160. *The Times* 20 Dec. 1933.
161. Smart (ed.), *Bernays Diary*, pp. 175–6.
162. *Liberal Magazine*, vol. XLII, no. 487, April 1934.
163. *The Times* 20 Dec. 1933.

3 Years of Consolidation, 1935–39

1. Speech to the Lancashire and Cheshire Women's Liberal Council 4 October 1932, *The Times* 5 Oct. 1932.

2. *The Times* 24 Oct. 1935.
3. N. Smart (ed.), *The Diaries and Letters of Robert Bernays, 1932–1939* (Lampeter, 1996), p. 12.
4. Bodleian Library, Oxford, Simon MSS, SP 7, fos 18–20, diary 14 Feb. 1935.
5. Cambridge University Library, Baldwin MSS, vol. 47, fo. 14, Ormsby-Gore to Baldwin n.d. [Feb. 1935].
6. M. Gilbert, *Winston S. Churchill*, vol. 5, companion pt 2 (London, 1981), p. 1140.
7. N. Thompson, *The Anti-Appeasers: Conservative Opposition to Appeasement in the 1930s* (Oxford, 1971), p. 65.
8. University of Birmingham Library, Chamberlain MSS, AC 5/1/698, Chamberlain to Hilda Chamberlain 5 May 1935.
9. Baldwin MSS, vol. 47, fo. 1, T. Jones to Baldwin 16 May 1935.
10. Ibid., vol. 121, fos 74–6, Ormsby-Gore to Baldwin 1 Oct. 1933.
11. Lord Avon, *Facing the Dictators* (London, 1962), p. 219.
12. Simon MSS, SP 82, fo. 9, Simon to Lord Willingdon 5 March 1935.
13. Chamberlain MSS, NC 2/23, diary 17 May 1935.
14. D. Marquand, *Ramsay MacDonald* (London, 1977), p. 774.
15. MacDonald diary 13 May 1935, cited Marquand, *MacDonald*, p. 775.
16. A.J.P. Taylor (ed.), *Off the Record: C.P. Crozier Political Interviews 1933–1943* (London, 1973), p. 47.
17. Flintshire Record Office, Morris-Jones MSS 16, diary 10 May 1935.
18. Churchill Archives Centre, Cambridge, Hore-Belisha MSS, HOBE 1/2, diary 21 May 1935.
19. J. Barnes and D. Nicholson (eds), *The Empire at Bay: the Leo Amery Diaries 1929–1945* (London, 1988), p. 395.
20. Simon MSS, SP 7, fo. 31, diary 28 May 1935.
21. Ibid., SP 7, fos 31–2, diary 4 June 1935.
22. R. Jenkins, *The Chancellors* (London, 1998), p. 353.
23. Barnes and Nicholson (eds), *Empire at Bay*, p. 396. See also C. Bridge, *Holding India to the Empire: The British Conservative Party and the 1935 Constitution* (London, 1986), p. 99.
24. T. Stannage, *Baldwin Thwarts the Opposition* (London, 1980), p. 201; N.J. Crowson (ed.), *Fleet Street, Press Barons and Politics: The Journals of Collin Brooks, 1932–1940* (London, 1998), p. 135.
25. Smart (ed.), *Bernays Diaries*, p. 191.
26. G. Lane Fox to Lord Irwin 28 Jan. 1931, cited Gilbert, *Churchill*, vol. 5, companion pt 2, p. 252.
27. D. Dutton, "'A mad hatter contest from beginning to end": Randolph Churchill and the Wavertree by-election, February 1935', *Transactions of the Historic Society of Lancashire and Cheshire*, 142 (1992), pp. 179–202.
28. Simon MSS, SP 7, fo. 31, diary 28 May 1935.
29. Chamberlain MSS, NC 18/1/934, Chamberlain to H. Chamberlain 22 Sept. 1935.
30. Simon MSS, SP 7, fo. 38, diary 22 Oct.1935.
31. J. Ramsden, *The Making of Conservative Party Policy: The Conservative Research Department since 1929* (London, 1980), pp. 83–4.
32. Simon MSS, SP 7, fo. 38, diary 24 Oct. 1935.

33. J. Ramsden (ed.), *Real Old Tory Politics: The Political Diaries of Robert Sanders, Lord Bayford 1910–1935* (London, 1984), p. 251.
34. Stannage, *Baldwin Thwarts Opposition*, p. 122.
35. T. Jones, *A Diary with Letters 1931–50* (London, 1954), pp. 155–6.
36. M. Cowling, *The Impact of Hitler* (Cambridge, 1975), p. 93.
37. *Liberal Magazine*, vol. XLII, no. 484, Jan. 1934.
38. House of Lords Record Office, Samuel MSS, A/84/7, Sinclair to Samuel 3 Nov. 1932.
39. *Liberal National Magazine*, vol. 1, no. 7, Feb. 1937.
40. Ramsden, *Making*, pp. 85–6.
41. Stannage, *Baldwin Thwarts Opposition*, p. 179.
42. *The Times* 5 Oct. 1935.
43. Manchester Central Library, papers of the Manchester Liberal Federation, M 283/1/3/6, executive committee meeting 6 Nov. 1935.
44. *The Times* 8 Nov. 1935.
45. Election address, cited J.G. Jones, 'Montgomeryshire politics: Clement Davies and the National Government', *Montgomeryshire Collections*, vol. 73 (1985), p. 106.
46. H. Morris-Jones, *Doctor in the Whips' Room* (London, 1955), p. 100.
47. *North Wales Times* 26 Jan. 1935; *Manchester Guardian* 19 Jan. 1935.
48. *Denbighshire Free Press* 9 Nov. 1935.
49. Ibid.
50. *Oldham Chronicle* 13 July 1935.
51. Ibid., 19 Oct. 1935.
52. Ibid., 25 Oct. 1935.
53. Ibid.
54. Ibid., 2 Nov. 1935.
55. Ibid., 26 Oct. 1935.
56. Kirklees District Archives, papers of the Huddersfield Liberal Association, WYK 1146/1/1/5, executive committee meeting 28 Oct. 1935.
57. Walsall Local History Centre, papers of the Walsall Liberal Association, 31/1/3, general committee meeting 24 Oct. 1935.
58. *Walsall Observer* 26 Oct. 1935.
59. Ibid., 2 Nov. 1935.
60. Manchester Central Library, papers of the Lancashire, Cheshire and North-Western Liberal Federation, M 390/1/9, committee meeting 16 March 1934.
61. Stockport Central Library, papers of the Stockport Liberal Association, B/NN/2/9, special meeting of executive committee 12 Oct. 1931.
62. Ibid., B/NN/2/10, various meetings of executive committee 1935.
63. Baldwin MSS, vol. 47, fos 129–30, Bernays to Baldwin 24 Oct. 1935.
64. Denbighshire Record Office, Glyndŵr MSS, DD/G/188, Hughes to Roberts 16 Oct. 1935.
65. Simon MSS, SP 7, fo. 40, diary 5 Dec. 1935.
66. Ibid., diary 16 Nov. 1935.
67. *Montgomeryshire Express* 9 Nov. 1935, cited Jones, 'Montgomeryshire politics', p. 105.
68. *Wrexham Leader 9 Nov. 1935.*
69. Glyndŵr MSS, DD/G/184ii, Morris-Jones to E. Hughes 27 May 1936.

70. Morris-Jones MSS 16, diary Nov. 1935.
71. *The Times* 28 Nov. 1935.
72. *Oldham Chronicle 16 Nov. 1935*.
73. *Liberal Magazine*, vol. XL111, nos 506–7, Nov-Dec. 1935.
74. Simon MSS, SP 7, fo. 38, diary 22 Oct. 1935.
75. *Liberal National Magazine*, vol. 1, no. 1, March 1936.
76. *The Times* 28 April 1936.
77. Morris-Jones MSS 17, diary 12 June 1936.
78. *The Times* 13 June 1936.
79. *Liberal National Magazine*, vol. 2, no. 1, Nov. 1936. In March 1938 it was announced that the Liberal National Organisation had moved to 'more commodious premises' in Matthew Parker Street. *The Times* 25 March 1938.
80. *Liberal National Magazine*, vol. 1, no. 5, July 1936.
81. J. Stevenson, *Third Party Politics since 1945: Liberals, Alliance and Liberal Democrats* (Oxford, 1993), p. 18.
82. *Liberal National Magazine*, vol. 1, no. 5, July 1936.
83. *Liverpool Daily Post* 27 June 1936.
84. *Liberal National Magazine*, vol. 1, no. 1, March 1936. Emphasis in original.
85. *The Times* 21 May 1936.
86. *Liberal National Magazine*, vol. 1, no. 4, June 1936.
87. Ibid., vol. 1, no. 6, Aug. 1936.
88. Ibid., vol. 1, no. 1, March 1936.
89. Ibid., vol. 1, no. 3, May 1936.
90. *The Times* 23 May 1936.
91. *Liberal National Magazine*, vol. 1, no. 4, June 1936.
92. L. Hore-Belisha, 'The future of Liberalism', *Liberal National Magazine*, vol. 1, no. 1, March 1936.
93. *Liberal Magazine*, vol. XL1V, no. 513, June 1936.
94. *The Scotsman* 23 May 1936.
95. *Liberal Magazine*, vol. XL1V, no. 513, June 1936.
96. *Liberal National Magazine*, vol. 1, no. 4, June 1936.
97. *The Times* 20 May 1936; Smart (ed.), *Bernays Diaries*, pp. 399–400, Bernays to Simon 22 May 1936.
98. Chamberlain MSS, NC 7/11/29/45, Simon to Chamberlain 15 Sept. 1936.
99. *The Times* 20 Nov. 1936; I.G.C. Hutchison, *Scottish Politics in the Twentieth Century* (Houndmills, 2001), p. 47.
100. Morris-Jones MSS 17, diary 2 Nov. 1936.
101. R. Self (ed.), *The Neville Chamberlain Diary Letters*, vol. 4 (Aldershot, 2005), pp. 213–14, Chamberlain to H. Chamberlain 17 Oct. 1936.
102. Chamberlain MSS, NC 7/11/30/74, S. Hoare to Chamberlain 17 March 1937.
103. Ibid., NC 7/11/30/112, Runciman to Chamberlan 7 May 1937.
104. University of Newcastle Library, Runciman MSS, WR 285, Simon to Runciman 7 May 1937.
105. Barnes and Nicholson (eds), *Empire at Bay*, pp. 441–2.
106. Smart (ed.), *Bernays Diary*, pp. 295–6, 310; Morris-Jones MSS 18, diary 28 May 1937.
107. *Manchester Guardian* 21 June 1935.

108. *Spectator* 27 Nov. 1936.
109. S. Roskill, *Hankey: Man of Secrets*, vol. 3 (London, 1974), p. 277.
110. Morris-Jones MSS 17, diary 11 Nov. 1936.
111. Chamberlain MSS, NC 2/24, diary 17 Jan. 1937.
112. Morris-Jones MSS 18, diary 21 May 1937.
113. R. Bernays, 'Liberal Nationals and the future', *Liberal National Magazine*, vol. 2, no. 3, Jan. 1937.
114. W. Mabane, 'The Liberal view of the National Government', *Liberal National Magazine*, vol. 2, no. 5, April 1937.
115. S. Ball (ed.), *Parliament and Politics in the Age of Baldwin and MacDonald: The Headlam Diaries 1923–1935* (London, 1992), p. 330.
116. S. Ball (ed.), *Parliament and Politics in the Age of Churchill and Attlee: The Headlam Diaries 1935–1951* (London, 1999), pp. 124–5.
117. *The Times* 18 Nov. 1936.
118. Ibid., 9 Nov. 1936, letter from Frank Hall.
119. Papers of the Walsall Liberal Association, 31/1/3, meeting of general committee 17 Aug. 1938.
120. *The Times* 6 Jan. 1939.
121. Ibid., 16 Jan. 1939.
122. Ibid., 17 Jan. 1939.
123. Ibid., 14 Jan. 1939.
124. *Eastern Daily Press* 23 Jan. 1939.
125. *The Times* 18 Jan. 1939.
126. Churchill Archives Centre, Cambridge, Thurso MSS II, 71/2, Sinclair to Scott 8 May 1935.
127. Ibid., II, 73/1, Sinclair to R. Findlay 4 Feb. 1937.
128. Runciman MSS, WR 262, Runciman to Hutchison 5 April 1937.
129. *Liberal National Magazine*, vol. 2, no. 7, June 1937.
130. *News Chronicle* 6 July 1937.
131. *Huddersfield Daily Examiner* 5 April 1939.
132. Huntingdon Record Office, papers of the Huntingdon Liberal Association, 5051, annual general meeting 20 July 1938.
133. Ibid., annual general meeting 19 July 1939.
134. *Western Mail* 3 Dec. 1938, cited Jones, 'Montgomeryshire politics', p. 109.
135. National Library of Wales, Clement Davies MSS, CD I/1/1, resolution passed by the executive committee of the Montgomeryshire Liberal Association 14 July 1938; A. Wyburn-Powell, *Clement Davies: Liberal Leader* (London, 2003), p. 71.
136. *The Times* 7 July 1936.
137. *Cleckheaton and Spenborough Guardian* 5 Feb. 1937.
138. *Liberal National Magazine*, vol. 2, no. 3, Jan.1937; *The Liberal*, vol. 1, no. 6, Jan. 1937.
139. *Liberal National Magazine*, vol. 1 (new series), no. 7, April 1939.
140. Papers of the Manchester Liberal Federation, M 283/1/1/4, annual meeting of general council 30 March 1938.
141. R. Grayson, *Liberals, International Relations and Appeasement* (London, 2001), esp. chapter 5.
142. Glyndŵr MSS, DD/G/184ii, E. Hughes to W. Jones 2 Dec. 1935.

143. Simon MSS, SP 85, fos 77–8, Simon to Spender 10 Oct. 1938.
144. *Bradford Telegraph and Argus* 25 Oct. 1938.
145. Ibid., 5 Nov. 1938.
146. Clement Davies MSS, CD 1/1/5, Davies to Jano Davies 3 Jan. 1939.
147. National Library of Wales, papers of the Montgomeryshire Liberal Association, C 1988/27/3, meeting of reorganisation committee 10 Dec. 1938.
148. *Liberal National Magazine*, vol. 2, no. 8, July 1937.
149. *Manchester Guardian* 26 June 1937.
150. *The Liberal*, vol. 2, no. 1, Oct. 1937.
151. *Liberal National Magazine*, vol. 3, no. 8, July 1938; *The Times* 23 June 1938.
152. *Liberal Magazine*, vol. XLVI, no. 534, March 1938; Runciman MSS 262, Runciman and Hutchison to chairmen of Liberal National Area Councils 7 March 1938.
153. *Liberal Magazine*, vol. XLVII, no. 551, Aug. 1939.
154. *Manchester Guardian* 6 April 1938. In private, Chamberlain had conceded as early as 1934 that it would be 'useless' to propose the formation of a National party. 'There are too many vested interests in the present names and no Conservatives would give up their name for the pleasure of being in the same boat as MacDonald and Simon.' Chamberlain to Ida Chamberlain 29 April 1934, cited Self (ed.), *Neville Chamberlain Diary Letters*, vol. 4, p. 68.
155. *Liberal National Magazine*, vol. 1 (new series), no. 8, May 1939. Ironically, Simon himself had resigned as Home Secretary over the introduction of conscription back in January 1916. The issue had long been a divisive one for Liberals.
156. Ibid., vol. 1 (new series), no. 1, Oct. 1938.
157. See, for example, the polemical tract *Your MP* by 'Gracchus' (London, 1944) which details in a selective and tendentious manner the voting records of a number of Liberal National MPs alongside those of Conservatives.
158. *Liberal National Magazine*, vol. 1 (new series), no. 1, Oct. 1938.
159. Barnes and Nicholson (eds), *Empire at Bay*, p. 526.
160. Smart (ed.), *Bernays Diaries*, pp. 299, 372.
161. *Liberal National Magazine*, vol. 1 (new series), no. 3, Dec. 1938.
162. Simon MSS, SP 11, fos 6–7, diary 2 Sept. 1939.
163. Ibid.

4 The War Years and Beyond, 1939–47
1. University of Birmingham Library, Chamberlain MSS, NC 7/11/32/62, Davies to Chamberlain 14 Dec. 1939.
2. D.M. Roberts, 'Clement Davies and the Fall of Neville Chamberlain 1939–40', *Welsh History Review* 8 (1976–7), pp. 188–215; Lord Boothby, *My Yesterday, Your Tomorrow* (London, 1962), pp. 253–5.
3. *The Times* 29 Jan. 1940.
4. *Liberal Magazine*, vol. XLVIII, no. 557, March-April 1940.
5. H. Dalton, *The Fateful Years* (London, 1957), p. 282.
6. *Punch* 29 May 1940.
7. *The Times* 1 Dec. 1939.
8. J. Colville, *Footprints in Time* (London, 1976), p. 73.

9. Chamberlain MSS, NC 18/1/1139, Chamberlain to Ida Chamberlain 20 Jan. 1940.
10. A.J. Trythall, 'The Downfall of Leslie Hore-Belisha', *Journal of Contemporary History* 16,3 (1981), pp. 391–411.
11. Flintshire Record Office, Morris-Jones MSS 21, diary 16 Jan. 1940.
12. Ibid., diary 8 Jan. 1940.
13. Ibid., diary 11 Jan. 1940.
14. House of Lords Record Office, Percy Harris MSS, HAR 1/1, diary 15 Jan. 1940.
15. A.J.P. Taylor (ed.), *W.P. Crozier: Off the Record, Political Interviews 1933–1943* (London, 1973), p. 133.
16. Morris-Jones MSS 21, diary 20 March 1940.
17. *The Times* 4 May 1940.
18. Morris-Jones MSS 21, diary 9 May 1940.
19. M. Pottle (ed.), *Champion Redoubtable: The Diaries and Letters of Violet Bonham Carter 1914–45* (London, 1998), p. 213.
20. House of Lords Records Office, Ernest Brown MSS, BRO/1, L. Burgin to Brown 16 May 1940; Morris-Jones MSS 21, diary 22 May and 5 June 1940.
21. Morris-Jones MSS 21, diary 4 Dec. 1940.
22. C. Stuart (ed.), *The Reith Diaries* (London, 1975), p. 253.
23. Morris-Jones MSS 21, diary 13 May 1940.
24. Ibid., diary 31 July 1940.
25. Ibid., diary 20 Nov. 1940.
26. Ibid., 22, diary 24 April 1941.
27. R.R. James (ed.), *Chips: The Diaries of Sir Henry Channon* (London, 1967), p. 304.
28. M. Gilbert, *Winston S. Churchill*, vol. 6 (London, 1983), p. 1105.
29. House of Commons Debates, 5th Series, vol. 371, col. 914.
30. *The Times* 2 Aug. 1941.
31. Morris-Jones MSS 22, diary 15 June 1941.
32. Ibid., diary 1 Aug. 1941.
33. Ibid., diary 7 Aug. 1941.
34. *Liberal Magazine*, vol. XLIX, no. 566, Sept-Oct. 1941.
35. House of Lords Record Office, Lloyd George MSS, G/24/2/158, report by Sylvester 19 Sept. 1941.
36. *The Times* 18 Sept. 1941.
37. Morris-Jones MSS 22, diary 9 Sept. 1941.
38. Ibid., 36, R.W. Williams Wynn, president Denbigh Conservative Association, to Morris-Jones 17 Sept. 1941.
39. *Liberal Magazine*, vol. XLIX, no. 567, Nov.-Dec. 1941.
40. Morris-Jones MSS 22, diary 23 Sept. and 2 Oct. 1941.
41. Ibid., 23, diary 19 Jan. 1942; K. Jefferys (ed.), *Labour and the Wartime Coalition: From the Diary of James Chuter Ede 1941–1945* (London, 1987), p. 50.
42. H. of C. Debs, 5th Series, vol. 377, cols. 725–7; *The Times* 29 Jan. 1942.
43. H. of C. Debs, 5th Series, vol. 377, col. 877.
44. Morris-Jones MSS 23, diary 29 Jan. 1942.
45. Ibid., diary 11 Feb. 1942.
46. Ibid., diary 12 Feb. 1942; *The Times* 13 Feb. 1942.

47. Ibid., diary 13 Feb. 1942.
48. *The Times* 18 March 1942.
49. D. Dutton, 'A surfeit of Liberals: the Eddisbury by-election of April 1943', *Transactions of the Historic Society of Lancashire and Cheshire* 155 (2006), pp. 121–38.
50. Morris-Jones MSS 23, diary 10 Sept. and 2 Dec. 1942.
51. Ibid., 24, diary 24 Feb. 1943.
52. Ibid., diary 31 March 1943.
53. *The Times* 18 March 1942.
54. *Liberal Magazine*, vol. L, no. 569, March-April 1942.
55. *Western Sunday Independent* 29 March 1942.
56. Note by Layton on 'talk with the Prime Minister' 24 June 1943, cited M. Baines, 'The survival of the British Liberal party', Oxford D. Phil. (1991), p. 54; Pottle (ed.), *Champion Redoubtable*, p. 273.
57. *The Times* 14 July 1943.
58. Ibid., 17 July 1943.
59. Morris-Jones MSS 24, diary 7, 13 and 28 July 1943.
60. Ibid., diary 13 July 1943.
61. *The Times* 19 July 1943.
62. National Library of Wales, Megan Lloyd George MSS 20475, C3173, Foot to Lloyd George 7 Aug. 1943; I. Hunter, 'The final quest for Liberal reunion 1943–46', *Journal of Liberal Democrat History* 32 (2001), p. 13.
63. Pottle (ed.), *Champion Redoubtable*, p. 284.
64. *The Times* 1 Nov. 1943.
65. Pottle (ed.), *Champion Redoubtable*, p. 284.
66. Manchester Central Library, papers of the Lancashire, Cheshire and North-Western Liberal Federation, M 390/1/2, minutes of executive committee meeting 26 May 1944.
67. G. de Groot, *Liberal Crusader: The Life of Sir Archibald Sinclair* (London, 1993), p. 215.
68. *The Times* 20 Nov. 1944.
69. Morris-Jones MSS 24, diary 22 Nov. 1943.
70. The other component of the National Government, the National Labour party, wound itself up five weeks before the General Election and took on the rather meaningless guise of the 'National Campaign Committee'.
71. Pottle (ed.), *Champion Redoubtable*, p. 350, Bonham Carter to Churchill 1 June 1945.
72. University of Birmingham Library, Avon MSS, AP 20/42/83, Mabane to Eden 12 May 1945.
73. Liberal and Liberal National candidates opposed one another in 12 seats. In no instance did the Liberal candidate finish higher in the poll than his Liberal National opponent.
74. Bradford District Archives, papers of the Bradford South Liberal National Association, 36D78/29, officers meeting 6 Sept. 1944.
75. Denbighshire Record Office, Glyndŵr MSS, DD/G/2550, Liberal National secretary's report 19 March 1946.
76. *The Times* 5 July 1943.
77. Ibid., 14 July 1943.

NOTES   235

78. Ibid., 9 May 1944.
79. Ibid., 5 Dec. 1942.
80. *New Horizon*, no. 31, April 1945.
81. *The Times* 3 July 1945.
82. Sinclair, speaking in Edinburgh, *The Times* 11 July 1945.
83. *The Times* 18 June 1945; *Liberal Magazine* July 1945.
84. *The Times* 3 July 1945.
85. *Liverpool Daily Post* 4 July 1945.
86. Radio broadcast, quoted in *Huddersfield Daily Examiner* 16 June 1945.
87. *Huddersfield Daily Examiner* 1 June 1945.
88. *Walsall Observer* 23 June 1945.
89. The outcome in three further constituencies should be noted. In Inverness, Murdoch Macdonald was returned, without Conservative opposition, as an Independent Liberal pledged to support Churchill. In the adjoining constituency of Ross and Cromarty, formerly held by Malcolm MacDonald for the National Labour party, John 'Jacko' MacLeod was the nominee of the local Liberal association which was affiliated neither to the Liberal Party Organisation nor the Liberal Nationals. He, too, declared himself a supporter of Churchill, defeated his Labour opponent and, in the Commons, aligned himself with the Liberal National group. But there was a suggestion that he would have joined the Sinclair Liberals had Sinclair himself not lost his seat (J. Grimond, *Memoirs* (London, 1979), p. 129). And in Pembrokeshire, Lloyd George's son Gwilym, who had held office in the Caretaker Government, styled himself a 'National Liberal and Conservative', secured the support of local Tories and held off the challenge of his Labour opponent. It was rumoured that he was later offered the leadership of the Liberal National parliamentary group.
90. Kirklees District Archives, Mabane MSS, DD/WM/1/9, Mabane to Hickman 10 Aug. 1945.
91. Mabane MSS, DD/WM/1/9, Sellars to Mabane 9 Aug. 1945.
92. Mabane MSS, DD/WM/1/9, Hickman to Mabane 9 Aug. 1945.
93. Papers of the Bradford South Liberal National Association, 36D78/29, officers meeting 4 Dec. 1945.
94. Bodleian Library, Oxford, Simon MSS, SP 96, fos 137–40, Simon to Churchill 2 Aug. 1945.
95. Bodleian Library, Oxford, Conservative Party Archive, CCO 3/1/63, Col. P.J. Blair, Scottish Unionist Political Secretary, to T.F. Watson, Conservative Central Office, 18 May 1946.
96. Glyndŵr MSS, DD/G/2544, Edna Hughes to Mulholland, Liberal National agent, Manchester, 18 May 1945.
97. Conservative Party Archive, CCO 3/1/63, Blair to Watson 18 May 1946.
98. Ibid., CCO 3/1/64, report of meeting held at 24 Old Queen Street 21 March 1946.
99. *Yorkshire Post* 15 July 1946.
100. Conservative Party Archive, CCO 3/1/63, Blair to Watson 18 May 1946.
101. Ibid., CCO 3/1/63, Blair to Pierssené 14 June 1946.

102. Glyndŵr MSS, DD/G/2550, 'The future of Liberalism', published by Liberal National Organisation.
103. Hunter, 'Final quest', p. 14.
104. Conservative Party Archive, CCO 3/1/63, Blair to Watson 18 May 1946.
105. Avon MSS, AP 11/12/38, Thomas to Eden 29 May 1946.
106. Conservative Party Archive, CCO 3/1/64, report of meeting held at 24 Old Queen Street 21 March 1946. Emphasis added.
107. Sinclair to G. Mander 6 Dec. 1945, cited Hunter, 'Final quest', p. 14.
108. Sinclair to Samuel 20 May 1946, cited ibid.
109. Samuel to Montrose 17 May 1946, cited ibid.
110. *The Times* 18 March 1946.
111. D. Dutton, 'Liberalism Reunited: The Huddersfield Experience 1945–47', *Journal of Liberal History* 52 (2006), pp. 32–7.
112. Manchester Central Library, papers of the Manchester Liberal Federation, M 283/1/4/3, minutes of general committee meeting 9 July 1946.
113. *New Horizon*, no. 46, Sept. 1946; *Liberal Magazine* Aug. 1946.
114. *The Times* 3 July 1946.
115. Hunter, 'Final quest', p. 15.
116. 'Declaration on Liberal Reunion' 28 June 1946, published by Liberal National Organisation.
117. *The Times* 11 July 1946.
118. Hunter, 'Final quest', p. 16.
119. *Manchester Guardian* 28 Oct. 1946.
120. Bolton Central Library, papers of the Bolton Conservative Association, FDC 1/1/9, minutes of the final meeting of the Election Committee 27 July 1945.
121. Conservative Party Archive, CCO 3/1/63, Churchill to Woolton 3 Aug. 1946.
122. R. Douglas, *The History of the Liberal Party 1895–1970* (London, 1971), p. 253.
123. *The Times* 18 Nov. 1946.
124. A. Horne, *Macmillan, 1894–1956* (London, 1988), p. 298.
125. Conservative Party Archive, CCO 3/1/63, Blair to Pierssené 14 June 1946.
126. Bodleian Library, Oxford, Woolton MSS 21, fos 52–3, memorandum of conversation with Teviot and Mabane 25 Oct. 1946 and draft (not sent) of Woolton to Churchill 26 Oct. 1946.
127. Woolton to Churchill 4 Dec. 1946, cited M. Kandiah, 'Lord Woolton's chairmanship of the Conservative party, 1945–1951', University of Exeter Ph.D. (1992), pp. 85–6.
128. Woolton MSS 21,fo. 58, Stuart to Woolton 25 Jan. 1947.
129. Conservative Party Archive, CCO 3/1/63, Pierssené to Blair 8 March 1947.
130. Churchill Archives Centre, Cambridge, Hore-Belisha MSS, HOBE 1/10, diary 29 Jan. 1947.
131. Woolton MSS 21, fo. 62, Woolton to Churchill 25 March 1947; Conservative Party Archive, CCO 3/1/64, statement issued jointly by Woolton and Teviot; *The Times* 12 May 1947.

5 The Long Road to Extinction, 1947–68

1. J. Ramsden, *An Appetite for Power: A History of the Conservative Party since 1830* (London, 1998), p. 535.

2. *The Times* 14 May 1962.
3. Ibid., 12 May 1947.
4. Bodleian Library, Oxford, Conservative Party Archive, CCO 3/1/63, Pierssené to Blair 21 April 1947. Emphasis in original.
5. *The Times* 12 May 1947.
6. Ibid., 17 May 1947.
7. *Liberal Magazine* Oct. 1948.
8. British Library of Political and Economic Science, Rhys Williams MSS, J/11/5/1, Juliet Rhys-Williams to Robin Hall 6 Feb. 1947. I am grateful to Dr Matt Cole for bringing this reference to my attention.
9. *Liberal News* 8 April 1949.
10. *Liberal Magazine* Jan. 1949.
11. *The Times* 24 Nov. 1949, letter from Fred Hardman.
12. Minutes of the Edinburgh South Liberal Association 12 Nov. 1947, cited M. Cole, 'The Identity of the British Liberal Party 1945–62', University of Birmingham Ph.D. (2006), p. 93.
13. *Manchester Guardian* 16 Nov. 1949.
14. Ibid., 21 Nov. 1949.
15. *West Wales Weekly News* 7 April 1949, cited J.G. Jones, 'Major Gwilym Lloyd-George and the Pembrokeshire election of 1950', *Journal of the Pembrokeshire Historical Society* 11 (2002), p. 103.
16. Jones, 'Gwilym Lloyd-George', p. 110.
17. Ibid., p. 112.
18. Conservative Party Archive, CCO 1/7/70, 'Basic Report' on Newcastle East 8 June 1949.
19. Denbighshire Record Office, papers of the Denbighshire Conservative Association, DD/DM/80/6, minutes of finance and general purposes committee meetings 3 June and 23 Oct. 1947.
20. Ibid., report of conference with representatives of the Liberal National Organisation 11 Oct. 1947.
21. Ibid., emergency general meeting 19 Nov. 1948.
22. National Library of Wales, papers of the Wrexham Conservative Association, A 1985/92/2, executive committee meetings 12 March and 2 April 1947.
23. Ibid., 4 June 1947.
24. Ibid., Conservative association divisional council meetings 16 July 1948 and 22 Feb. 1949.
25. Denbighshire Record Office, Glyndŵr MSS, DD/G/2572, Edna Hughes to Ensor Walters 20 July 1949.
26. Papers of the Wrexham Conservative Association, A 1985/92/2, executive council meeting 3 June 1949.
27. Bradford District Archives, papers of the Bradford Liberal National Association, 36D78/29, officers' executive committee meeting 24 Nov. 1947; *Bradford Telegraph and Argus* 25 Nov. 1947.
28. Ibid., 36D78/29, H. Lees, Conservative Agent, to A. Geoffrey Peel, Liberal National Secretary, 25 Oct. 1948.
29. Ibid., special general meeting 28 Feb. 1949.

30. Conservative Party Archive, CCO 1/7/164, J.W. Sutcliffe to Lord Woolton 11 March 1949.
31. Ibid., Woolton to Mrs E.L. Hartley 29 April 1949 and Woolton to Sutcliffe 25 March 1949.
32. Ibid., Sutcliffe to Woolton 11 March 1949.
33. Ibid., Sutcliffe to Thomas Dugdale 22 March 1949.
34. *Liberal News* 27 July 1951.
35. Conservative Party Archive, CCO 3/1/63, Blair to Pierssené 18 March 1949.
36. W.S. Churchill, *His Father's Son: A Life of Randolph Churchill* (London, 1996), p. 295.
37. Ibid., p. 293.
38. Lord Hill, *Both Sides of the Hill* (London, 1964), pp. 10, 14–15.
39. H. Nicholas, *The British General Election of 1950* (London, 1951), p. 107.
40. Bedfordshire Record Office, papers of Sir Herbert Janes, JN 326, Hill to Janes 2 Nov. 1949.
41. *The Times* 25 May 1948.
42. Woolton to Macmillan 18 March 1948, cited M.D. Kandiah, 'Lord Woolton's chairmanship of the Conservative party, 1945–1951', University of Exeter Ph.D. (1992), p. 74.
43. *The Times* 21 June 1948.
44. Maclay at National Liberal Conference in Bournemouth, reported in *Denbigh Free Press* 4 June 1949.
45. *The Times* 23 May 1949.
46. House of Lords Debates, 5th Series, vol. CLXIV, col. 254.
47. Bodleian Library, Oxford, Simon MSS, SP 98, fos 3–5, Simon to Teviot 26 July 1949.
48. Ibid., SP 97, fos 161–3, Simon to Churchill n.d., but Nov. 1948.
49. Ibid., SP 97, fo. 140, Churchill to Simon 13 Nov. 1948.
50. Ibid., SP 97, fos 169–71, Simon to Churchill 18 Jan. 1949.
51. Conservative Party Archive, CCO 3/1/63, Blair to Sir Arthur Young 15 June 1949. Maclay served as chairman of the parliamentary party from 1947 to 1956.
52. Maclay to Woolton 9 Jan. 1950, cited Kandiah, 'Lord Woolton', p. 165.
53. Conservative Party Archive, CCO 3/1/63, Pierssené to Blair 20 June 1949.
54. Pierssené to Woolton 29 Dec. 1949, cited Kandiah, 'Lord Woolton', p. 164.
55. University of Birmingham Library, Avon MSS, AP 16/1/193A, Butler to Eden 13 June 1949.
56. Conservative Party Archive, CRD 2/49/14, Maclay to Butler 9 June 1949.
57. Nicholas, *General Election of 1950*, p. 123; *The Times* 20 Jan. 1950.
58. Simon MSS, SP 98, fo. 7, Teviot to Simon 27 July 1949.
59. S. Ball (ed.), *Parliament and Politics in the Age of Churchill and Attlee: The Headlam Diaries 1935–1951* (Cambridge, 1999), p. 615.
60. See, for example, National Library of Wales, papers of the Cardiganshire Liberal Association, file 24, for evidence of an unsuccessful attempt to secure an agreement in Cardiganshire. 'This Association ... cannot depart from the independent position always maintained by it in the past in relation to its candidates for the County': David Thomas, Secretary Cardiganshire Liberal

Association, to Sir Arthur Harford, Chairman Cardiganshire Conservative Association, 7 June 1948.
61. D. Dutton, 'Liberalism reunited: the Huddersfield experience 1945–47', *Journal of Liberal History* 52 (2006), p. 37.
62. These figures subsume the National Liberal vote within the Conservative total.
63. Kandiah, 'Lord Woolton', p. 169.
64. Simon MSS, SP 98, fo. 106, Simon to Woolton 6 Jan. 1950.
65. Nicholas, *General Election of 1950*, pp. 83–4.
66. A. Watkins, *The Liberal Dilemma* (London, 1966), p. 50.
67. Nicholas, *General Election of 1950*, p. 85.
68. Hill, *Both Sides*, pp. 128–9.
69. These figures, which follow the details given in the leaflet 'The Liberal-Unionist Group', issued by the National Liberal Organisation for the General Election of 1951, may understate the group's Liberal component.
70. Simon MSS, SP 98, fo. 130, 'The Problem of the Next Election' 27 Feb. 1950.
71. Nicholas, *General Election of 1950*, p. 299.
72. K. Young (ed.), *The Diaries of Sir Robert Bruce Lockhart 1939–1965* (London, 1980), p. 704.
73. *The Times* 27 Feb. 1950.
74. Simon MSS, SP 98, fos 130–1, 'The Problem of the Next Election' 27 Feb. 1950.
75. Woolton MSS 21, fo. 103, Woolton to Churchill 9 March 1950.
76. M. Gilbert, *Winston S. Churchill*, vol. 8 (London, 1988), p. 529.
77. House of Commons Debates, 5th Series, vol. 472, col. 592.
78. Simon MSS, SP 98, fos 225–6, Simon to Macmillan 9 May 1950.
79. Gilbert, *Churchill*, vol. 8, p. 529.
80. H. Macmillan, *Tides of Fortune 1945–1955* (London, 1969), p. 318.
81. N. Fisher, *Harold Macmillan* (London, 1982), p. 132.
82. 'What do the Tories want?', *Liberal News* 11 Aug. 1950.
83. Woolton MSS 21, fos 73–83, Woolton to Salisbury 28 Sept. 1950.
84. Ibid., fo. 116, Teviot to Woolton 19 Sept. 1950.
85. Ibid., fo. 125, Woolton to Teviot 28 Sept. 1950.
86. G. Tregidga, *The Liberal Party in South-West Britain since 1918* (Exeter, 2000), p. 142.
87. Conservative Party Archive, CCO 3/3/103, Lord Milverton and Eight Former Independent Liberal Parliamentary Candidates, 'Why National Liberal?'
88. House of Lords Record Office, Samuel MSS A/129/17, Milverton to Willingdon 16 April 1950.
89. *Liberal News* 24 April 1950.
90. Conservative Party Archive, CCO 4/4/43, T.F. Watson, Chief Organisation Officer, to Conservative agents 8 Aug. 1951.
91. *The Times* 26 Feb. 1951.
92. Woolton MSS 21, fo. 145, Maclay to Woolton 8 June 1951.
93. *The Times* 19 Oct. 1951.
94. Ibid., 13 Oct. 1951.
95. *Liberal News* 28 Sept. 1951.
96. D. Butler, *The British General Election of 1951* (London, 1952), p. 198.

97. *Denbigh Free Press* 13 Oct. 1951.
98. *The Times* 6 Oct. 1951.
99. Ibid., 9 Oct. 1951.
100. National Library of Wales, Davies MSS, J/3/59, M. O'Donovan to Davies 5 Oct. 1951.
101. *The Times* 25 Oct. 1951.
102. *Liberal News* 12 Oct. 1951.
103. *The Times* 1 Oct. 1951.
104. The *Evening Standard* (17 Oct. 1951) described him as one of the three dominant personalities of the campaign.
105. P. Goodhart, *The 1922: The Story of the 1922 Committee* (London, 1973), p. 148.
106. *The Times* 6 May 1950.
107. Ibid., 5 June 1945.
108. R.R. James, *Anthony Eden* (London, 1986), p. xi.
109. Butler, *General Election of 1951*, pp. 242, 266–7.
110. Conservative Party Archive, CCO 4/5/52, memorandum by T.F. Watson for Pierssené 29 Jan. 1954.
111. Papers of the Denbighshire Conservative Association, DD/DM/80/9, 'Future Policy' by Lt-Col. J.C. Wynne-Edwards, submitted to the Denbigh Conservative Central Council 10 Nov. 1951.
112. Ibid., DD/DM/80/10, executive committee meeting 19 Nov. 1959.
113. Ibid., central council meeting 19 Nov. 1959.
114. *Liverpool Daily Post* 2 and 4 May 1955.
115. Sheffield City Archives, papers of Mrs M. Murfin, MD 7348/1/1, meeting of Sheffield and District Liberal Council 20 Aug. 1952.
116. Lord Heseltine to author 1 April 2005.
117. Janes MSS, JN 326, Janes to C. Hill 26 Oct. 1959.
118. Papers of the Wrexham Conservative Association, A 1985/92/3, Conservative and National Liberal Association executive council meeting 31 July 1952.
119. Glyndŵr MSS, DD/G/2586, Edna Hughes to Ensor Walters n.d.
120. *Liverpool Daily Post* 25 Aug. 1953.
121. *Wrexham Leader* 26 March 1954.
122. Glyndŵr MSS, DD/G/2564, Edna Hughes to Mrs Pritchard 29 March 1954.
123. *The Times* 28 Sept. 1954; M. Baines, 'The survival of the British Liberal party 1932–1959', Oxford D. Phil. (1991), p. 120.
124. K.O. Morgan, *The People's Peace: British History 1945–1990* (pb. edn, Oxford, 1992), p. 155.
125. *Norfolk News* 3 May 1957, cited R. Jackson, *Rebels and Whips: Dissension, Discipline and Cohesion in British Political Parties since 1945* (London, 1968), pp. 282–3.
126. Woolton MSS 21, fos 197–8, Maclay to Woolton 10 Dec. 1951.
127. M. Pottle (ed.), *Daring to Hope: The Diaries and Letters of Violet Bonham Carter 1946–1969* (London, 2000), p. 128.
128. K. Young, *Harry, Lord Rosebery* (London, 1974), p. 174.
129. *New Horizon* Dec. 1952, article by N.P. Thomas.
130. Rea to Samuel 2 Nov. 1953, cited Baines, 'Survival of Liberal party', p. 70.
131. Davies MSS, J/18/125, T. Muirhead to Davies 30 Sept. 1956.
132. H. Morris-Jones, *Doctor in the Whips' Room* (London, 1955), p. 87.

133. *Liverpool Daily Post* 17 March 1955, letter from G.W. Madoc Jones.
134. D. Butler, *The British General Election of 1955* (London, 1955), p. 28.
135. *The Times* 31 May 1955, letter from W.P. Wood.
136. Ibid., 7 June 1955.
137. M. Fry, *Patronage and Principle: A Political History of Modern Scotland* (Aberdeen, 1987), p. 224; J. Kellas, 'The Party in Scotland', in A. Seldon and S. Ball (eds), *Conservative Century* (Oxford, 1994), p. 674.
138. *The Times* 27 March 1958.
139. A. Cyr, *Liberal Party Politics in Britain* (London, 1977), p. 101.
140. *The Times* 29 March 1958.
141. Ibid., 31 March 1958.
142. Organisation Officer to General Director 22 Dec. 1958, cited Baines, 'Survival of Liberal party', p. 119.
143. *The Times* 21 Sept. 1959; see also 'About the National Liberals', published by the National Liberal Organisation, 3rd edn, 1962: 'Only by putting aside all Party prejudice, by dismissing from their minds the recollections of "old forgotten far off things and battles long ago" and giving their full support to the Government can Liberals make an effective contribution to maintaining in Britain the free way of life which is their pride and their traditional heritage.'
144. *The Times* 10 Nov. 1961.
145. M. Egan, 'The grass-roots organisation of the Liberal party, 1945–64', Oxford D. Phil. (2000), p. 97.
146. *The Times* 14 May 1962, '21 Tory banners with an outdated device'.
147. *The Times* 16 May 1962.
148. Ibid., 18 May 1962.
149. 'The Councillor' autumn 1961, cited Cole, 'Identity of Liberal Party', p. 95.
150. *Conservative Campaign Guide*, Conservative Central Office (London, 1964), p. 611.
151. *The Times* 14 May 1962.
152. D. Dutton, 'Anticipating "the Project": Lib-Lab relations in the era of Jo Grimond', *Contemporary British History* 20, 1 (2006), pp. 101–17.
153. *The Times* 14 May 1962.
154. Lord Muirshiel to author 21 March 1990.
155. Macmillan diary 14 July 1962, cited A. Horne, *Macmillan 1957–1986* (London, 1989), p. 345.
156. Interview, Lord Renton 6 March 2002.
157. *Daily Telegraph* 15 Aug. 1962.
158. Ibid., 17 Aug. 1962, letter from Herbert Butcher.
159. Ibid., 15 Aug. 1962.
160. Janes MSS, JN 326, Hill to Janes 26 Jan. 1961.
161. Lord Gilmour to author 28 May 2005.
162. Janes MSS, JN 326, Hill to Janes 2 Nov. 1959.
163. *Western Mail* 1 Oct. 1964.
164. M. Gillard and M. Tompkinson, *Nothing to Declare: The Political Corruptions of John Poulson* (London, 1988), p. 89.
165. R. Fitzwalter and D. Taylor, *Web of Corruption: The Story of J.G.L. Poulson and T. Dan Smith* (London, 1981), pp. 166–7; J. Poulson, *The Price* (London, 1981), p. 27.

166. Glyndŵr MSS, DD/G/1511, H.J. Whittick, Conservative election agent, to Edna Hughes 11 March 1966.
167. Interview, Sir John Nott 22 March 1992.
168. Lord Renton to author 3 March 1992.
169. Interview, Lord Renton 6 March 2002; J. Nott, *Here Today, Gone Tomorrow* (London, 2002), pp. 125–6.

Conclusion
1. D. Le Foe, 'Mission accomplished', *New Horizon*, no. 274, June 1968.
2. D. Renton, 'From start to finish', *New Horizon*, no. 274, June 1968.
3. *Liberal Magazine*, vol. XLIII, no. 501, June 1935.
4. G. Tegai Hughes to the author 17 May 2006.
5. *Liberal Magazine*, vol. XL, no. 462, March 1932.
6. *The Times* 3 July 1946.
7. *Liberal Magazine*, vol. XLV, no. 521, Feb. 1937.
8. *Liberal National Magazine*, vol. 1, no. 4, June 1936.
9. House of Lords Record Office, Samuel MSS, A/155/9, Muir to Samuel 19 Nov. 1935.
10. Ibid., A/155/10, Spender to Samuel 9 July 1939.
11. R. Toye, *Lloyd George and Churchill: Rivals for Greatness* (London, 2007), pp. 249–50.
12. H. Macmillan, *The Middle Way* (London, 1938), p. 8.
13. K. Middlemas (ed.), *Thomas Jones: Whitehall Diary*, vol. 2 (London, 1969), p. 229.
14. R. Evans, 'Why we are Liberal Nationals', Liberal National Organisation (London, 1939).
15. D. Steel, *Against Goliath: David Steel's Story* (London, 1989), pp. 87–8.
16. *Montgomeryshire Express* 2 Nov. 1935, cited J.G. Jones, 'Montgomeryshire politics: Clement Davies and the National Government', *Montgomeryshire Collections*, vol. 73 (1985), p. 105.
17. D. Jarvis, 'The shaping of Conservative electoral hegemony, 1918–39' in J. Lawrence and M. Taylor (eds), *Party, State and Society: Electoral Behaviour in Britain since 1820* (Aldershot, 1997), p. 143.
18. Middlemas (ed.), *Whitehall Diary*, vol. 2, p. 187.
19. *The Times* 28 Nov. 1935.
20. N. Smart (ed.), *The Diaries and Letters of Robert Bernays, 1932–1939* (Lampeter, 1996), p. 203.
21. Bodleian Library, Oxford, Conservative Party Archive, CCO 500/12/1, note by T.F. Watson for S. Pierssené 29 May 1946.
22. M. Kandiah, 'Conservative leaders, strategy – and "consensus"? 1945–1964' in H. Jones and M. Kandiah (eds), *The Myth of Consensus* (Houndmills, 1996), p. 63.
23. E.H.H. Green, *Ideologies of Conservatism: Conservative Political Ideas in the Twentieth Century* (Oxford, 2002), p. 253.
24. Conservative Party Archive, CCO 500/12/1, Woolton to P. Hannon 27 May 1947.
25. Ibid., CCO 500/12/1, note by T.F. Watson for S. Pierssené 29 May 1946.
26. Kandiah, 'Conservative leaders', p. 63.
27. *Manchester Guardian* 21 Nov. 1949, letter from F.J. Chambers.

28. Conservative Party Archive, CCO 500/12/1, 'Relations with Liberal Nationals, England and Wales', n.d.
29. R. Toye, '"I am a Liberal as much as a Tory": Winston Churchill and the memory of 1906', *Journal of Liberal History* 54 (March 2007), pp. 38–45.
30. Green, *Ideologies*, pp. 252, 254; N. Birch, *The Conservative Party* (London, 1949), p. 34.
31. Viscount Simon, *Retrospect* (London, 1952), p. 172.
32. *Liberal Magazine* Jan. 1948.
33. Letter from Dingle Foot, Wilfrid Roberts and Philip Hopkins to Hugh Gaitskell, published in *The Times* 10 July 1956.
34. P. Dean, 'The Liberal party' 26 Oct. 1962, cited E.H.H. Green, 'The Conservative party, the state and the electorate, 1945–64' in Lawrence and Taylor (eds), *Party, State and Society*, p. 193.
35. Conservative Party Archive, CCO 500/12/5, L. Wolstenholme, Central Office Agent for Wales, to R.J. Webster 24 Oct. 1967.
36. Ibid., CCO 500/12/5, Webster to Wolstenholme 26 Oct. 1967.
37. A.H. Taylor, 'The effect of electoral pacts on the decline of the Liberal party', *British Journal of Political Science*, vol. 3 (1973), p. 247.
38. J. Stuart, *Within the Fringe* (London, 1967), between pp. 90–1.
39. *The Times* 6 Oct. 1951.
40. G. Pierce, 'The decline of parliamentary democracy', *New Horizon*, no. 274, June 1968.

A Note on Sources

No central archive of the Liberal National party appears to have survived. The collection previously noted as being in the possession of Lord Drumalbyn (Niall Macpherson, 1908–87, National Liberal and later National Liberal and Conservative MP for Dumfriesshire 1945–63) cannot now be traced. Among important constituency papers attention is drawn to those of the Bradford Liberal National Association (Bradford District Archives), the Walsall Liberal Association (Walsall Local History Centre), the Huddersfield Liberal Association (Kirklees District Archives), the Denbighshire Conservative Association (Denbighshire Record Office) and the Wrexham Conservative Association (National Library of Wales). There is also important material in the Conservative Party Archive (Bodleian Library, Oxford).

Significant information may be found in the private papers of Sir John Simon (Bodleian Library, Oxford), Walter Runciman (University of Newcastle-upon-Tyne Library), Leslie Hore-Belisha (Churchill Archives Centre, Cambridge), Clement Davies (National Library of Wales), Sir Henry Morris-Jones (Flintshire Record Office), William Mabane (Kirklees District Archives), Sir Herbert Janes (Bedfordshire Record Office), Alderman Edward Hughes (Denbighshire Record Office) and Lord Woolton (Bodleian Library, Oxford). Among published diaries there are N. Smart (ed.), *The Diaries and Letters of Robert Bernays, 1932–1939* (Lampeter, 1996) and R.J. Minney (ed.), *The Private Papers of Hore-Belisha* (London, 1960). Much valuable information may be derived from the successive periodicals published by the party, namely *The Liberal National Magazine* and *The Liberal* before the Second World War and *New Horizon* after it. The memoirs of prominent Liberal Nationals include Viscount Simon, *Retrospect* (London, 1952), Geoffrey Shakespeare, *Let Candles Be Brought In* (London, 1949), Sir

Henry Morris-Jones, *Doctor in the Whips' Room* (London, 1955) and David Renton, *The Spice of Life* (London, 2006). Among biographies, see D. Dutton, *Simon: A Political Biography of Sir John Simon* (London, 1992) and A. Wyburn-Powell, *Clement Davies: Liberal Leader* (London, 2003). There are useful entries on a number of Liberal Nationals, including Walter Runciman, Ernest Brown, Leslie Hore-Belisha, Geoffrey Shakespeare, George Lambert, Lord Teviot and Jack Maclay in the *Oxford Dictionary of National Biography* (Oxford, 2004).

There is as yet remarkably little secondary literature specifically on the Liberal National party. But see G. Goodlad, 'The Liberal Nationals, 1931–1940: the problems of a party in partnership government', *Historical Journal* 38, 1 (1995), N. Cott, 'Tory cuckoos in the Liberal nest?', *Journal of Liberal Democrat History* 25 (1999–2000), I. Hunter, 'The Final Quest for Liberal Reunion 1943–46', *Journal of Liberal Democrat History* 32 (2001), J. Reynolds, 'Impacts of Reunification?', *Journal of Liberal Democrat History* 32 (2001) and, by the present author, 'John Simon and the Post-War National Liberal Party: an Historical Postscript', *Historical Journal* 32, 2 (1989), '1932: A Neglected Date in the History of the Decline of the British Liberal Party', *Twentieth Century British History* 14, 1 (2003), 'William Mabane and Huddersfield Politics, 1931–1947', *Northern History* XL111, 1 (2006) and 'Liberalism in Crisis: Liberals, Liberal Nationals and the Politics of North-East Wales 1931–5', *Welsh History Review* 23, 1 (2006). The origins and early history of the National Government have been expertly traced by P. Williamson, *National Crisis and National Government: British Politics, the Economy and Empire 1926–1932* (Cambridge, 1992) and S. Ball, *Baldwin and the Conservative Party* (New Haven, 1988). N. Smart, *The National Government, 1931–1940* (Basingstoke, 1999) offers a serviceable study of the government as a whole. There is valuable material in T. Stannage's account of the 1935 General Election, *Baldwin Thwarts the Opposition* (London, 1980), while the whole issue of multi-party government and co-operation is thoughtfully discussed in G.R. Searle, *Country Before Party: Coalition and the Idea of 'National Government' in Modern Britain 1885–1987* (Harlow, 1995). The National Liberal party's relations with the Conservative party are considered by J. Ramsden, *The Age of Balfour and Baldwin 1902–1940* (London 1978) and *The Age of Churchill and Eden 1940–1957* (London, 1995) and in M.D. Kandiah's unpublished thesis 'Lord Woolton's Chairmanship of the Conservative Party, 1945–1951' (University of Exeter, 1992).

Index

Abdication crisis (1936), 105, 107
Aberdeen, 89
Abingdon Street, 53
Abyssinia, 117
Acton, 188
Agincourt, battle of, 120
All Saint's (Manchester), 66
All Souls Oxford, 31
Allied War Production Council, 130
Alternative vote, 13, 23-4
Amery, L.S., 13, 31, 38, 61, 73, 84, 106
Appeasement, 117, 119, 122
Ashdown, Paddy, 17
Ashford, 26, 40, 50, 71
Aske, Robert, 34, 40
Asquith, Herbert Henry, 9, 14, 70, 77, 98, 100, 101, 117, 181, 193, 201, 207; puts Labour into power, 11, 12, 13, 18; and split with Lloyd George, 8, 10, 19, 42, 43
Asquith, Margot, 10, 45
Atlantic Charter, 131
Attlee, Clement, 140, 144, 153, 172, 174, 178, 180, 182, 196, 212
Auden, W.H., 4
Ayr, 158

Baldwin, Stanley, 13, 25, 50, 60, 74, 79, 83, 86, 87, 94, 105, 107, 203, 209; and Liberal Nationals, 61, 64, 73, 75, 103, 120, 183, 206; liberalism of, 46, 62-3, 65, 82, 84, 89, 97, 208; and National Government, 6, 36, 73, 84, 85; and tariffs, 10, 37
Ball, Joseph, 89
Barlow, Sir John, 110

Barrie, Charles, 43, 116
Beauchamp, 7th Earl, 16, 20
Bedfordshire, 180, 200
Beechman, Alec, 113-4, 138
Bentley, Michael, 73
Bernays, Robert, 65, 74, 80, 94, 95, 99, 103-4, 106, 107-8, 122
Beswick (Manchester), 67
Bethnal Green, 12, 22
Bevan, Aneurin, 45, 72, 75
Beveridge, William, 142, 214
Bideford, 159
Bishop Auckland, 55
Blackpool, 61-2
Blindell, James, 40
Bodmin, 96, 113
Boer War, 42
Bolton, 153, 176
Boothby, Robert, 2, 4
Bosworth, 40
Boult, Capt. Frederick, 120
Bow Group, 214
Bracken, Brendan, 5
Bradford, 117, 141, 145-6, 163, 185, 186, 191, 200, 202
Bradford Conservative and National Liberal Association, 185-6
Bradford Onlooker, 185
Bradford Telegraph and Argus, 118
Branson, Noreen, 4
Brighouse and Spenborough, 163
Brighouse and Spenborough Liberal Association, 164
Bristol, 17, 65, 94, 95, 99, 103, 200, 202
Britain and the Next Five Years, 179
Britain's Future: Socialism or Liberty, 194

INDEX

Britain's Industrial Future, 15
British Broadcasting Corporation, 133
British Union of Fascists, 2, 106
Brooks, Colin, 84
Brown, Ernest, 31, 32, 33, 34, 35, 40, 43, 48, 53, 84, 105, 125, 149, 156; and party leadership, 128. 129, 130, 133, 136-7, 138-9, 140, 142, 144, 145
Brown, William, 93
Budget (1940), 126
Burgin, Leslie, 31, 40, 61, 68, 105, 125, 131
Burnley, 151, 185
Butcher, Herbert, 128, 129, 145, 177, 181,198, 200, 202
Butler, R.A., 126, 175, 182, 187, 202
Buxton, 32
By-elections, Bradford South (1949), 161; Brighouse and Spenborough (1960), 200; Central Norfolk (1962), 199; Dumfries (1963), 199; East Fife (1933), 69; East Fife (1961), 195, 199; East Norfolk (1939), 110-2; Eddisbury (1943), 135; Edinburgh East (1947), 160; Galloway (1959), 192; Greenock (1936), 104; Lambeth Norwood (1935), 87; Motherwell (1954), 185; North Cornwall (1932), 69; Paisley (1920), 9; St Ives (1937), 113-4; Scottish Universities (1946), 155; Torquay (1955), 192; Torrington (1958), 192-4; Walsall (1938), 110; Wavertree (1935), 85
Byers, Frank, 151, 152, 205

Callaghan, James, 196
Cambridge University, 165
Campbell Case, 12
Cannock, 159
Cannock Liberal Association, 160
Carmarthenshire, 213
Carter, Mark Bonham, 192-3
Carter, Violet Bonham, 70, 128, 138, 139, 140-1, 168, 175, 176, 180, 188, 189, 193
Caxton Hall, 128, 200
Chamberlain, Austen, 28, 83
Chamberlain, Neville, 5, 6, 45, 53, 73, 83, 103, 107, 111, 125, 126, 129, 208; commitment to National Government, 104, 105, 106, 121; foreign policy of, 109, 117, 122; and fusion with Liberal Nationals, 64, 75; and Liberal defections, 25, 26, 27, 28, 29, 31, 32, 36, 57, 59; and rearmament, 85-6
Cheetham (Manchester), 66

Cheshire, 93, 135
Chesterfield, 100, 109
Churchill, Randolph, 85, 130, 165
Churchill, Winston S., 5, 51, 61, 82, 124, 128, 129, 130, 132, 135, 140, 141, 143, 144, 149, 165, 173, 179, 180, 189, 192, 207, 214; and anti-Labour front, 153, 155, 158, 166, 171, 175, 176, 181; and Liberal reunion, 136, 137; Liberalism of, 142. 170, 182, 198, 212; and National Government, 73, 85; and National Liberals, 146, 167, 168, 172, 174, 213
Mr Churchill's Declaration of Policy to the Electors, 143
Churt, 35,
Clacton, 55
Clayton (Manchester), 109, 211
Cleckheaton, 27, 48
Clwyd, Lord, 90
Coal Mines Bill (1929), 20, 21
Cobb, Capt. Edward, 110
Cole, N.J., 180, 200
Collard, Richard, 199
Collins, Godfrey, 34, 35, 40, 43, 48, 61, 104
Colne Valley, 176, 180
Colville, John, 126
Colwyn Bay, 90
Common Wealth party, 135
Conservative Business Committee, 37
Conservative Central Office, 50, 56, 86, 158, 175, 186, 193, 210, 213
Conservative party, and absorption of National Liberals, 162-3, 165, 166, 167-9, 177, 182, 184-6, 191-4, 198-200, 202, 204, 213; and Liberal party, 13-14, 25-6, 27, 28, 29, 31, 34, 36, 37, 50, 51, 153-4, 158-61, 171-2, 173-6, 178-9, 188, 190, 196-7, 207, 210; and Liberal Nationals, 3, 6, 42, 50, 52, 56, 58, 59, 60-1, 64, 68, 71-2, 79, 86, 91-2, 93-4, 101-3, 107-9, 110-2, 120-1, 139, 141, 146-50, 183, 208-9, 211; Liberal tendencies of, 46, 62-3, 97, 142, 146, 166, 170, 182-3, 188, 189, 208, 209, 212-3; and Lloyd George Coalition, 9-10; and National Government, 1, 4, 54, 57, 63-4, 72, 73, 78, 82, 84-5, 86-7, 105, 106, 143; and Woolton-Teviot Agreement, 154-7, 161-2, 211
Conservative Research Department, 86, 89
Cooper, Alfred Duff, 5
Cornelius, Vivian, 104
Cornwall, 52, 67, 113, 132

Council of Action, 96
The Councillor, 196
Cowdray, Lord, 77
Crewe, Marquess of, 35
Cripps, Sir Stafford, 132
Croft, Henry Page, 61
Cumberland, 16
Curry, Aaron, 55
Czechoslovakia, 117, 122.

Daily Telegraph, 154, 198
Dalton, Hugh, 13
Dangerfield, George, 8
Darwen, 49, 50, 96
Davies, Clement, 21, 34, 43, 47, 68, 89, 115, 118, 208; leaves Liberal Nationals, 125, 132, 135; as Liberal party leader, 146, 164, 172, 175, 176, 180, 181, 182. 190, 197
Davies, John C., 90-1
Davies of Llandinam, Lord, 118
Dawson, Geoffrey, 36
Day, John, 72
De La Warr, Earl, 103, 106
Denationalisation, 166
Denbigh, 19, 40, 54, 88, 89, 91, 96, 100, 120, 132, 144, 161, 162, 179, 184, 185, 188, 190, 200, 205
Denbigh Conservative Association, 132, 161, 185
Denbigh Liberal Association, 90
Derby, 17th Earl of, 25
Derbyshire, 100
Design for Freedom, 154
Devizes, 89
Devon and Cornwall Liberal Federation, 136, 151
Dewsbury, 96, 109, 185
Doctor's Mandate, 39
Dodd, John S, 91, 96
Doncaster, 109
Dorset, 43, 50
Douglas Roy, 3, 16
Dudgeon, Cecil, 40
Dumfriesshire, 55, 76, 94, 145, 147, 148
Duncan, James, 184, 200
Dundee, 113, 164, 168, 176
Dunstable, 159
Durham, 65

East Fife, 9, 69, 70, 71, 119, 125, 168, 178, 199
East Fife Liberal National Association, 100

East Norfolk Conservative Association, 111
East Norfolk Liberal Association, 111
economic liberalism, 158, 201, 214
Eddisbury, 40, 93, 95
Eddisbury Liberal National Association, 135
Eden, Anthony, 5, 78, 83, 129, 140, 173, 182, 188, 191, 198
Edge, William, 34, 40, 43, 48
Edinburgh, 98, 148, 152, 168
Edinburgh Declaration (1946), 152
Education Act (1944), 143
Edward VIII, 105
electoral reform, 23, 27
Electoral Reform Bill (1931), 30
Elland, 163
Elliot, Walter, 76, 104, 155
Elmley, Viscount, 111
England, Abraham, 31, 40
Ethelred the Unready, 5
Evans, Emlyn Garner, 162, 179
Evening Standard, 44
Eye, 48, 119, 130, 132, 205

Factories Act (1937), 106, 119
Family Allowances, 143
Federation of British Industries, 46
Felixborough, 1
Fildes, Henry, 93-4
Finance Bill (1931), 34
First World War, 7, 15, 18, 31, 44, 83, 95, 136, 140, 156
Fisher, H.A.L., 63
Fisher, Nigel, 175
Flintshire, 40, 49
Flintshire Liberal Association, 49
Foot, Dingle, 113, 138
Foot, Isaac, 4, 96, 113, 114, 136, 204
Foot, Michael, 165
Forester, C.S., 121
Fothergill, Philip, 152, 180
Fox, George Lane, 28
free trade, 29, 44, 46, 47, 49, 55, 58, 60, 64, 65, 69, 71, 74, 91, 94, 204
Freedom for the Future, 191
Fulford, Roger, 1, 2, 200, 212

Gaitskell, Hugh, 196
Galloway, 40
Garvin, J.L., 25
Gateshead, 178, 185
General Agreement on Tariffs and Trade, 204

INDEX 249

General Election (1906), 147; (1918), 8, 95; (1922), 8, 10, 70, 110; (1923), 10, 11 70, 110, 194; (1924), 14, 18; (1929), 15, 17, 70, 91, 110, 188, 194, 205, 209; (1931), 2, 3, 48, 50-2, 77, 101, 209; (1935), 2, 65, 71, 82, 84-8, 92, 93, 95, 99, 101-2, 109, 113, 116, 141, 205, 206, 209; (1945), 135, 140, 141, 145, 147, 154, 162, 164, 205, 210, 211; (1950), 3, 161, 162, 164, 169, 171, 173, 176, 212; (1951), 178, 180, 184, 189, 205, 214; (1955), 190-1, 195; (1959), 2, 185, 190, 194-5; (1964), 171, 196, 198-9; (1966), 157, 202, 214; (1997), 17
General Strike (1926), 14, 42
Geneva, 78
George V, 62
George VI, 105
George, David Lloyd, 11, 45, 46, 63, 65, 70, 83, 90, 91, 96, 130, 132, 165, 166, 207; and Labour party, 12, 13, 18-31, 33, 34, 37, 209; as Liberal party leader, 14, 15, 16, 17; and Liberal Nationals, 44, 131; and National Government, 35, 38, 49, 51, 61, 87; and Political Fund, 14, 43, 76-7; and split with Asquith, 8, 9, 10, 39, 42, 43
George, Megan Lloyd, 137, 138, 189
Germany, 47, 122, 143
Gestapo speech (1945), 182
Gilmour, Ian, viii, 199
Gilmour, Sir John, 199
Gladstone, Herbert, 10, 17
Gladstone, William E., 181, 207
Gladstonian Liberalism, 9, 15, 93, 165, 214
Glamorganshire, 185
Glasgow, 98
Glasgow Herald, 149
Glassey, Alec E, 43
Glen-Coats, Lady, 151
Gloucester, 185
Glyn, Ralph, 20
Gold Standard, 36, 38
Government of India Act (1935), 85
Gower, 109, 185
Graham, W., 92-3
Grand National, 188
Granville, Edgar, 48, 75, 77, 119, 130-5
Great Yarmouth, 40
Greece, 130
Greenock, 40, 61
Greenock Unionist Association, 104
Grey, Sir Edward, 15, 16, 17, 49

Grimond, Jo, 189, 190, 196, 197, 201, 213
Guest, Frederick, 17
Guildford, 173, 199
Guilty Men, 4

Hackney, 109
Hackney, Walter, 48
Hailsham, 1st Viscount, 54, 117
Halifax, 1st Earl of, 129
Hamilton, Sir Frederick, 138
Hanley, 109, 120
Hanmer, Trevor, 186-8
Hansard, 85
Harbord, Arthur, 40
Harris, Percy, 12, 79, 137-8
Harrogate, 123, 165
Harwich, 48, 196, 200, 202
Hastings, 187
Hastings Group, 187-9, 214
Headlam, Cuthbert, 109
Heath, Edward, 201, 203
Heinemann, Margot, 4
Henderson, Hubert, 47
Henderson, James, 168
Hereford, 22, 132
Heseltine, Michael, viii, 185
Hexham, 15
Heywood and Radcliffe, 40
Hickman, Stanley, 68
Hill, Dr Charles, 165, 172, 181, 184, 192 197-8, 199
Hitler, Adolf, 83, 117, 122, 142
Hoare, Samuel, 63, 105, 107
Hoare-Laval crisis, 66, 116
Hobhouse, Charles, 14
Hogg, Quintin, 145, 153-4
Holdsworth, Herbert, 117-8, 129, 141, 146, 163
Holidays with Pay Act (1938), 119
Holland-with-Boston, 40, 145, 200, 202
Holt, Richard D., 15, 16
Home Counties Liberal Federation, 102
Hopkins, Alan, 200
Horabin, Thomas L., 132, 137. 146. 150, 151
Hore-Belisha, Leslie, 83, 99, 165, 191; leaves Liberal Nationals, 134-6; and Liberal National party, 76, 77, 100, 101, 120, 129; and National Government, 53, 56, 59, 61, 75, 102, 104, 105, 125, 127, 128; opposes Churchill Coalition, 130, 131; and origins of Liberal Nationals, 30-5, 38, 40, 43, 48, 54, 67

Horne, Robert, 28
Howard, Greville, 200
Huddersfield, 49 67, 68, 92, 93, 95, 106, 108, 114, 144, 145, 148, 151, 171. 176
Huddersfield Borough Liberal Association, 114
Huddersfield Daily Examiner, 114-5
Huddersfield Liberal Association, 67, 92, 114, 144
Hughes, Edna, 163, 186-8, 202
Hughes, Alderman Edward, 94, 99, 100, 117
Hughes, Glyn Tegai, viii
Hunt, Rowland, 142
Hunter, Dr Joseph, 55, 76
Huntingdonshire, 48, 115, 161, 178, 200, 202
Huntingdonshire Liberal Association, 115
Hutchison, Robert, 23, 26, 29, 31, 32, 33, 34, 40, 43, 48, 50, 56, 62, 68, 76, 77, 98, 102, 113, 120, 122, 139

Import Duties Bill (1932), 54
Independent Television Authority, 199
India, 78, 85, 168
Invergordon Mutiny, 36
Inverness-shire, 40 132, 135, 148
Irwin Declaration (1929), 85
Isis, 44

Janes, Sir Herbert, 68, 186
Japan, 78, 132, 140, 143
Jarrow Hunger March, 143
Jenkins, Roy, 84
Jennings, Sir Ivor, 41
Johnson, Donald, 136
Johnstone, Harcourt, 77, 129
Jones, Leif, 26
Jones, Alderman Oswald, 161
Jones, Thomas, 64, 209
Jowitt, William, 17

Kedward, Roderick, 26, 35, 40
Keir, David, 70-1
Kent, 71
Kerr, Hamilton W., 96
Keynes, John M., 47, 214
Kristallnacht, 122

Labour party, vii, 3, 6, 7, 8, 9, 10, 15, 16, 17, 48, 50, 51, 52, 75, 86, 89, 95, 97, 109, 112, 124, 140, 144, 152, 153, 160, 166, 171, 173, 182, 183, 202, 214; minority government of (1924), 11, 12, 13; minority government of (1929-31), 18-28, 30, 32, 33, 34, 35, 42-3, 45, 208; threat of, 64, 91, 94, 143, 146, 166, 194, 198, 203-4, 208-11
Lamb, Richard, 162
Lambert, George, 19, 22, 26, 29, 31, 40, 43, 48, 128, 192
Lambert, George, jnr, 192-3
Lambeth Palace Road, 145
Lancashire, Cheshire and North-Western Liberal Federation, 70, 93, 109
Land and the Nation, 15
land taxes, 31-2
Langford, E.W., 111
Lansbury, George, 27
Laski, Harold, 78
Layton, Walter, 136
Le Foe, Dominic, 203-4
League of Nations, 78, 116
Leckie, Joseph, 49-50, 55, 65, 92-3, 95 110
Leith, 33, 40, 144, 180
Levenshulme (Manchester), 66
The Liberal, 98
Liberal Candidates Association, 24
The Liberal Case, 2
Liberal-Conservative joint associations, 155, 159, 160, 164, 177, 178
Liberal Council, 15, 17, 41, 66
Liberal Imperialists, 42
Liberal Magazine, 47, 71, 76, 87, 205
Liberal National Convention (1936), 98; (1937), 119; (1938), 119; (1939), 123; (1941), 131; (1948), 165
Liberal National Council, 56, 75, 98, 119, 125
Liberal National Forum, 121
Liberal National League of Youth, 98, 121
Liberal National Magazine, 97-8, 100, 103, 108, 121, 122
Liberal National Organisation, 98, 116, 122, 145
Liberal National party, changes name (1948), 166; composition of, 43-4; decline of during Second World War, 124-35; finances of, 76-7; and foreign policy, 116-9; and formalisation of split with Liberals, 48-72; and free trade, 46-8; and General Election (1935), 85-96; and General Election (1945), 141-5; growing dependence on Conservatives, 145-6; 153-65; organisational development of, 97, 107-12, 121-3; origins of, 7-40; popular support for, 102; and renewed challenge of Liberal party, 112-6;

reputation of, 1-6; reunion with Liberal party, 135-40, 146-53; role in National Government, 72-80, 81-4, 104-7. See also National Liberal party.
Liberal National View, 76
Liberal News, 175, 177
Liberal party, attitude to minority Labour governments, 7, 11-13, 18-34; belated challenge to Liberal Nationals, 112-6; crosses floor (1933), 64-5; damaged by Liberal Nationals, 6, 205-7; decline and fragmentation of, 8-11, 14, 27, 41-3, 52-8, 66-71; determines Liberal National historiography, 3; finances of, 76-7; and formation of National Government, 34-5; and free trade, 46-7, 55; and General Election (1929), 15-18; and General Election (1931), 36-40, 48-52; and General Election (1935), 87-96; and General Election (1945), 141, 143-4; and General Election (1950), 171-2; and General Election (1951), 178-81; increasing irrelevance of, 79-80, 177-9, 211; loss of identity of, 65-6; and National Government's foreign policy, 116-9; position in late 1930s, 99-100, 121; and possible absorption by Conservatives, 153-4, 158-61, 166, 174-6, 189-90, 210-11, 212-13; and possible reunion, 87, 125, 127, 135-40, 146, 148-53, 169; resignation from National Government, 57-60, 72; revival of 192-4, 196-7, 213; ridicules Liberal Nationals, 102, 204
Liberal party conference (1943), 137
Liberal Party Organisation, 99, 114, 115, 136, 151, 152, 172, 197
Liberal reunion, 10, 136, 135-40, 146-53, 169, 189, 190
Liberal Summer Schools, 11
Liberal-Unionist parliamentary group, 173, 177, 182, 183-4, 188, 191, 192, 195, 198, 199, 200, 212
Liberal Unionists, 28, 103, 135, 156, 166, 207
Liberal vote, 62, 75, 87, 97, 144, 154, 167, 173-4, 177, 184, 203, 209
Liberal Year Book, 66, 112
Liberalism As I See It, 16
Limehouse, 33
Lindsay, Sir Ronald, 5
Liskeard, 136
Llewelyn-Jones, Frederick, 34, 40, 49

Lloyd-George, Gwilym, 160-1, 173, 180, 181, 185, 212
London, 95, 121
London County Council, 76
Longsight (Manchester), 66
Lothian, 11th Marquess of, 48, 65, 99, 129
Louth, 160
Luton, 40, 68, 121, 148, 165, 172, 178, 184, 186
Lyndhurst, Lady, 1

Mabane, William, 49, 67, 92, 95, 106, 108, 114, 122, 140, 141, 142, 144, 145, 148, 152, 154, 155, 156
MacDonald, Malcolm, 109,132
MacDonald, Murdoch, 31, 34, 40, 128, 129, 131, 132, 134, 135, 136,150
MacDonald, Ramsay, 20, 28, 54, 72, 86, 203; attitude to Liberal Nationals, 53, 60, 62, 79; attitude to Liberals, 12, 13, 18, 21, 23, 24, 57; as Prime Minister, 6, 7, 8, 34, 36, 37, 38, 39, 40, 42, 43, 48, 50, 52, 73, 82, 83, 85
McKeag, William, 65
McKibbin, Ross, 13
Maclay, Jack (Lord Muirshiel), viii, 150, 168, 170, 178, 181, 184, 189, 191, 192, 197, 198
Maclay, Joseph P., 65
Maclean, Donald, 9, 53
Macleod, John 'Jacko', 150, 173, 180
Macmillan Committee, 47
Macmillan, Harold, 20, 154, 165, 174-5, 182, 187, 192, 195, 197, 198, 201, 207
Macpherson, Ian (Lord Strathcarron), 19, 26, 40, 48, 109
Macpherson, Niall (Lord Drumalbyn), 145, 148, 197, 199, 203
'MacStanleyism', 84
Making Britain Great Again, 170
Manchester, 19, 29, 46, 47, 69, 89
Manchester Exchange Liberal Association, 57
Manchester Guardian, 23, 63, 106, 153, 160
Manchester Liberal Federation, 48, 66, 69, 89, 116, 151
Manchester Reform Club, 89
Manchuria, 78
Mander, Geoffrey, 58
Margesson, David, 61, 111
Marquand, David, 46, 72
Martell, Edward, 3
Marwick, Arthur, 4

Masterman, Charles, 9
Maudling, Reginald, 200-1
Meadowcroft, Michael, 197
Medlicott, Frank, 111, 128, 188
Merionethshire National Liberal Association, 185
Meston, Lord, 136
Midland Liberal Federation, 206
Millar, Duncan, 69
Milverton, Lord, 177
Mitchell, Ashley, 114
Monmouth, 154
Montgomeryshire, 21, 43, 68, 89, 96, 115, 125, 205
Montgomeryshire Liberal Association, 68, 118
Montrose, 40, 147, 150, 159, 168
Montrose, Duke of, 149
Moore, D.E., 185
Moran, Lord, 141
Morgan, Geraint, 200
Morley, John, 165
Morning Post, 84
Morris, Rhys Hopkin, 213
Morris-Jones, Dr Henry, 58, 59, 64, 77, 98, 144, 161; challenged by Liberals, 89-90, 96; and Conservatives, 56, 120, 190; and origins of Liberal Nationals, 19, 21, 22, 27, 30, 35, 37, 38, 40, 54; leaves Liberal Nationals, 130-1, 132, 133, 134, 135; returns to Liberal Nationals, 135; on Simon, 28, 79, 107, 127, 128, 129
Moscow, 132
Mosley, Oswald, 33, 46, 106
Motherwell, 109
Mowat, C.L., 72
Moynihan, Lord, 172
Muir, Ramsay, 4, 11, 50, 54, 70, 72, 115, 206
Munich Conference (1938), 117-8, 122
Mussolini, Benito, 78

Nathan, Harry, 22
National Coal Board, 187
National Co-ordinating Committee, 108
National Farmers Union, 111, 135
National Government, 1, 3-6, 25, 34-7, 40, 48-9, 51, 56, 59, 60, 62-5, 72-3, 76-7, 79-82, 84-8, 90-2, 94-8, 101-2, 104-5, 108-9, 114, 116, 119-22, 124, 128, 136, 143, 145, 204, 2067, 209-10
National Insurance, 143
National Labour party, 4, 5, 73-4, 86, 102-4, 106, 109, 132, 209

National Liberal Assembly (1954), 187
National Liberal Club, 66
National Liberal Council, 157, 177, 183, 191, 201, 202, 203
National Liberal Federation, 32, 50, 55, 69, 72, 92, 97, 99, 112
National Liberal Forum, 200-1, 203
National Liberal Organisation, 177, 183, 188, 203
National Liberal party, achievements and significance of, 203-15; in Conservative governments, 181-3, 192, 197-8; and General Election (1950), 169-73; and General Election (1951), 177-81; and General Election (1955), 190-1; and General Election (1959), 194-5; and General Election (1964), 199-200; and General Election (1966), 200; and Liberal recruits, 176-7; and Liberal revival, 195-7; position in constituencies, 183-7, 192-4, 195, 199; and possible reunion, 189-90; seeks clarification of relations with Conservatives, 167-8; and survival of economic liberalism, 214-5; sustained by Poulson, 200-2; wound up, 202, 203. See also Liberal National party.
National Service Bill (1939), 121
nationalisation, 145
A New Climate for Industry, 165
New Deal, 90
New Horizon, 142, 183, 189, 198, 199, 201, 203, 214
New Liberalism, 9, 15
New Party, 33, 46
New Statesman, 47
News Chronicle, 70
Newcastle, 40, 148, 161, 180, 185, 213
Nicolson, Harold, 5, 33
'Night of the Long Knives' (1962), 197
1922 Committee, 125, 175, 181
Norfolk, 110, 178, 188, 199
Norman, Montagu, 126
Normanton, 185
North, Lord, 4
North Angus, 159, 200
North Mearns and Angus, 195
Norwegian campaign (1940), 128
Norwich, 40, 55, 68, 121
Nott, Sir John, viii, 202
Nottingham, 158
Nuffield, Lord, 76
Nugent, George R.H., 173, 199

INDEX

Nuneaton, 50

Observer, 25, 33
Old Queen Street, 98, 145
Oldham, 28, 88, 89, 91, 96, 114, 121
Oldham Chronicle, 91
Oldham Liberal Association, 112
Orkney and Shetland Islands, 213
Ormsby-Gore, William, 78, 83
Osborn, Alderman J.D.H., 161-2
Osborn, John, 200
Osborne, Cyril, 160
Ottawa Agreements (1932), 57, 58, 60, 61, 64, 67
Overlap Prospectus of Principles, 175
Owen, Frank, 22, 132
Oxford, 44, 47
Oxford Liberal Club, 114

Paddington, 165
Paisley, 14, 64, 65
Passchendaele, battle of, 114
Pembrokeshire, 160, 173, 212
Pembrokeshire Conservative Association, 161
Pembrokeshire Liberal Association, 161
Peterborough, 89
Peters, Sidney, 48, 115
Phoney War, 125
Pierce, Griffith, 202, 214
Pierssené, Stephen, 158, 169
Plymouth, 40, 43, 121, 150, 165, 191, 200
Poland, 122
Pontefract, 121
Postwar Policy Committee, 136
Poulson, John, 200-1, 203
Powell, Enoch, 201
Preston, 110
Preston Liberal National Association, 110
Progressive Alliance, 8, 12, 13, 19
proportional representation, 13, 175, 194
protection, 46, 90, 204
Public Order Act (1936), 106
Punch, 28, 126
Pybus, Percy, 3, 48, 53

Radical Group, 14-15, 41
Ramsay, Thomas, 40
Ramsden, John, 157
Rashleigh, Elizabeth, 177
Rathbone, John, 113
Rea, Lord, 190
Rea, Walter, 52, 96

Reading, 1st Marquess of, 24-5, 29, 34, 37, 53
Reading, 2nd Marquess of, 177
rearmament, 86, 89, 99
Reith, John, 129
Rennell, Lord, 177
Renton, David, viii, 47, 197-8, 200, 202, 203, 204
Republic of Ireland Act (1949), 168
Reynolds, Sir John, 153
Ridsdale, Julian, 196, 200, 202
The Right Honourable Gentleman, 1
The Right Road for Britain, 169-70
Roberts, Aled, 94, 95, 100
Roberts, Sir Peter, 200
Rome, 78
Rosebery, 5th Earl of, 59
Rosebery, 6th Earl of, 140, 143, 145, 166, 172, 189, 195
Ross and Cromarty, 40, 99, 109, 173, 180
Rowe, Richard, 158
Rowse, A.L., 5
Royle, Anthony, 193
Runciman, Lady, 119
Runciman, Walter, 20, 43, 50, 54, 57, 64, 89, 125; and Liberal Nationals, 58, 60, 61, 67, 73, 80, 119, 140; and National Government, 105, 113, 117, 120; and opposition to Lloyd George, 14, 16, 17, 35; and John Simon, 77; and tariffs, 38, 47, 53, 55, 63
Russell, Richard J., 34, 40, 93, 95

St Ermin's, 48, 138
St George's (Manchester), 67
St Ives, 50, 67, 113, 200, 202
St Ives Liberal Association, 113
Salisbury, 3rd Marquess of, 207
Samuel, Herbert, 14, 16, 17, 23, 67, 79, 88, 95, 180; and appeasement, 117; on Liberal Nationals, 2, 6, 81, 97, 150, 166; and Liberal split, 21, 54, 76, 144; and National Government, 34, 36, 37, 38, 39, 49, 50, 53, 57, 58, 60, 61, 94
Samuelite Liberals, 39, 48, 55, 58, 64, 65
Sandys, Duncan, 175
Sankey, Viscount, 60, 73, 74
Sassoon, Philip, 28
Scandinavia, 128
Schuster, Sir George, 110, 144
Scotland, 144, 146, 147, 150, 151, 192
Scott, C.P., 17
Scottish Liberal Federation, 88

Scottish Liberal National Association, 119, 151
Scottish Liberal party, 160
Scrymgeour-Wedderburn, Henry, 164-5
Seager, Sir Leighton, 145
Seaham Harbour, 36
Second World War, 2, 6, 15, 72, 120, 122, 124, 142, 182, 204, 205, 207
Sellars, Ewart, 145
Shakespeare, Geoffrey, 31, 34, 38, 40, 43, 48, 53, 54, 58, 59, 60, 61, 68, 111, 129, 138, 139, 144, 177
Shaw, N.M., 200
Sheffield, 100, 178, 185, 200
Sheffield Hillsborough, 109
Shinwell, Emanuel, 130
Shoreditch, 95
Silent Column Club, 129
Simon, Ernest D., 11, 12, 19, 21, 22, 47
Simon, Sir John, 16, 66, 67, 76, 79, 80, 93, 110, 115, 120, 130, 144, 164, 173, 180, 200; as Chancellor of the Exchequer, 105, 122, 125-7; character and career, 4-5, 44-6; and Conservative party, 82, 119, 142-3, 146, 167-8, 171, 172, 174-5, 212; as Foreign Secretary, 52-3, 77-8, 83, 94, 95; and formation of Liberal National party, 32-6, 39-40, 42, 43, 48, 203; and General Strike, 14; as Home Secretary, 83, 106, 107; as Liberal National Leader, 77, 81, 97, 98, 101, 102, 117, 119, 121; and Liberal reunion, 56-7, 60; as Lord Chancellor, 128, 129, 140, 167, 181; and National Government, 26, 31, 59-60, 61-2, 71, 73, 74, 84, 85-6, 89, 104, 105; and opposition to Lloyd George, 15, 22-3, 24, 25, 26, 27-8, 30, 45; and tariffs, 29, 36-7, 38, 46, 54-5
Simon, Lady, 89
Simonds, Gavin, 181
Sinclair, Sir Archibald, 22, 31, 51, 55, 65, 71, 88, 168; as Liberal chief whip, 26, 30; as Liberal Leader, 3, 99, 102, 112, 117-8, 127, 137, 139, 140, 207; and National Government, 58, 61
Sinclair Liberals, 121, 129, 131, 142, 143, 144, 149-150, 151, 161, 210
Skidelsky, Robert, 3
Smith, J.D. Eaton, 68
Snowden, Philip, 32, 53, 58, 60, 70
South Angus, 178, 184, 200
South Bradford Liberal Association, 118
South Molton, 22, 40, 43, 192

South Shields, 109
Southampton, 115, 129, 178, 180, 185
Southampton Liberal Association, 115-6
Soviet Union, 133
Spectator, 106, 153
Spen Valley, 36, 40, 42, 45, 48, 54, 89, 95, 115, 144, 163-4, 200
Spen Valley Liberal Association, 115
Spender, J.A., 117, 207
Stamp, Lord, 126
Stanley of Alderley, Lord, 70
The State and Personal Liberty, 142
Steel, David, 208
Stevenson, Frances, 16, 18
Stewart, James Henderson, 69, 70, 101, 119, 125, 128, 129, 138, 145, 148-9, 151, 168, 181, 199
Stockport, 93
Stockport Liberal Association, 93
Stonehaven, Lord, 75
Stryver, Augustus, 1
Stuart, James, 156
Sudetenland, 117
Suez Crisis (1956), 182, 188, 190, 192
Sunday News, 29
Sutcliffe, J.W., 164
Sutherland, Sir William, 65
Swansea, 109, 179, 199
Sylvester, A.J., 131

tariffs, 10, 11, 29, 35, 36, 37, 38, 47, 48, 50, 55, 57, 64, 90, 91, 94, 113, 179
Tavistock, 72
Taylor, Sir William, 200
Teviot, Lord, 138, 145, 150, 154, 155, 158, 166, 167, 168, 170, 171, 173, 176, 180, 191
Thatcher, Margaret, 215
This is the Road, 169
Thomas, J.H., 73
Thomas, J.P.L., 149
Thomas, Dr Russell, 99
Thorneycroft, Peter, 154
Thornton-Kemsley, Colin, 200
Thorpe, Jeremy, 189, 201
Tiley, Arthur, 186, 191, 200
The Times, 5, 30, 31, 32, 36, 37, 39, 40, 53, 65, 70, 79, 80, 96, 98, 112, 125, 126, 173, 178, 191, 193, 195, 197, 209, 214
Topping, Robert, 87
Torrington, 177, 195
Tory Reform Committee, 153-4
Towns and the Land, 15

INDEX

Trades Disputes Act (1927), 27
Trades Union Bill (1930), 29
Trades Union Congress, 46
Trades Union political levy, 26-7
Trent, Lord, 206

unemployment, 7, 15, 16, 22, 29, 37, 46, 47, 94
United Nations Organisation, 143
United States of America, 90, 131, 133, 143, 194

Versailles, Treaty of (1919), 77
Vickers, Joan, 191, 199

Wade, Donald, 196
Wales, 98
Walsall, 49, 55, 65, 92, 93, 95, 110, 144, 185
Walsall Conservative Association, 50, 92
Walsall Liberal Association, 92, 110
Walters, Tudor, 19
Ward, W. Gretton, 91-2, 96
Washington, 129
Webb, Beatrice, 5, 45
Welfare State, 201
West Midlands Liberal Federation, 160
Western Isles, 50, 95, 147, 205
Western Mail, 200
Westminster Newsletter, 115
Wheatley, John, 19
Who are the National Liberals?, 177
Williams, Lady Rhys, 159
Williamson, Philip, 73
Wilson, Harold, 196, 202, 203, 214
Wilson, Horace, 126

Windsor, Duke of, 107
Winterton, Lord, 61, 130
Withington (Manchester), 19, 47
Wolverhampton, 58
Woodford, 172, 174
Woodhead, Ernest, 114
Woolley, William, 164
Woolton, Lord, 153, 154-5, 158, 163, 164, 165, 168, 169, 171, 172, 175, 176, 189, 210
Woolton-Teviot Agreement (1947), 156-8, 161, 162, 164, 167, 178, 198, 211
World Disarmament Conference (1932), 78
World Economic Conference (1933), 57
Worthing, 186
Wrexham, 94, 95, 99, 100, 117, 141, 143, 147, 162, 186, 187, 188, 189, 202, 214
Wrexham Conservative and National Liberal Association, 162
Wrexham Liberal National Association, 117, 163
Wright, J.F., 111
Wynne-Edwards, Lt-Col. J.C., 184-5

Yellow Book, 15
Yorkshire, 100, 164
Yorkshire Liberal Federation, 66
Young, Lady Hilton, 60

www.ingramcontent.com/pod-product-compliance
Lightning Source LLC
Chambersburg PA
CBHW061439300426
44114CB00014B/1744